Perspectives in The Vedic and The Classical Sanskrit Heritage

Perspectives in The Vedic and The Classical Sanskrit Heritage

G.V. Davane

D.K. Printworld (P) Ltd.
NEW DELHI-110015

Cataloging in Publication Data — DK

Davane, G.V., (Gulab Vinayak), 1921-
Perspectives in the Vedic and the classical Sanskrit heritage.
Includes bibliographical references (p.).
Includes index.

1. Vedic literature — History and criticism.
2. Sanskrit literature — History and criticism.
I. Title.

ISBN 81-246-0031-7

First Published in India in 1995

Published in India by:
D.K. Printworld (P) Ltd.
Regd. office: H-12, Bali Nagar
New Delhi-110015
Phones: (011) 546-5926, 546-6019; *Fax*: (011) 546-5927

Printed by : **RAINBOW Processors & Printers**
C-159, N.I.A.-1, New Delhi-110028 Telephone : 5467547

Gratefully dedicated
to
The All India Oriental Conference,
which has been the source of inspiration
in my research pursuits

Foreword

THE present Volume of studies by Professor Dr. Ms Gulab V. Davane brings into limelight her contributions spread over a thirty-year long career of researches in Sanskrit literature.

It should be stated here that these periodical writings have to be viewed as *milestones* in the History of studies in particular branches; and their (renewed) publication in a collected form today does not demand updating of their contents in the light of further researches in the interregnum.

The methodology adopted throughout Dr. Davane's writings is excellent and unquestionable. Under every theme of her enquiry are to be found up-to-date readings in earlier writings on the topic of study, unsparing work at thorough collection of evidences, their minute and rigorous analysis, their logical and objective interpretation coupled with original suggestions, and finally a systematic presentation of the conclusions arrived at.

Such an activity of disciplined search is exactly in consonance with the spirit that motivated the band of scholars of resurgent India in the first quarter of the present century, who in 1917 founded the Bhandarkar Oriental Research Institute and, through it, in 1919 founded a national forum for scholars in the form of the (present) All-India Oriental Conference. This act was animated by an urge to put a stop to the West's monopoly of reaping away the harvest after tilling the 'soil' that properly belonged to Indians, namely the Ancient Literature of India. It is a matter of unmixed joy to see that this premier forum, functioning for the last three quarters of the present century, has fruitfully served the cause of co-ordinating and promoting the academic strivings of Indians young and old, by reviving the old Indian scientific spirit, through free, honest and objective discussion and dialogue that was the glorious tradition of the soil, as was recorded by *Ṛgvedic* sages in the famous words: set every five words *saktum iva titaunā punanto yatra dhīrā manasā vācam akrata* (X. 71. 2ab).

One of the aspirants who got inspired and attracted to the assemblies of scholars at the periodical sessions of the All-India Oriental Conference is Prof. Dr. G.V. Davane, through whose long-spread and active participation therein has emerged the present rich volume of studies as an index of her lifelong dedication to Sanskrit learning. I have every confidence that the world of scholars will be quick to discover the sterling value of the varied contributions made by Dr. Davane in the advancement of learning.

10-03-1994

S.D. Laddu
Director,
Post-Graduate & Research Department,
Bhandarkar Oriental Research Institute,
Pune - 411004

Preface

ORIGINALLY most of these essays were written for the various sessions of the All India Oriental Conference. I had taken a lot of pains for every article and there is an attempt to make out some significant elements in each one. The Sanskrit research-scholars of the younger generation are not likely to have read them for they were published long before. Moreover, such collection is convenient and becomes available to more readers. These are some reasons which made me very happy to have my papers and articles published in a book form.

While reading the book one comes accross a few words, which are not likely to be understood by those, who are not acquainted with Indian culture. For the sake of such readers a 'Glossary' has been provided at the end.

I am heartily thankful to Dr. S.D. Laddu for having written 'Foreword' to this book. It was really very kind of him to have written it in spite of his heavy engagements.

I am happy that M/s D.K. Printworld (P) Ltd. have enabled me to publish my collection.

If this book inspires Sanskrit students and research scholars to take great pains over every research-article, I shall feel amply rewarded.

G.V. Davane

Preface

Contents

Acknowledgements

OUT of the essays appearing here five entitled 'Influence of the *Meghadūta* on Sanskrit Literature', '*Utprekṣās* of Bāṇabhaṭṭa,' 'The Goddess Sarasvatī in Sanskrit Literature,' 'Good and Bad Verbal Borrowing according to Rājaśekhara', and 'Sītā in Sanskrit Plays' were published in *Journal of the University of Bombay*, in September 1964, September 1965, October 1968, October 1971, and 1978, respectively. The article 'M M. Dr. P. V. Kane's Contribution to Sanskrit Poetics' appeared in *M.M. Dr. P.V. Kane's Commemoration Monograph*, brought out by the University of Bombay in 1974. There are five presentations, viz., 'Poetic Conventions in Sanskrit Literature', 'The Fourteen Gems in the Legend of *Samudra-Manthana*', 'The Moon in the *Vedic* Literature', '*Apavārya* and *Jānāntikam* in Theory and Practice' and '*Uśijaḥ* in the *Ṛgveda*', published in *Journal of the Asiatic Society of Bombay* in 1974, 1976, 1978, 1980 and 1986, respectively. Bharatiya Vidya Bhavan, Bombay, in their '*Bharatīya Vidyā*' published a couple of articles, i.e., 'The Process of *Rasaniṣpatti*' in 1979 and '*Ṛgvedic Ṛṣi* Nābhānediṣṭha' (as 'A Note on the *Ṛgvedic* seer Nābhānediṣṭha') in 1988. A presentation 'The Rāhu-Ketu Myth' appeared in the *Journal of the Vishveshvaranand Vishva Bandhu Institute of Sanskrit and Indological Studies*, in 1975. The essay 'A Critical Study of Dhanvantari' appeared in *Annals of the Bhandarkar Oriental Research Institute*, in 1976. Another article 'Dreaming-sleep and Deep-sleep in the *Vedic* Literature' was published in the *Proceedings of the 31st Session of the All India Oriental Conference*, in 1984. Another essay entitled 'The Legend of Udayana' first appeared in *Bulletin of the Deccan College Post-graduate and Research Institute*, in 1958. The article entitled '*Samudra* in the *Ṛgveda*' appeared as 'An Analytical

Study of *Samudra* in the *Ṛgveda*' in *Vaidika Saṁśodhana Maṇḍala, Golden Jubilee Volume*, in 1981.

I feel my duty to mention the dates of original readings of these papers, which are mentioned below with chapter details:

1. Vikram University, Ujjain, October 1960.
2. Seminar organised by Sanskrit Deptt., University of Bombay, March 1973.
3. AIOC, Guwahati, January 1965.
4. AIOC, Aligarh, October 1968.
5. AIOC, Jadavpur, October 1969.
6. International Congress of Orientalists, Delhi, January 1964.
7. AIOC, Dharwar, November 1976.
8. AIOC, Jaipur, October 1982.
9. AIOC, Ahmedabad, October 1985.
10. AIOC, Calcutta, October 1986.
11. AIOC, Delhi, December 1957.
12. AIOC, Srinagar, October 1960.
13. AIOC, Kurukshetra, December 1974.
16. AIOC, Bhuvaneshvar, October 1959.
18. AIOC, Pune, June 1978.
19. Seminar organised by Bharatiya Vidya Bhavan, Bombay, 1978.

I am heartily thankful to the Editors, Publishers and concerned Authorities for having allowed me to include these articles in this composite volume.

G. V. Davane

Abbreviations

Ā	*Ānandavardhana*
A.Ā	*Aitareya Āraṇyaka*
ABORI	*Annals of the Bhandarkar Oriental Research Institute*
Ā.C.	*Āścaryacūḍāmaṇi*
Ai. Br.	*Aitareya Brāhmaṇa*
Ak	*Aṭṭhakathā*
Ap	*Apavārita* or *Apavārya*
AŚā	*Abhijñānaśākuntala*
AV	*Atharvaveda*
Bh.	*Bhāmaha*
BKM	*Bṛhatakathāmañjarī*
BKSS	*Bṛhatkathāślokasaṅgraha*
Br.	*Bṛhadāraṇyakopaniṣad*
BR	*Bālarāmāyaṇa*
Ch.	*Chāndogyopaniṣad*
DP	*Dhammapada*
DR	*Daśarūpa (Daśarūpaka)*
G.Br.	*Gopatha Brāhmaṇa*
HC	*Harṣacarita*
HSP	*History of Sanskrit Poetics*

Ja.	*Janāntika*
J.Br.	*Jaiminīya Brāhmaṇa*
JRAS	*Journal of the Royal Asiatic Society*
Kān. S	*Kāṇva Saṁhitā*
Kap. S	*Kapiṣṭhala Saṁhitā*
Kath.	*Kaṭhopaniṣad*
Kau. Br.	*Kauṣītakī Brāhmaṇa*
Kau. Up.	*Kauṣītakī Upaniṣad*
KP	*Kāvyaprakāśa*
KPP	*Kumārapālapratibodha*
KS	*Kathāsaritsāgara*
KSV = KSV-I	*Kāvyalaṅkārasūtravṛtti*
Ku.	*Kumārasambhava*
MA	*Mālavikāgnimitra*
Mad. S. = Madhy. S.	*Mādhyandina Saṁhitā*
Mai. S	*Maitrāyaṇī Saṁhitā*
Mai. Up.	*Maitryopaniṣad*
MB	*Mahābhārata*
MBNR	*Mahābhārata Northern Recension*
MBSR	*Mahābhārata Southern Recension*
MBNWR	*Mahābhārata North-Western Recension*
MD = Megha	*Meghadūta*
MM	*Mālatīmādhava*
Mṛ	*Mṛcchakaṭika*
MSVV	*Mūlasarvāstivādavinaya*
MVC	*Mahāvīracarita*
NS	*Nāṭyaśāstra*
NSP	*Nirṇayasāgara Press*
P	*Purāṇa*
Pañ. Br	*Pañcaviṁśati Brāhmaṇa*

PD	*Priyadarśikā*
Pr.	*Praśnopaniṣad*
PY	*Pratijñāyangandharāyaṇa*
R	*Rāmāyaṇa*
Rā	*Rājaśekhara*
Raghu	*Raghuvaṁśa*
ṚV	*Ṛgveda*
Ṣad. Br.	*Ṣadviṁśa Brāhmaṇa*
Ś. Br.	*Śatapatha Brāhmaṇa*
SV	*Svapnavāsavadatta*
SV	*Sāmaveda*
Sāṁkh. Ar.	*Sāṁkhyayana Āraṇyaka*
Tai. Ā.	*Taittirīya Āraṇyaka*
Tai. Br. = T. Br.	*Taittirīya Brāhmaṇa*
Tai. S = T.S.	*Taittirīya Saṁhitā*
Tan. Br = Tandy Br.	*Tāṇḍya Brāhmaṇa*
URC	*Uttararāmacarita*
Vaj. S	*Vājasaneyī Saṁhitā*
Vi = V	*Vikramorvasīya*
Vj	*Vakroktijīvita*
VP	*Viṣṇu Purāṇa*
VV	*Vīṇāvāsavadattā*
YV	*Yajurveda*

1

Influence of the *Meghadūta* on Sanskrit Literature

THE *Meghadūta* of Kālidāsa has been receiving covetable admiration from Indian as well as Western literary critics. As Prof. S.K. De[1] puts it, "The editions, as well as translations in various languages (of the *Meghadūta*), are numerous." No wonder if this work has been translated into all Indian languages. Its Tibetan version is available in *Tanjur*. This version was translated into German by Hermann Beckh in 1907. It has a Sinhalese rendering also. Its first English rendering was given by Prof. H.H. Wilson in 1813. Since then it has been attracting attention of European poets and critics. Prof. A.B. Keith[2] glorifies the *Meghadūta* in these words: "Indian criticism has ranked it, highest among Kālidāsa's poems, for brevity of expression, richness of content and power to elicit sentiment; and the praise is not undeserved".

Shri Hajariprasada Dvivedi places this work on par with the *Bhagavad Gītā* in this respect. He says,[3]

> *dharma aura ādhyātmika upadeśa denevāle hara eka vidvān aura ācārya gītā kī eka vyākhyā avaśya likha jātā hai. aura sāhityarasika kavi aura sahṛdaya koi na koi ṭīkā, vyākhyā, kavitā yā ālocanā meghadūta ke sambandha meṁ avaśya likha jāte haiṁ. ye donoṁ grantha viśvanāthajī ke mandira ke ghaṇṭe ke samāna haiṁ.*

According to him every Indian student of Metaphysics would

feel like writing something on the *Gītā;* and so would every Indian literary critic try his hand at the *Meghadūta.*

This tremendous influence exercised by the *Meghadūta* on later Sanskrit literature can be studied under the following different heads:

I. Literature explaining or supplementing the *Meghadūta.*
II. The *Dūtakāvyas* or the Messenger-poems.
III. Delineation of *Vipralambha Sṛṅgāra* or love in separation.
IV. Description of Nature.
V. Ideas and expressions parallel to those in the *Meghadūta.*

I. Literature Explaining or Supplementing the *MD*

1. Commentaries

Like the *Bhagavad Gītā* this poem has got a vast number of commentaries. As Prof. De[4] points out, "The popularity and currency of the work are shown by the existence of some fifty commentaries." In addition to *Pañjikā* of Vallabhadeva (8th century A.D.), *Pradīpa* of Dakṣiṇāvarta, *Sañjīvanī* of Mallinātha (14th cent. A.D.), *Vidyullatā* of Pūrṇa Sarasvatī (end of 14th cent. A.D.), *Bālabodhinī* of Sthīradeva, *Sumanoramaṇī* of Parameśvara (15th cent. A.D.) *Tātparyaṭīkā* of Sanātana Gosvāmī, *Subodhā* of Bharatamallika, *Mālatī* of Kalyāṇamalla, *Muktāvalī* of Rāmanātha Tarkālaṅkāra, *Saṅgatā* of Haragovinda Vācaspati, *Kavipriyā* of Śāśvata, Prof. De[5] adds that there are some manuscripts which have not yet appeared in print, e.g., *Vidvajjanānurañjanī* of Sarasvatītīrtha (latter half of the 12th and the 13th cent. A.D.) *Sāroddhāriṇī* (15th or 16th cent. A.D. according to Shri K.B. Pathak), *Meghalatā* (anonymous), *Subodhikā* of Megharāja etc.

Meghadūta has been also commented upon by Jain authors like Caritravardhana, Sumativijaya, Mahimasiṁhagaṇi, Lakṣmi-nivāsa, Kanakakīrtigaṇi, etc.

2. Supplements to the *Meghadūta*

(i) There is a work known as *Yakṣollāsa* belonging to the

seventeenth century. It has been composed by a poet named Kṛṣṇamūrti, who calls himself 'Abhinava Kālidāsa'.

In the nineteenth century there have been a few attempts at supplementing the *Meghadūta* of Kālidāsa.

(ii) Mandikai Ramshastri composed his *Meghapratisandeśa* in which Yakṣapatnī sends her return-message through the same cloud.

(iii) In the *Meghadautya* of Trailokyamohana the Yakṣapatnī sends the cloud with a plea to Kubera, that the curse be withdrawn.

(iv) *Yakṣamīlanakāvya*[6] describing the happy union of the separated couple has been composed by Mahāmahopādhyāya Parameshwara Jha.

(v) Shri Koraḍa Rāmachandra has composed a poem known as *Ghanavṛtta*.[7]

(vi) Though not in the form of independent works, commentators of the *Meghadūta* have tried to find out the cause of Kubera's curse.

According to Bharata, Sanātana, Rāmanātha, Haragovinda and Kalyāṇamalla the Yakṣa was to look after the pleasure park of Kubera. He was so much engrossed in enjoyment with his wife that he became negligent in keeping a watch over the park. Once Indra's elephant Airāvata entered there and routed the whole of the park. Hence he was cursed by Kubera.

According to *Sāroddhāriṇī*, Vallabha, Sumantavijaya and other Jain commentators it was the Yakṣa's job to bring every morning fresh golden lotuses, which Kubera used for Śiva's worship.

The Yakṣa found it difficult to leave his bed and wife so early. One evening he brought the buds to be used for the worship next morning. Unfortunately a bee was sitting in one of these buds. The next day, when Kubera was using these lotuses his finger was bitten by the bee. Kubera could now guess as to what had happened and therefore he cursed the Yakṣa.

Out of these explanations the former one has been accepted by Shri Hajariprasada Dvivedi in his *Meghadūta Eka Purāṇī Kahānī*.

3. Attempts at Utilising the text of the *Meghadūta* for Jain Literary Works

(i) In the latter half of the eighth century Jinasena composed his *Pārśvābhudaya,*[8] giving in glorious language the biography of Pārśvanātha, the 23rd *Tīrthaṅkara.* In this work the whole of the *Meghadūta* consisting of 120 verses, has been preserved in the manner of *Samasyāpūraṇa.* Each stanza in the *Pārśvābhudaya* borrows one or two lines from the *Meghadūta,* the remaining lines being composed by Jinasena himself. The *Meghadūta* easily lent itself to Jinasena's purpose as the story of the exiled Yakṣa presents a striking resemblance to certain incidents in the life of Pārśvanātha. He closes the poem with the remark:

> *taccoditena jinasenamunīśvareṇa,*
> *kāvyaṁ vyadhāyi pariveṣṭitameghadūtam.*

(ii) Vikrama composed his *Nemidūta* of 126 verses in which Rājimatī the wife of Nemi, the 22nd *Tīrthaṅkara,* sends a message for him. In this poem the fourth quarter of every verse is identical with the fourth quarter of the corresponding verse in the *Meghadūta.* According to his version the *Meghadūta* has 123 verses.

(iii) Exactly similar is the nature of *Śīladūta* of Caritrasundaragaṇi (1431 A.D.). The work describes how Sthūlabhadra converted his wife Kośā to Jain asceticism.

(iv) Similarly *Meghadūtasamasyālekha* of Meghavijaya (1669 A.D.) has preserved Kālidāsa's poem in the manner of *Samasyāpūraṇa.*

(v) In the fourteenth century Merutuṅga composed his Jạin *Meghadūta* dealing with the events in the life of Neminātha.

(vi) One *Meghadūta* of Mantri Vikrama has been mentioned in the *Jain Granthāvalī* of the '*Śvetāmbara* Jain Conference'.

(vii) *Cetodūta* of an unknown Jain poet has been composed in the manner of *Samasyāpūraṇa,* fourth line of every verse being identical with the fourth line of the corresponding verse of the *Meghadūta.*

II. The *Dūtakāvyas* or the Messenger-poems

The *Meghadūta* has been addressed to a cloud, which is

expected to carry a message of the Yakṣa from Rāmagiri to his beloved in Alakā.

Hence this lyric is known as a *Dūtakāvya* according to the manuscripts in the Northern India, and as a *Sandeśakāvya* according to the manuscripts in the Southern India. The *Meghadūta* is the first known *Dūtakāvya* or Messenger-poem and is followed by numerous poems belonging to the class. As Shri Chintaharana Chakravarti puts it "The new type of poetic composition, introduced by Kālidāsa in his *Meghadūta* works an epoch in the history of Sanskrit literature and it was fruitful in catching the imagination of the people."

Pofessor S.K. De[9] has explained how there was bumper crop of these *Dūtakāvyas* in the period following tenth century A.D., a period, which, this great scholar rightly calls as 'unoriginal epoch', a period in which there was 'no absorption of new influences, nor any attempt to deviate from the beaten track'. He mentions that the number of these *Dūtakāvyas* is above 50.

Shri Krishnamachariar[10] gives a list of 56 *Sandeśakāvyas*. Earlier in 1927 Shri Chintaharana Chakravarti had enlisted 48 Messenger-poems.

With the help of these lists already available and taking into account a few messenger-poems published recently let us classify these in different groups as follows:

With a view to imitate Kālidāsa whose Yakṣa is *cetanācetaneṣu kṛpaṇaḥ* most of these poems are using *mānavetaradūtas*. These can be classified as follows:

1. Birds as Messengers

(i) A Swan is the most popular with the poets of these *Dūtakāvyas*. It had already appeared in the capacity of a messenger in the *Nalopākhyāna* in the *Mahābhārata*.

The following *Dūtakāvyas* have used Swan as a messenger:

(a) *Haṁsasandeśa* of Veṅkatanātha or Vedāntadeśika (14th century): Here Rāma in bereavement sends a swan to Sītā in Laṅkā. It is divided into two *Āśvāsas* of 60 and 50 verses. The route extends from the mountain Mālyavat to Laṅkā via East coast of Madras.

(b) *Haṁsadūta* of Vāmanabhaṭṭa Bāṇa (First half of the 15th century): In this poem a Yakṣa separated from his wife for the period of one year is staying on the mountain Malaya. He sends a swan with a message for his beloved in Alakā.

(c) *Haṁsadūta* of Rūpagosvāmin (16th century): Here Rādhā's friend Lalitā sends a swan as a messenger on behalf of all the *Gopīs* in Vṛndāvana, particularly on behalf of Rādhā, to Kṛṣṇa in Mathurā. The message refers to Kṛṣṇa's fond places in Vṛndāvana, the sufferings of the *Gopīs* in separation and the pathetic condition of Rādhā. Kṛṣṇa is requested to come and save her life. The metre used is *Śikhariṇī*.

(d) *Haṁsasandeśa* of Raghunāthadāsa: The original Sanskrit work is not available now; but its Bengali translation, dated seventeenth century is available. Here also as in (c) above Lalitā is sending a swan to Mathurā. It describes the message first and then the route from Vṛndāvana to Mathurā.

(e) *Haṁsasandeśa* of Vidyānidhāna Kavīndrācārya Sarasvatī: This short poem of 40 verses deals with the same topic as (c) and (d) above.

(f) *Haṁsadūta* by an anonymous poet: This philosophical poem has 50 verses in the *Pūrvabhāga* and 51 in the *Uttarabhāga*. A *Śaiva* devotee sends his soul in the form of a swan to his beloved, viz., Rudrabhakti.

The separation has been caused by wordly attachment. Hence detachment of *karma* is desired for. The poem gives philosophy of *Vedānta, Yoga* and *Śaiva* schools.

(g) *Haṁsadūta* of Pūrṇasarasvatī[11]: Shri J.B. Chaudhari records that its manuscript is available in the Trivandrum Manuscripts Library.

(h) Another *Haṁsasandeśa* is an incomplete work by an anonymous poet. According to the list given by Shri Chaudhari it exists in a manuscript form in the Government Oriental Manuscripts Library, Madras.

The poem ends with the *Pūrvakhaṇḍa* only. Here a swan is sent by a lover to his beloved.

(i) *Haṁsadūta* of Haṁsayogin[12] is a communication between *Jivātman* and *Bhakti*.

(ii) A Parrot plays the role of messenger in the following 5 poems:

(a) *Śukasandeśa* of Lakṣmīdāsa has 74 verses in the

Pūrvasandeśa and 87 in the *Uttarasandeśa,* the metre used being *Mandākrāntā.*

The hero experiences separation from his beloved in dream only and sends a message — again in dream — from Rameswara to Guṇapura (Trikkanapur).

(b) *Kīradūta* of Rāmagopāla: It contains 104 verses in *Mandākrāntā* metre. Here a parrot appears as messenger sent by the *Gopīs* of Vṛndāvana to Kṛṣṇa in Mathurā.

(c) *Śukasandeśa* of Karingapalli Nambudri has been mentioned in the list of Sanskrit manuscripts in the private libraries of Southern India.

(d) *Śukasandeśa* of Raṅgācārya has been enlisted by Shri Chintaharana Chakravarti.

(e) *Śukadūta* of Yādavacandra Vidyāratna, has been mentioned by Shri Chakravarti among the *Dūtakāvya* of lesser importance.

(iii) The following 2 poems use a Peacock, the conveyance of Sarasvatī, as a messenger:

(a) *Mayūrasandeśa* of Raṅgācārya has been noted in a list of the manuscript in Adyar Library.

(b) *Mayūrasandeśa*[13] of Udaya (14th century): The hero is Śrīkaṇṭha, King of Annakara, who is mistaken to be god Śiva by the Vidyādharas. The king laughs at their mistake and consequently is cursed by them that he shall be separated from his beloved for a period of one month. He requests them that he may be allowed to stay somewhere near a temple of Viṣṇu. Granting his wish they take him to the city Syānadūra (Trivandrum). The time of seperation was rainy season. The king in his love-lorn condition sees a peacock there and requests it to be his messenger. The *Pūrvabhāga* describes the route in details and the *Uttarabhāga* depicts the pathetic condition of the heroine Māracemantikā and gives the actual message like that delivered by the Yakṣa of Kālidāsa.

(iv) A Cuckoo, called as *Madanadūtī* by Kālidāsa, plays the role of a messenger in the following five poems:

(a) *Kokilasandeśa* of Uddaṇḍa *kavī* (beginning of 15th century): Here the hero, while sleeping with his wife was suddenly taken away by a celestial being and was left near the Canjeevaram temple. He had to undergo that separation for five months. After about three months the spring beings. He sees a cuckoo, whom he sends with a message for his beloved in Kerala.

(b) *Kokilasandeśa* of Nṛsiṁha.[14]

(c) *Kokilasandeśa* of Veṅkaṭācārya.[15]

(d) *Pikadūta* is a poem of 31 verses in *Śārdūlavikrīḍita* metre. In it a cuckoo is sent as messenger by the *Gopīs* in Gokula to Kṛṣṇa in Mathurā.

(e) In *Pikasandeśa* of Dadhīci Brahmadevaśarman a cuckoo appears not as a messenger, but as one who delivers the message. A bee is selected as the messenger and the addressee is a poet. The poem describes the deteriorating conditions in India by the end of the nineteenth century.

(v) A *Cātaka* has been used for sending a message, as Shri Chakravarti mentions in *Cātạkasandeśa*, by a poor brāhmaṇa to King Ramavarman of Trivandrum. This brāhmaṇa, originally a native of Malabar, was staying in Trivandrum after Tippu's invasion. Due to his illness he has to return home and stay there. While staying there he sends this message-poem with a view to win the king's patronage.

(vi) One *Cakorasandeśa* also has been enlisted by Shri Chakravarti.

Prof. De[16] remarks that there are numerous *Cātakadūtas* and *Cakoradūtas.*

(vii) A *Cakravāka* appears as a messenger in *Rathāṅgadūta* mentioned in the introduction to the Jain *Meghadūta.*

(viii) A Crow appears as a messenger in *Kākadūta*, a parody composed in the twentieth century by Shri Chintamanarao Sahasrabudhe of Dharwar. Here a prisoner who has been in the prison for few months sends a message through a crow to his beloved *Kādambarī*, i.e., wine. Obviously this *Dūtakāvya* is a parody meant to give a satire on the society. This poem describes the topography of the region around Dharwar in Karnatak.

2. Insects as Messengers

After birds insects like bees also start coming in this field of the messenger-poems.

(i) A Bee figures as a messenger in the following three poems:

(a) *Bhṛṅgasandeśa* of Vāsudeva: Here the sleeping hero is carried away by a Yakṣa. When he gets up, he finds himself far away from home. He feels so much exhausted that he cannot return home immediately. He sees a bee there and requests it to carry his message to his beloved.

(b) *Bhramaradūta* of Rudra Nyāyavācaspati: In this poem Sītā sends a message to Rāma through a bee in the Aśokavana.

(c) *Bhramarasandeśa* of Shri Mahalinga Sastri[17] (1954 A.D.): The hero in this poem is Indra, who is sending a message for his beloved Śacī through a bee. The incident of their separation has been taken from the *Śivalīlārṇava* of Shri Nilakantha Dikshita. Indra had incurred severe sin in killing Vṛtra, who was a sage in his former birth. This sin of *Brahmahatyā*, assuming the form of a horrible spectre persues Indra, wherever he goes. At last Indra goes to the bank of Gaṅgā and hides himself inside the stalk of a lotus, growing in the holy water. Now a bee from the Nandanavana has been following Indra because of the fragrance of the flowers in the garland worn by him. Indra sees this bee and requests it to carry his message to Śacī. The route of the bee, which lies northwards along the course of Gaṅgā, has been described in poetic terms. The bee has been advised to pay a visit to the Mānasa-lake on the mountain Kailāsa, via the Gandhamādana. The elephant Airāvata had formerly offended the irritable sage Durvāsas. Since then it had undertaken the vow of worshipping daily the image of Śiva installed by Indra on the bank of Mānasa. Hence Airāvata comes there every morning, worships the image with a golden lotus that grows in the lake, and then takes the lotus as *nirmālya* to be offered to his beloved Abhramū.

The bee is, therefore, advised to sit in that lotus and reach the heaven.

In the course of describing the route Indra frequently expresses his reverence for god Śiva. Hence while the message is being delivered Indra is purged of his sin due to his repentence and devotion to god Śiva. Bṛhaspati appears there and advises him as to how to regain his glory. He does accordingly. Hence he is restored to the former glory and reunited with Śacī.

The poem has 110 verses in the *Mandākrāntā* metre.

The *Pikasandeśa* of Dadhīci Brahmadevaśarman mentioned

under [II.1.(iv) (e)] should be in fact calculated here.

3. Inanimate Objects as Messengers

Probably all later poets realised that it was impossible to compete with the Master-poet Kālidāsa. Hence in no other independent *Dūtakāvya* the cloud has been used as messenger. *Meghapratisandeśa, Meghadautya*, etc. have already been discussed under 'Literature supplementing the *Meghadūta*'. There are two *Dūtakāvyas* using cloud as the messenger, viz., the Jain *Meghadūta* of Merutuṅga and the *Meghadūta* of Mantri Vikrama. These have been already noted in (I.3).

(i) Wind that comes nearest to the cloud very easily presented itself to be employed as a messenger. The first well-known messenger of the *Rāmāyaṇa*-fame has been referred to by Kālidāsa as *Pavanatanaya*. Moreover the Yakṣa has been described[17] as clapsing the breeze that comes from the North. Hence the wind readily offered itself as a messenger. It is worthnoting that after the *Meghadūta* the first well-known Sanskrit *Dūtakāvya*, composed by Dhoyī, employes wind as the messenger.

The following is a list of the *Dūtakāvyas* employing the wind as messenger:

(a) *Pavanadūta* of Dhoyī, the court poet of King Lakṣmaṇasena of Bengal (12th century): This poem with 104 verses in the *Mandākrāntā* metre deals with the love affair of Kuvalayavatī with the King Lakṣmaṇasena. Kuvalayavatī, a *Gandharvakanyā* in Kanakanagarī sees King Lakṣmaṇasena, while he is on his 'world-conquest-tour', and falls in love with him. When he returns to his capital she is overpowered with the pangs of separation and requests the *Dakṣināila* to convey her message to the Gauḍa King in Vijayapura.

(b) *Pavanadūta* of Vādicandrasūri (17th century): Here Vidyānareśa, the King of Ujjayinī sends the wind with a message to his wife Tārā, who has been kidnapped by a Vidyādhara.

(c) *Vātadūta* of Kṛṣṇanātha Nyāyapañcānana (towards the end of the 19th century): In this poem the wind has been sent by Rāma from the mountain Mālyavat to Sītā in Laṅkā.

(d) *Dakṣiṇāniladūta* of Dr. Bholashankara Vyasa of Banārasa

University, is a *Khaṇḍakāvya*. The theme is erotic like that of the *Meghadūta*. The Southern breeze has been employed as the messenger. The metre used is *Mandākrāntā*.

He has illustrated[19] three verses from the same in his *Saṁskṛta-Kavi-Darśana*.

(ii) The Moon plays the role of a messenger in the following poems:

(a) In the *Indudūta* of Vinaya Vijayagaṇi (1653 A.D.), the poet, who is in Yodhapura (Jodhpur) requests the moon to carry his *Vijñaptipatra* to his preceptor in Surata (Surat).

(b) In *Candradūta* of Jambukavi (10th century) a lady sends her message to her lover through the moon.

(c) *Candradūta* of Kṛṣṇacandra Tarkālaṅkāra has the separation between Rāma and Sītā as the topic.

Prof. De remarks that there are many *Candradūtas* known to Sanskrit literature.

(iii) In *Padāṅkadūta* of Kṛṣṇa Sārvabhauma (1723 A.D.) the *Gopīs* in Vṛndāvana request the Foot-prints of Kṛṣṇa to take their message to Mathurā.

(iv) In *Tulasīdūta* of Vaidyanātha Bhaṭṭācārya, the *Tulasī*-plant has been chosen by the *Gopīs* to carry their message to Kṛṣṇa.

(v) This fascination for the *Dūtakāvyas* is indeed led to an absurdity when in the *Nemidūta* of Vikrama, Rājīmatī, the wife of Nemi, the 22nd *Tirthaṅkara,* requests the Mountain Rāmagiri (which, in fact is the Mt. Abu) to play the role of a messenger and to persuade Nemi to return home.

The poem has been composed in the manner of *Samasyāpūrti* as explained in the former part of this chapter.

4. Abstract Concepts used as Messengers in Some of the *Dūtakāvyas*

(i) Mind appears as a messenger in the following poems:

(a) *Manodūta* of Viṣṇudāsa (15th century): Here the poet sends his mind with a message, full of devotion for Viṣṇu, to that deity.

(b) *Manodūta* of Tailaṅga Vrajanātha (1757 A.D.): When Draupadī is in a helpless condition in the *Kauravasabhā,* she sends her mind to Kṛṣṇa requesting him to come to her rescue.

(c) *Manodūta* of Rājarāma: Here also the poet, a devotee of

Viṣṇu, sends his mind to the deity.

(d) *Manodūtikākāvya* is a philosophical poem which discusses the relation between *Jīvātman* and *Paramātman.*

(e) There is a Jain *Manodūta* mentioned in *Jain Granthāvalī* of the *Śvetāmbara* Jain conference.

(f) In the *Cetodūta* of an unknown Jain poet the mind is sent by the poet to his preceptor. It has been composed in the manner of *Samasyāpūrti* as already explained in (I.3).

(g) *Hṛdayadūta* of Bhaṭṭa Harihara has been noted by Shri Chakravarti.

(ii) *Śīla* (Pious Conduct) is made to appear as the *Dūta* in *Śīladūta* of Caritrasundaragaṇi. In fact it is not a *Dūtakāvya;* but it embodies the text of the *Meghadūta* in the manner of *Samasyāpūraṇa* as we have already noted.

(iii) The poets belonging to the *Bhakti*-cult, especially the *Vaiṣṇavas,* have used *Bhakti* (Devotion) as a messenger in their works, e.g., in *Bhaktidūtī* of Kāliprasāda the poet sends a message through *Bhakti* to his beloved *Mukti* (liberation).

5. Mythological Messengers in Some of the *Dūtakāvyas*

(i) In *Uddhavasandeśa* of Rūpagosvamin, Uddhava is sent as a messenger by Kṛṣṇa in Mathurā to the *Gopīs* in Vṛndāvana.

(ii) *Uddhavadūta* of Mādhavaśarman has the same topic.

(iii) In *Kapidūta*[20] Hanumat goes to Sītā with a message from Rāma.

6. Human and Superhuman Beings as Messengers in some of the Poems

(i) *Pānthadūta* of Bholānātha. Here the *Gopīs* deliver a message for Kṛṣṇa to a traveller, who is proceeding to Mathurā.

(ii) In *Viprasandeśa* of Lakṣmaṇasūri, Rukmiṇī, before her marriage, is sending a message describing her longing for Kṛṣṇa through a brāhmaṇa.

(iii) In *Subhagasandeśa*[21] of Nārāyaṇa a *Snātaka* is sent as a messenger.

(iv) In the *Siddhadūta*[22] of Avadhūta, Rāma, a *Siddha* figures as a messenger.

So far we have had a list of 53 *Dūtakāvyas.* If we add to it

12 from section 2 and 4 from section 3, the total will be 69. With a more critical study of Sanskrit literature and with greater efforts of procuring more manuscripts, the list may be enlarged still further.

Let us now analyse these *Dūtakāvyas* in order to study in the case of each, the nature of the messenger, the cause of separation, the duration of separation, the topic of description, and the route to be traversed by the messenger.

The categories in which the messengers of these poems can be divided have already been noticed in sub-sections 1 to 6.

The Causes of Seperation

In the Rādhā-Kṛṣṇa episode it is Kṛṣṇa's going away to Mathurā in order to save people from Kaṁsa's harrasment [II.1 (i) (c); II.1 (ii) (b); II.1 (iv) (d); II. 3 (iii); II. 5 (i); II. 5 (ii)].

In the Rāma-Sītā episode the separation is caused because of Sītā being abducted by Rāvaṇa. Exactly like that the separation is caused because of Tārā being kidnapped by a Vidyādhara in [II.3 (i) (b)].

In philosophical poems the worldly attachment is naturally an impediment on the way of Salvation [II. 1 (i) (f)].

In the Jain *Dūtakāvyas* like [II.3 (ii) (a)] there is no separation as such. The disciple is away from the preceptor due to his religious tour. In the *Nemidūta* it is due to Nemi's renunciation.

The curse of Kubera, with which Kālidāsa's *Dūtakāvya* begins, also forms the cause of separation in the *Haṁsa-dūta* of Vāmanabhaṭṭa. Parallel to this curse there is the curse of Vidyādharas in the *Mayūrasandeśa* of Udaya. In the *Bhramara-sandeśa* of Mahalinga Sastri the separation is caused by another misfortune, viz., Indra incurring the sin of *Brahmahatyā*.

In the rest of the *Dūtakāvyas* the cause is not such as would invite the reader's sympathy, e.g., in *Śukasandeśa* of Lakṣmīdāsa separation is not real. It is experienced in dream only.

In *Pavanadūta* of Dhoyī, the king has just returned to his capital after his *Digvijaya*.

In the *Cātakasandeśa* the purpose is just mercenary. Thus no cause of separation is as poetic as the curse of Kubera in Kālidāsa's *Meghadūta*.

The Durations of Separation

In Kālidāsa's *Meghadūta* the Yakṣa-couple is suffering this sort of separation for the first time, and its duration of one full year, is really too long. Their pangs of separation become simply unbearable after the weary period of eight months has elapsed. Vāmanabhaṭṭa's *Haṁsadūta,* which comes closest to Kālīdāsa's poem, has the same duration of curse. Nearly same is the duration of Rāma's separation from Sītā. In rest of the love-poems it is just a few months [II.1(i) (c); II.1(ii)(b); II.1(iv) (a); etc.] or even a few days [II.2(i); II.3(i) (a)].

The Topics of Description

(a) A glance at the foregoing sections will show that *Vipralamba-śṛṅgāra* (Love in separation) which is the topic of Kālidāsa's *Meghadūta* is the most popular with these *Dūtakāvyas.* In most of these poems a separated lover is sending a message to his beloved. In a few cases a lady is the speaker, the addresse being her lover, like, [II.2(i) (b); II.3(i); II.3(ii) (b); I.3(ii) etc.]. In Rādhā-Kṛṣṇa episode the message is sent by Rādhās̄ friend Lalitā or by all the *Gopīs.*

(b) The *Vaiṣṇava* schools of *Bhakti* cult, especially the Bengal schools of Vaiṣṇavism, which followed Rādhā-Kṛṣṇa worship utilised the *Dūtakāvyas* for describing the pangs of separation suffered by the *Gopīs* in Vṛndāvana and made the *Gopīs* or Rādhā's friend Lalitā send a message to Kṛṣṇa through a swan [II.1(i) (c)-(e)], a parrot [II.1(ii) (b)], a cuckoo [II.1(iv) (d)], the foot-prints of Kṛṣṇa [II.3(iii)], a *Tulasī*-plant [II.3(iv)] or a traveller [II.6(i)].

Uddhava is made to bring a message from Kṛṣṇa in [II.5(i)-(ii)].

A similar motif has been used by Rāma-worshippers in [II.1(i) (a); II.2(i) (b); etc.] by making a swan, the wind or a bee play the role of a messenger.

After Bengal schools of Vaiṣṇavism other *Bhakti*-schools also started using the *Sandeśakāvyas* for propounding their own doctrines [II.4(i); II.4(iii); etc.]. The *Śaivas* also used it as can be seen from [II.1(i)(f)]. The fascination for these *Dūtakāvyas* attracted the philosophers also as in [II.1(i) (i); II.4(i) (d)].

(c) Jains composed their *Dūtakāvyas*, which were in fact nothing but *Vijñaptipatras* by the disciples to their preceptors, informing them of the progress of religious activities [II.4(ii)]. The *Śīladūta* of Caritrasundaragaṇi describes how Sthūlabhadra converted his wife Kośā to asceticism. *Nemidūta* of Vikrama refers to an important incident in the life of Nemi, the 22nd *Tīrthaṅkara*.

(d) The *Kākadūta*, [II.1(viii)], is a parody, teaching morals to the society.

(e) There are a few of these poems which can be placed under the head miscellaneous topics [II.1(iv)e; II.1(v); etc.].

The Routes to be Traversed

These *Dūtakāvyas* that describe in details the routes to be followed by the respective messengers have naturally a great topo- graphical importance. These cover the topography of the different regions from Rāmagiri (Ramtek near Nagpur) according to Prof. Wilson, MM. Mirashi etc. and Ramgad in Madhya Pradesha (according to some modern critics) to fabulous city Alakā (the *Meghadūta*); from Kanakagiri, another fabulous place, to Vijayapura in Bengal (*Pavanadūta* of Dhoyī); from Ujjayinī to a fabulous Vidyādharanagarī [II.3(i)(b)]; Vṛndāvana to Mathurā [II.1(i)(c)-(e), II.1(ii)(b); etc.]; the mountain Mālyavat to Laṅkā [II.1(i)(a); etc.;] Rameśvara to Guṇapura (Trikkanapur near Craganore) [II.1(ii)(a)]; Syānandūra (Trivandrum) to Annakara (a village near Trichur) [II.1(iii) (b)]; Kāñcī to Kerala [II.1(iv) (a)-(c)]; Malabar to Trivandrum [II.1(v)]; Jodhpur to Surat [II.3(ii) (a)]; Hastināpura to Maturā [II.4(i) (b)]; etc.

Thus a study of these *Dūtakāvyas* is bound to be interesting for a student of Geography of Ancient and Modern India, though it is true that this poetic geography is not always reliable.

Ideas and Expressions Found in the *Dūtakāvya* Literature

These messenger-poems have made some contribution to Sanskrit poetry also. The ideas and expressions that they have borrowed from the *Meghadūta* will be discussed in a later section. Let us note down here by way of illustration, some of the beautiful ideas and expressions found in the *Dūtakāvya* literature.

In *Pavanadūta* of Dhoyī we come across the following notable ideas:

In verse 18, the mountain Mālyavat has been fancied to be dishevelled traces of the hair of Lady-Earth.

Similarly the streams of water trickling through the rocks of the mountain, the poet says, are suggesting the flow of tears of Rāma on Sītā's abduction.

In verse 84 *nidrā* (sleep) is called *svapnasaṅketadūtī*. Like the *Meghadūta* this poem also gives beautiful *Arthāntaranyāsas*:

karyottapte manasi labhate nāvakāśam vilāsaḥ
kim vā nāryo ramaṇavirahe sāhasam nācaranti?
yat satyam na tribhuvanamapi prītaye duḥkhitānām.
jāyante hi praṇayini sudhāvīcayo vācikāni.

Haṁsasandeśa of Vāmanbhaṭṭa Bāṇa contains the following beautiful ideas:

In verse 46 the river Gaṅgā has been looked upon as the autumnal moon, removing the darkness of ignorance prevailing among people, or the pearl-decoration used by lady-liberation, or the stream of merit of sages accumulated together.

In verse 95 the Yakṣa calls his wife *Prasavadhanuṣaḥ kalpanā-cāpavallī.*

In *Mayūrasandeśa* of Udaya, verse 44 in the *Uttarabhāga*, describes the eye of Māracemantikā as a cloud, that bathes the earth with showers of tears.

In verse 71 of the *Uttarabhāga* the message is described as the stream of honey to be enjoyed by the bee of the beloved's mind.

This poem gives us some intelligent etymologies of certain words and names. In verse 52 in the *Pūrvabhāga* the name of the city Kolamba (Quilon) has been explained as:

ko'lam vaktuṁ kaviranupamāmṛddhimityarthaśaṁsaḥ,
kolambeti dhruvamavikalo yatra jāgarti śabdaḥ.

Verse 36 of the *Uttarabhāga* explains the name of the heroine as:

mārasyāstram munijanamanojitvaraṁ pauṣpamanyat,

pañcabhyosaviti kaviganọ māracemantiketi.

Verse 91 of the *Uttarabhāga* glorifies *kekā*, the cry of a peacock as follows:

viśleṣārtā vayī sati jagatyāptamitre yuvānaḥ,
ke kā vā syuḥ striya iti yathārtho hi kekānavaste.

This poem also gives *Arthāntaranyāsas* like the following:

mahadavamatiḥ kasya nārtiṁ prasūte ?
bhrātṛprītyai vyavasitadhiyāṁ ko vilambaprasaṅgaḥ ?

Similarly in *Bhramarasandeśa* of Mahalinga Sastri verse 32 describes how lady mango-creeper will hold fast the bee to her breast, since the bee is *svadanarasika* and *cāṭuvādapravīṇa.*

Verse 36 explains how when the bee rests and hums in water at night, it will remind others of Brahmadeva, arising from the lotus growing from the naval of Viṣṇu, and loudly chanting the *Vedas.*

Verse 50 says if the bee falls upon the fragrant and golden coloured *Ketakī,* regardless of the thorns:

āsvādajñaḥ ka iha bhavatāṁ sāhasaṁ nādriyeta ?

Verse 63 describes how *Vāsantī Śrīḥ,* the beauty of the spring', i.e., the Lady-Spring, with her smiling face of lotus, blooming eyes of the blue lotuses, plump breasts of the swarms of bees, will be singing sweetly with the cooing of the cuckoos; and how wearing the bright yellow dress of *karṇikāra* flowers she will be constantly engaged in dancing.

This poem also gives *Arthāntaranyāsas* like:

nirviṣṭam yadyuvabhirajaram yauvanam taddhi dhanyam.

In every *Dūtakāvya* we will comes across some beautiful ideas as above, but even then a general survey of these poems justifies the following[23] remarks of Prof. S.K. De:

"The general tendency in an unoriginal epoch to produce imitations or counterfoils is responsible for more than 50 *Dūtakāvyas,* which derive their impetus, but not inspiration from Kālidāsa's *Meghadūta.* Their interest lies not so much in their poetical worth as in their utilisation of the original form and motif in different ways and for different purposes, furnishing illuminating illustrations of the variations that can be worked by ingenious and industrious talents, which could scarcely imbibe the poetic spirit of the original work.

The *Mandākrānta*-metre is generally accepted, but we have also *Śikhariṇī, Vasantatilakā, Mālinī* and even *Śārdūlavikrīḍita.* Not only the inamimate objects like the wind, the moon, foot-steps, and the sacred *Tulasī*-plant, but also various birds and animals, like the parrot, cuckoo, bee, swan, peacock, *cakora, cātaka, cakravāka,* as well as mythological beings like Uddhava and Hanumat are selected as messengers for imaginary journeys over various places in India, the topographical information being of variable value. The limit is reached when even abstract objects like the mind and devotion are made to discharge the function, the poems tending to become abstract and allegorical. Mythological subjects, such as the well-known stories of Rāma and Sītā, Kṛṣṇa and Rādhā, Pārśvanātha and Neminātha are utilised, besides those of historical personalities in a few rare cases. In the hands of Jain and *Vaiṣṇava* authors the device easily becomes the means of religious instruction, reflection or propaganda. A curious literary application is also seen in the adoptation of the trick of *Samasyāpūraṇa* in the composition of some *Dūtakāvyas.* The Jain imitations sometimes adopt and incorporate one or two *Pādas,* usually the fourth *Pāda,* of Kālidāsa's verses into the corresponding *Pādas* of their own verses, the rest being composed by the poets themselves as a kind of clever filling up of the entire stanza. It is ingenious, but the literary exercise naturally leads to artificiality and straining of language. The original object of sending a love-message is also replaced in some works by the intention of making the poem a kind of descriptive *Vijñapatipatra* sent by a disciple to his preceptor, to report progress in religious activities in a distant land. This finds parallel to the *Vaiṣṇava* effort to make the poems vehicles for conveying devotional ideas, the sentiment of love being replaced by those of tranquillity and devotion. The process reaches its climax as the *Dūtakāvya* becomes a nominal form for conveying abstract philosophical ideas, as when a devotee sends the swan of his mind with a philosophical message to his beloved, *Bhakti,* for an imaginary flight to the world of Śiva".

III. Delineation of *Vipralambha śṛṅgāra* or Love in Separation

The whole of the *Meghadūta* is a lyric describing 'love in separation'. In the *Pūrvamegha* nature has been described in the language of love, e.g., the rivers on the way have been described as suffering due to separation from the cloud.

The *Uttaramegha* describes *Vipralambha śṛṅgāra* in details. The Yakṣapatnī is leading a hard life of a *Proṣitabhartṛkā.* She has become thin and pale like a lotus plant blasted by frost. She presents a pathetic appearance with eyes swollen due to constant weeping, hair dishevelled and lower lip turned pale; she passes sleepless nights, though the days can somehow be passed with the worship of deities, by talking to the Sārikā, by painting the resemblance of the Yakṣa, by trying in vain to remember melody set to the tunes of her *vīṇā,* counting the days of separation, or enjoying union with her lord in imagination. Her life is sustained by the tie of never-ending hope only. Even the cloud would be shedding tears of water on seeing this love-lorn lady.

Similarly the Yakṣa finds the pangs of separation simply un-bearable. He too has been frequently enjoying union in his fancy only. He resorts to the means of diversion like *virahiṇī-sadṛśāvalokana, citrakarma, svapnasamāgama* and *tatspṛṣṭa sparśana*. He is cherishing happy memories of every small incident in their married life.

This description of *Vipralambha śṛṅgāra*, given by Kālidāsa became very popular with later Sanskrit poets. The heroes and heroines in all love plays in Sanskrit experience similar agonies due to separation. Bānabhaṭṭa (7th century) has given an exaggerated picture of the pangs of separation in describing the *virahāvasthā* of Puṇḍarīka, Mahāśvetā, Candrāpīḍa, and Kādambaṛī. Bhavabhūti (1st half of the 8th century) has described the conditions of Mādhava-Mālatī, Makaranda-Madayantikā in similar language. Mādhava is made to undergo separation from his beloved once more after the marriage. Jayadeva, in his *Gītagovinda,* is throughout singing songs describing the *vipralambha śṛṅgāra* of Rādhā and Kṛṣṇa. He was the first to use description of *Vipralambha śṛṅgāra* for the purpose of *Bhakti*-cult, and in this respect his *Gītagovinda* exercised a strong influence on later Sanskrit poets. Of course we cannot say that every poet, who described the *Vipralambha* had a copy of the *Meghadūta* in his hand; but the popularity of Kālidāsa's poems must have exercised an indirect influence on their mind.

IV. Description of Nature

While describing the route to be followed by the cloud, Kālidāsa has given an exquisitely beautiful description of the various spots and different phenomena of nature. He personifies nature and endows her with human emotions, e.g., the vapour produced by contact of the cloud with the mountain Rāmagiri is the outburst of joy that the mountain experiences on meeting its friend. The various rivers on the way are the *Nāyikās* pining to meet the *Nāyaka,* viz., the cloud. The Day-lotus-plant is a *Nāyikā* offended during night by the *Nāyaka,* viz., the sun. Hence early morning he is hurrying up in order to wash off the dew-drop-tears from her lotus-eyes, with his hands, the rays.

Kālidāsa has embellished the description of nature by using appropriate *Upamās, Rūpakas, Utprekṣās, Arthāntaranyāsas* and other Figures of Speech. With all these enticing features the description of nature given by Kālidāsa in his *Meghadūta* became a model to be followed by later Sanskrit poets. The *Dūtakāvyas,* discussed in Section II described the routes of their respective messengers in all details in imitation of the *Meghadūta,* though they could not attain that poetic height, e.g., *Pavanadūta* of Dhoyī describes Mt. Mālyavat as the dishevelled locks of the hair of lady-Earth. Gaṅgā has been described as proceeding to her lord the Ocean, her heart tremulous with love. She has used white swans as ear-decorations and is carrying in her hand a bouquet of buds of the clusters of foam.

Haṁsasandeśa of Vāmanabhaṭṭa describes the mountain Kailāsa with its dark forests as possessing the charms of god Śiva, who besmears his body with ashes and wears his *Yogapaṭṭa* having the dark cobras on it.

In *Mayūrasandeśa* of Udaya the Night-lotus-grove has been described as shedding tears of the dew-drops and groaning with the humming of bees, since her lord the moon has departed. Similarly young creepers are described as embracing the trees; the honey-drops are their *romāñca,* the bees their side-long glances and the foliage waved by the breeze, their red lips.

In *Bhramasandeśa* of Mahaling Shastri the forest-grove is described as welcoming the bee, singing welcome-songs with the notes of the cuckoos.

The mango-creeper and other creepers are described as the *Nāyikās* eargerly awaiting the arrival of their *Nāyaka,* the bee. The bee should not ignore the affection of Mālatī and should undertake the adventure of testing the *rasa* from *Ketakī.*

The description of nature given in Kālidāsa's *Meghadūta* has been thus imitated not only in the *Dūtakāvyasa,* but in many other places in Sanskrit literature. Bāṇabhaṭṭa, in his *Kādambarī* and *Harṣacarita,* has vividly described various spots and scenes of nature in the language of the *Meghadūta.* While describing the hour of sunset in the *Ratnāvalī,* Śrīharṣa makes the sun bid farewell to his beloved, the Day-lotus-plant, with the words:

yato'smi padmanayane samayo mamaiṣa
suptā mayaiva bhavatī pratibodhanīyā.

The idea of attributing human feelings to the scenes of nature was so fascinating that even Viśākhadatta has used it in his political play, the *Mudrārākṣasa.* In Act III of that play he describes the Śarad as a teacher bringing under discipline the whole world, and as a *ratikathācaturā dūtī,* leading the offended Gaṅgā to the ocean and reconciling her to her lord.

V. Ideas and Expressions Parallel to Those in the *Meghadūta*

Ideas

The central idea of the poem is sending an inanimate object, viz., a cloud as the messenger. It has been followed by numerous poets as we have already seen in Section II. Kālidāsa himself has used the idea of the hero addressing different birds and objects in the *Vikramorvaśīya,* Act IV. He seems to be fond of it.

(i) The idea of employing a cloud as a messenger has been used by Bhavabhūti in his *Mālatīmādhava.* In Act IX Mādhava first addresses the cloud as follows:

> *kaccit saumya priyasahacarī vidyudāliṅgati tvā-*
> *māvirbhutapraṇayasumukhāścātakā vā bhajante,*
> *paurastyo vā sukhayati marut sādhusaṁvāhanāni*
> *viṣvag bibhrat surapatidhanurlakṣma lakṣmīṁ tanoti.*
> (*MM,* IX. 25)

The first line in this verse is imitating the idea that the lightning is the cloud's beloved, as mentioned more than once in the *Meghadūta,* e.g., the verse[24] 38 refers to the cloud as *ciravilasanāt-khinnavidyutkalatraḥ.* The last verse blesses him that he be never separated from his beloved, the lightning.

The second line in the above verse is in imitation of *vāmaścāyaṁ nadati madhuraṁ cātakaste sagandhaḥ.* The last line refers to the rainbow mentioned in verse 15 of the *MD.*

After having called attention of the cloud, Mādhava requests it as follows:

> *bhagavan jimūta,*
> *daivāt paśyerjagati vicarannichayā matpriyāṁ ce-*

dāśvāsyādau tadanu kathayermādhavīyāmavasthām,
āśātanturna ca kathayatātyantamucchedanīyaḥ
prāṇatrāṇam kathamapi karotyāyatākṣyāḥ ya ekaḥ.

The second line of this verse reminds us of the following instructions imparted by the Yakṣa to the cloud:

tāmutthāpya svajalakaṇikāśītalenānilena
pratyāśvastām samamabhinavairjālakairmālatīnām.

The third and the fourth lines follow the popular lines from the *Meghadūta:*

āsabandhaḥ kusumasadṛśaḥ prāyaśe hyaṅganānām,
sadyaḥpāti praṇayi hṛdayaṁ vipryoge ruṇaddhi.

In this part of the play Bhavabhūti is closely imitating Kālidāsa's *Meghadūta,* hence the metre used for these two verses is *Mandākrāntā.* Earlier in Act I Mādhava addresses the breeze saying:

tāmiśatpracalavilocanāṁ natāṅgī-
māliṅgan pavana mama spṛśāṅgamaṅgam.
(*MM,* VII.38)

Here Bhavabhūti, is imitating the idea of *MD,* 104. In the same Act in verse 35 he complains how he cannot complete the portrait of Mālatī as the eyes are flooded with tears. This reminds us of *MD,* 102.

(ii) There is a short poem *Ghaṭakarpara,* by a poet having the same name. In it *Proṣitabhartṛkā* sees a cloud in the beginning of rainly season, describes to it her pangs of separation and requests it to convey her condition to her lover in a distant land.

According to some critics Kālidāsa took his idea of the *Meghadūta* from this poem; but probably *Ghaṭakarpara* belongs to a much later date. It is possible that the idea of a cloud being addressed by a separated lover has been used in these two poems quite independently of each other, whichever is earlier.

Expressions

(i) According to some scholars like Shri Hamsaraj Agrawal[25] it can be inferred on the basis of Mandasor Inscription (473 A.D.) that Vatsabhaṭṭi in his *Praśasti* is imitating Kālidāsa's *Meghadūta*.

Earlier Shri Chintaharan Chakravarti has said that in his opinion Vatsabhaṭṭi cannot be pointed out as the first imitator of Kālidāsa's *Meghadūta*.

However the resemblance in the descriptions is notable. Moreover in this *Praśasti*, which was composed on the occasion of the construction of a *Sūryamandira* in Daśapura, the place has been described in 44 verses. It is possible that in the course of its composition Vatsabhaṭṭi was reminded of the *Meghadūta*, which refers to the *Daśapuravadhūs*[26] the ladies in the Daśapura.

Here Vatsabhaṭṭi describes the houses in *Daśapura* as follows:

calatpatākānyabalāsanāthānyatyarthaśuklānyadhikonnatāni,
taḍillatācitrasitāmrakūṭatulyopamāni gṛhāṇi yatra.
kailāsatuṅgaśikharapratimāni cānyānyābhānti dīrghavalabhīni savedikāni,
gāndharvaśabdamukharāṇi niviṣṭacitrakarmāṇi lolakadalīvanaśobhitāni.

The verse reminds us of the first verse of the *Uttaramegha*, describing the palatial mansions in Alakā.

(ii) The vast literature of the *Dūtakāvyas* is replete with expressions parallel to those in the *Meghadūta*.

Like the Yakṣa of Kālidāsa the Yakṣa in *Haṁsasandeśa* of Vāmanabhaṭṭa says, *ājñābhaṅgāt kupitamanasā dattaśāpo'smi rājñā*. *prītaḥ prītipramukhavacanaṁ svāgataṁ vyājahāra* in *MD*[27] has been imitated in *Bhramarasandeśa* of Mahalinga Shastri as *bandhuprītyā kimapi maghavā svāgatenājuhāva*.

The 5th verse, viz., *dhūmajyotiḥsalilamarutām . . . cetanācetaneṣu* has been popularly imitated in many *Dūtakāvyas* e.g.:

(1) *Haṁasandeśa* of Vedāntadeśika:

viśleṣena kṣapitamanasām meghaśailadrumādau yāñcādainyaṁ bhavati kimuta kvāpi saṁvedanārhe

(2) *Pavanadūta* of Vādicandrasūri:

dūtaṁ mohāt pavanasuhṛdaṁ prāhiṇodaśrunetraḥ,
prāyo moho bhavati bhavināṁ bodhaśūnyatvahetuḥ.

(3) *Haṁsadūta* of Rupagosvamin:

na tasyā doṣo'yaṁ yadi ca vihagaṁ prārthitavatī,
na kasmin viśrambhaṁ diśati haribhaktipraṇayitā ?

(4) *Bhramarasandeśa* of Mahalinga Shastri, verse 5:

puṣpaprekṣaṁ madhunavakaṇāsvādalolaḥ kva bhṛṅgaḥ
sandeśārthaḥ kva ca virahiṇāṁ prāpaṇīyaḥ prabuddhaiḥ,
dūtyenainaṁ tadapi kṛpaṇaḥ preṣayiṣyan yayāce
yuktāyukteṣvakuśaladhiyaḥ prāyaśo hyārtimantaḥ.

Even the Jain *Meghadūta Samasyālekha* copies it in verse No. 5 as follows:

kveyaṁ prāyaḥ pavanasalilajyotiṣāṁ sannikāyaḥ
kvārthaścāyaṁ pravarakaraṇairyo vidheyaḥ samarthaiḥ,
harṣōtkarṣāditi ca sahasācintayannucīvānstaṁ
kāmartā hi prakṛtikṛpaṇāścetanācetaneṣu.

Just as the cloud has been flattered by the Yakṣa of Kālidāsa so also all the *Dūtas* have been flattered by the persons concerned in these *Dūtakāvyas*, e.g., in verse II.15 in the *Pūrvabhāga* of *Mayūrasandeśa* the peacock has been flattered by Śrīkaṇṭha as:

śokadhvāntaṁ muhurapi nirākurvatī sarvato me
mūrtiḥ seyaṁ tava khagapate bhāti cāndrī kaleva,
vṛṣṭyā tuṣṭiṁ bhajati bhuvane hṛsyasi tvaṁ hi nṛtyan
manye tasmādvipulahṛdaya glāyati glayasīti.

The peacock is called *patatrīndravaṁśāvataṁsa* and the *Garuḍa* of Viṣṇu is referred to as belonging to the peacock's family.

In *Bhramarsandeśa* of Mahalinga Shastri Indra praises the bee as follows:

jātaṁ bhadra tridaśanagarīkalpavāṭīnikuñje
jānāmi tvāṁ manasijadhanurjyālatābhṛṅgavargyaṁ.

The poetic end of the *Meghadūta* has been copied by most of these messenger-poems, e.g., corresponding to *kaccit saumya vyavasitamidaṁ bandhukṛtyam tvayā me* Kuvalayavatī[28] bids farewell to the breeze with the words:

sandeśo'yam manasi nihitaḥ kaccidāyuṣmatā me
kiṁ vā bhūyastvayi viracitairaṅga bhikṣāprakāraiḥ,
parārthaikapraṇayamanasāstvadvidhā bāṣpamisrā-
nnāpannānām na khalu bahuśaḥ kākuvādān sahante.

Haṁsasandeśa of Vāmanabhaṭṭa ends with the words:

kṛtvā kāryam mama punaridaṁ kīrtimenām ca labdhvā
pratyāvṛttaḥ punarapi tayā saṅgataḥ saṅgataḥ san,
cetoramye vihara salile svecchayā nimnagānā-
mavyāpannā vihaga yuvayorstu saṁyogalakṣmīḥ.

Mayūrasandeśa of Udaya has the following concluding verse:

viśleṣartām mama sahacarīmitthamāśvāsya yuktyā
paścādacchāśaya paripata bhrātarāśāmabhiṣṭām,
smartavyohaṁ priyasakha punastatra tatrāntare te
mā bhūt kāntāvirahaghaṭanā kiñca janmantare'pi.

All beautiful expressions of the *Meghadūta* have been thus drawn upon by Sanskrit poets.

Verses 36-52 of Dhoyi's *Pavanadūta* describe the city in the manner of Kālidāsa's Alakā and Ujjayinī. Similar is the description of the city Annakara in Udaya's *Mayūrasandeśa,* II.1-14. Verses II.15-28 describe the house of the hero including the description of the garden in the compound. The whole of this description runs closely parallel to that of Yakṣa's house in *MD,*72-77.

Verses II.72-52 describe the pathetic condition of Māracemantikā exactly in the manner of *MD,* 80-90.

Verses II.71-90 contain Śrīkaṇṭha's message, which reminds one of Yakṣa's message in *MD,* 98-109.

Verse 87 gives an *abhijñāna* like the one in *MD,* 108.

The expression *yāñcā moghā varamadhiguṇe nādhame labdhakāmā* is found in poems like *Haṁsadūta* of Rūpagoasvāmin —

yañcā satpakṣe vrajati hi kadācidviphalatām. The expression *āśabandhaḥ kusumasadṛṣaḥ prāyaśo hyaṅganānām, . . . ruṇaddhi* is very popular with later poets. In *Śukasandeśa* of Laksmidasa it appears as *āśapāśaḥ kila caladṛśāmāśrayaḥ proṣitānām.*

In the *MM* of Bhavabhūti it occurs in the following form:

āśātanturna ca kathayatātyantamucchedanīyaḥ
prāṇatrāṇam kathamapi karotyāyatākṣyā ya ekaḥ.

The expressions used by Kālidāsa while describing the various spots on the route of the cloud have also been borrowed by later *Dūtakāvyakṛts* literally or with some verbal changes. There will be no end to a list of such similarities. Hence the above sections will be sufficient to bring out clearly the great hold that the *Meghadūta* had on the minds of later Sanskrit poets.

References

1. *History of Sanskrit Literature*, p. 132, f.n.2., Calcutta, 1947.
2. *Ibid.*, p. 86.
3. *Meghadūta, Eka Purāṇī Kahānī*, Hindi Granth Ratnakar, 1957.
4. Introduction to the *Meghadūta* edition, p.1 Sahitya Akademi.
5. *Ibid.*
6. Chintaharana Chakravrti, *IHQ*, III.
7. *Ibid.*
8. *NSP*, 1909.
9. *History of Sanskrit Literature*, pp. 372-75.
10. *Classical Sanskrit Literature*, pp. 358-68, Madras, 1937, 3rd edn.
11. Shri Chakravarti's article in *IHQ*, III.
12. *Ibid.*
13. Published by Oriental Book Agency, Poona, 1944.
14. Enlisted by Shri Chakravarti.
15. *Ibid.*
16. *History of Sanskrit Literature.*
17. Published by Oriental Book Agency, Poona, 1954.
18. *Meghadūta*, Sahitya Akademi, verse No. 104.
19. *Saṁskṛta Kavi-Darśana*, Published by Chaukhamba Vidya Bhavan, Banaras, 1958.
20. Enlisted by Shri Chakravarti.
21. *Ibid.*

22. *Ibid.*
23. *History of Sanskrit Literature*, pp. 372-75.
24. *Meghadūta*, Sahitya Akademi.
25. *Saṁskṛtasāhityetihāsa*, Śakti Prakāśana, Ludhiana, 1951.
26. *MD*, verse 47.
27. *MD*, Sahitya Akademi.
28. *Pavanadūta* of Dhoyī.

2

Definition of *Kāvya* and its Scope

DEFINING a thing is always a difficult task. Definition means "marking the outlines or characteristics of a concept or a thing" (Johnson's Dictionary) "the setting of bounds, limitations; a precise statement of the essential nature of a thing" (Oxford Dictionary). "A Clear statement about a thing on account of its exact limit or nature" (Webster Dictionary). Precisely a definition of any concept is expected, firstly to cover all that which distinguishes it from dissimilar things, belonging as it does to a class; and then to cover all that which distinguishes it from similar things of its own class. Sanskrit logicians use the word *lakṣaṇa* for definition. A logically correct definition has to avoid the three faults *avyāpti* (too narrow application), *ativyāpti* (too wide application) and *asambhava* (impossibility). No literary critic will be so very careless as to have *asambhava* in his definition of a literary concept; but he is often unknowingly involved in the faults of *avyāpti* and *ativyāpti*.

Scope of *Kāvya*

Now the term *kāvya* has a very wide connotation in Sanskrit. It is not confined to metrical form only. As Dr. S.K. De[1] puts it "But both theory and practice make *kāvya* extensive enough to comprehend in its scope any literary work of imagination and refuse to recognise metre as essential. It, therefore, includes poetry, drama, prose-romance, folk-tale, didactic fable, historical writing, philosophical verses, religious and gnomic stanzas; in fact every branch of literature, which may be contained within the domination of belles-letters in the widest sense, to the exclusion of whatever is purely technical or occasional." Defining such extensive *kāvya*, i.e., literature, is naturally a very difficult task.

Definitions by Different Indian Critics

Yet Sanskrit critics have tried their hands at this definition, each defining *kāvya* in his own way, Bharata (about 3rd century A.D.), the earliest of Sanskrit critics was concerned with the theatrical aspect of Sanskrit drama. Hence he has not defined *kāvya*. He calls[2] story-element 'the body of the dramatic script'. *Itivṛttam tu kāvyasya śarīram parikīrtitam.* Obviously the implication seems to be that *rasa* the aesthetic pleasure is the essence of *kāvya*.

Bhāmaha (last quarter of the 7th century A.D. and 1st quarter of the 8th century A.D.) the earliest of the critics of *kāvya*, defines[3] *kāvya* in his *Kāvyālaṅkāra* as follows:

Śabdārthau sahitau kāvyam, "Literature is the harmonious association of word and sense." It is obvious that literature is made up of words that form its essential element. These words that form literature must naturally possess some sense. They must be meaningful words. Later on Bhāmaha has been stamped as 'as exponent of the *Alaṅkāra*-School'; but in his treatise he does not say anything precisely about his concept of *alaṅkāra*.

Daṇḍin (end of the 8th century A.D.); knows that *śabda* and *artha* which constitute literature are no better than its body, the external form and not its real essence. Though he could not locate the soul of literature he clearly says,[4] *śarīram tāvadiṣṭārtha-vyavacchinnā padāvalī.* According to him the words in literature are *iṣṭārthavyavacchinna,* i.e., 'yielding the meaning intended by the poet'. His commentator Taruṇa Vācaspati explains *iṣṭārtha* as *kavivivakṣitārtha.*

Some scholars feel that *iṣṭārtha* of Daṇḍin is the same as *ramaṇīyārtha* of Jagannātha.

Udbhaṭa (end of the 8th century A.D. and beginning of the 9th century A.D.) does not give a definition of *kāvya* in his *Kāvyalaṅkāra.* Because of his treatment of the *alaṅkāras* it seems that *alaṅkaraṇa* is the most important aspect of *kāvya* according to him.

All these earlier critics are now referred to as 'belonging to the *Alaṅkāra*-school'. However it does not mean that according to them the figures of speech like *Upamā, Rūpaka, Utprekṣā* formed the essence of *kāvya*. Probably by the word *alaṅkāra* they understood the fundamental principle of figurative expression. It is the figurative mode of expression that distinguishes a poetic remark from an ordinary speech.

Vāmana's Views About *Kāvya*

All the earlier critics had defined *kāvya* on the basis of *śabda* and *artha*. Now Vāmana (middle of the 8th century to the middle of 9th century A.D.) for the first time explains as to what his predecessors meant by these terms. He says[5] *kāvyaśabdo'yaṁ guṇālaṅkārasaṁskṛtayoḥ, śabdārthayorvartate. Bhaktyā tu śabdārtha-mātravacano'tra gṛhyate.* "*Kāvya* means *śabda* and *artha* as refined by means of poetic merits and poetic figures. It is only figuratively that it has been described here as comprising of word and sense only." Taking a hint from Daṇḍin that *śabda* and *artha* form merely the body of poetry, he attempts to search for its soul and says, *rītirātmā kāvyasya* (*KSVI*, 2.6). By *rīti* he understands *viśiṣṭā padaracanā* (*KSVI*, 2.7). The arrangement of words must have a peculiarity, i.e., a peculiar charm according to him. The essence of this peculiar charm lies in *guṇas*, i.e., the poetic merits (*KSVI*, 2.8). Bhāmaha, Daṇḍin and Udbhaṭa dealt with the matter of *kāvya* only. It is Vāmana, who brings out the importance of 'poetic fiction' clearly.

According to him "what matters in poetry is not so much of the matter. It is the manner of expression which plays a vital role." Mr. Bradlay, the well-known critic of English Literature also says, "Matter is nothing; the form, the treatment is everything." According to Goethe also 'Style is the man'. It is to the credit of Vāmana that he had brought out the importance of 'diction' much earlier than these modern critics. However Rudraṭa (9th cent. A.D.) does not take any note of Vāmana's diction. He follows the time-honoured tendency of exalting authority and disregarding originality by repeating the definition of *kāvya,* given by Bhāmaha. Through 'diction' Vāmana draws our attention to the fact that the poet has a peculiar way of using words, though he cannot lay his finger exactly on what that peculiarity was. All the earlier critics are busy analysing the external aspects of poetry, without touching the essence. No doubt Daṇḍin had something of this in his mind when he refers to *iṣṭārtha,* i.e., *kavivivakṣitārtha.* Yet he cannot bring out clearly what the poet intends. When the critics started searching for 'the soul of poetry' it was a sort of intellectual revolution. From the reference in the *Dhvanyāloka* of Ānandavardhana, it seems that before him a few intellectuals had already started their research in this field; but the credit of giving the findings in the form of a theory rightly goes to Ānandavardhana (middle of the 9th to the middle of the 10th cent. A.D.), the author of *Dhvanyāloka.* In the beginning only he makes it clear that *dhvani,* the suggested sense has been already recognised as the soul of poetry by his learned predecessors and now he is expounding the nature of *dhvani.* He explains that this is something other than the obvious apparent meaning of the *kāvya:*

> *pratīyamānaṁ punaranyadeva vastvasti vāṇiṣu mahākavīnām yattatprasiddhāvayavātiriktaṁ vibhāti lāvaṇyamivāṅganāsu.* (I. 4)

"But the implicit is quite different from this. In the words of the first-rate poets it shines supreme and towers above the beauty of the striking external constituents even as charm in ladies" (Translation by Dr. K. Krishnamoorthy). Ānandavardhana explains that when a poet expresses some idea in words, he intends to convey through it some other additional meaning. He just suggests it. This meaning is over and above the beauty belonging to the external aspects like word, arrangement etc. just as the charm of a beautiful woman is over and above the sum-total of the beauty of her individual limbs and aspects. According to Ānandavardhana *kāvyasyātmā sa evārthaḥ* (I. 5). "It is this meaning that constitutes the soul of poety or literature." Ānandavardhana brings out the fact clearly that *kāvya* is not merely agreeable ideas which the poet intends and conveys through the power of suggestion. It is this additional intended meaning that appeals to the emotions of the readers. The poet himself feels some emotions and awakens these emotions in his readers. He produces the particular mood in the readers. The essence of poetry consists in the capacity to produce such moods. When this mood is produced the reader enjoys the *rasa* 'the aesthetic relish'. The *guṇas,* poetic merits, the *alaṅkāra,* the poetic figures, etc. are all subordinate to this.

All critics coming after Ānandavardhana are convinced about the importance of *dhvani* and *rasa,* which go to create 'beauty' in poetry. The credit of making the theory of *rasa* — an outcome of the poet's suggestive power — enchantingly popular goes to Abhinavagupta (end of the 10th century A.D.), the intellectual giant, the well-known commmentator of *Dhvanyāloka.* Abhinavagupta explained the theory in such a masterly manner that it had a very strong hold over all the later critics. e.g., Rājaśekhara (end of the 10th cent. A.D.), the author of *Kāvyamīmāmsā* makes Sarasvatī, say to her son Kāvyapuruṣa, "*Rasa* is your soul."

Now the literary critics had realised the importance of *rasa* and *dhvani;* but till now they had not taken any note of the poet's function of creating poetry, his mental condition while composing a literary piece. It is Kuntaka or Kuntala (950-1050 A.D.), who has rendered memorable service in this regard. For the first time he thinks of and discusses the creative imagination of a poet in his *Vakroktijīvita.* A striking mode of speech resulting from the creative imagination of a poet is the essence of literature according to him:

> *śabdārthau sahitau vakrakaviyaparaśālini*
> *bandhe vyavasthitau kāvyaṁ tadvidāhlādakāriṇi.* (*VJ*)

> Word and sense in a poetic composition, shining with the charm of a striking mood of a poet and delighting the minds of the aesthets, who are conversant with it, constitute *kāvya.*

This *vakrokti* striking mode of speech is a peculiar mode of speech resulting from the skill of the poet *vakroktireva vaidagdhyabhaṅgībhanitirucyate* (*VJ,* 2.11). This *vaidagdhya,* the poetic skill, is the poetic imagination. It depends upon his intuition and culture. Thus we can give Kuntala the credit of having discovered 'the poetic imagination' and can compare him to the English critic Addison.

Later critics like Bhoja (1010-55 A.D.), the author of *Sarasvatī-kaṇṭhābharaṇa* do not add anything new to the definition of literature.

Mahimabhaṭṭa (between 11th and 12th cent. A.D.), the author of *Vyaktiviveka* is an opponent of *dhvani*-theory and brings 'suggestion' under 'inference' only.

After that, Kṣemendra (11th cent. A.D.) clearly brought out the concept of 'propriety', *aucitya*, in literature in his work *Aucitya-Vicāracarcā*. Whatever is not in conformity with a particular *rasa* is stamped as *anucita* by him.

Mammaṭa's and Other Critics' Opinions

Then came Mammaṭa (11th and 12th cent. A.D.), the author of *Kāvyaprakāśa*, who proved to be a towering personality in the field of Sanskrit literary criticism. Though he did not add any new theory to this field, he was known as 'An incarnation of the goddess Sarasvatī' on account of his versatile scholarship and acumen. In his definition of poetry he tries to put together in a condensed form all that his predecessors had contributed. His oft-quoted definition runs as follows:

tadadoṣau śabdārthau saguṇavanalaṅkṛtī punaḥ kvāpi.

Poetry consists of word and sense, faultless (from the point of view of literature, grammer, logic) and possessed of poetic merits. In some cases the word and sense could be without figures of speech. Since Mammaṭa's definition touched all aspects of *kāvya* it immediately appealed to all his contemporaries and successors. His *Kāvyaprakāśa* had the honour of having numerous commentaries on it. His definition of *kāvya* was accepted and repeated by all critics like Hemacandra (11th and 12th cent. A.D.), Ruyyaka (12th cent. A.D.), Māṇikyacandra (12th cent. A.D.), Vāgbhaṭa (Senior, 12th cent. A.D.), Vāgbhaṭa (Junior, 14th cent. A.D.), Jayadeva (14th cent. A.D.) etc.

It was Viśvanātha (14th cent. A.D.), the author of *Sāhityadarpaṇa*, who first attacked the definition given by Mammaṭa. He finds fault[6] with every word in it. About *adoṣau* he feels that this will leave no scope for any *kāvya* since even the composition of master-minds do contain some defects. If *adoṣau* is taken in the sense of *alpadoṣam* an exceptional flawless *kāvya* shall cease to be a *kāvya*. *Saguṇau* according to Viśvanātha cannot go with *śabdārthau* since *guṇas* belong to *rasa* and not to word and sense. About Mammaṭa's instance of non-existence of a clear figure of speech he points out that the figure *Sandeha-Saṅkara* of *Vibhāvanā* and *Viśeṣokti* is clearly present therein. After Viśvanātha the definition was criticised by Jagannātha, (17th cent. A.D.), the author of *Rasagaṅgāndhara*.

The obvious flaw in Mammaṭa's definition of *kāvya* is that it does not refer to *rasa*, the most essential element in poetry. It is true that Mammaṭa knew the importance of *rasa* and held that *guṇas* belong to *rasa*. He has clearly said, *ye rasasyāṅigino dharmāh śauryādaya ivātmanaḥ* (*KP*, VIII. 1). Yet he has committed an error in not referring to *rasa* in his definition. Thus his definition cannot be said to be scientific and accurate; but in spite of this drawback it had a full sway on the minds of his successors. This is because "His definition has the merit of being easy and simple to understand" as Prof. A.B. Gajendragadkar says in his introduction to his edition of *Kāvyaprakāśa*, I, II, III & X.

Dr. K. Krishnamoorthy calls Mammaṭa's definition as 'serviceable'. Viśvanātha himself defines poetry as follows: *vākyaṁ rasātmakaṁ kāvyam* (*SD*, 1). The definition is quite short; but since the concept of *rasa* is too subtle it is very difficult for a layman. Moreover if *rasa* is the only criterion for judging a literary piece as *kāvya* or *akāvya* a heart-captivating realistic description of a thing or a situation shall have to be discarded as *akāvya* since it contains no *rasa*.

Jagannātha's definition *ramaṇīyārthapratipādakaḥ śabdaḥ kāvyam* is also difficult to understand. He explains *ramaṇīyatā* as *lokottarāhlādajanakajñānagocaratā*. Thus *ramaṇīya* according to him "is that which leads to a sensation producing extraordinary joy." He calls this extraordinary joy as *camatkāra*. He himself discusses his definition in details and comes to the conclusion that words in poetry yield some supra-mundane sensations of indescribable artistic delight.

Thus after Ānandavardhana, every critic is convinced of the fact that *rasa,* through *dhvani* is the essence of *kāvya;* but each one clothes his definition of *kāvya* in a different garb according to his own liking. MM. Dr.P.V. Kane[7] rightly comments upon all these definitions as follows: "Numerous definitions of *kāvya* have been offered by several writers. Many of these definitions are affected by the author's own view about the essence of poetry. Some of the definitions are no more than mere descriptions. The definitions of a few writers, particularly early ones treat *śabda* and *artha* as equally prominent, while others give more prominence to *śabda.* Some give a definition, which is more difficult than the thing to be defined (such as that of Viśvanātha."

About the attempts of these critics at a precise definition of *kāvya* Dr. S.K. De also has remarked[8], "They succeed less often than getting themselves involved in hopeless inconsistencies."

Dr. K. Krishnamoorthy[9] has put this more aptly as "with the utmost subtlety and hair-splitting distinctions, every rhetorician has come forward to justify his own definition of poetry and to reject the definitions of others."

Some Outstanding Western Critic's Views

One can cast a glance on the attempts made by the Western critics in defining poetry or literature. Hudson[10] and Entwistle[11] have discussed the various definitions of poetry as put forth by well-known Western critics. Wordsworth's definition is quite well-known, "Poetry is the spontaneous overflow of the powerful emotions of human heart. It takes its origin from or it is emotion in tranquillity." "It is the image of man and nature." John Stuart Mill calls poetry "Impassioned truth". According to Lasceles Aber Crombie "Poetry consists of words, which can transport the experience alive into our minds and make it veritably our experience as well as the poet's; and this experience confers immediate delight."

Shelley understands poetry to be "expression of imagination." According to Johnson "Poetry is the art of uniting pleasure with truth, by calling imagination to the help of reason."

For Carlyle it is 'musical thought', while for Edgar Alen Poe it is 'rhythmical creation of beauty'.

Mathew Arnold defines poetry as "a criticism of life under the conditions fixed for such a criticism, by the laws of poetic truth and poetic beauty."

Mecalay says, "A poet produces an illusion. He does by means of words what a painter does by means of colours." According to Coleridge poetry is "an antithesis of science, having for its object pleasure, not truth."

Having discussed these definitions Hudson concludes, "Poetry interprets life through imagination and feeling."

Entwistle comments upon this variety of definitions as: "Many of them are arresting and significant; not one is completely satisfactory and taken together they are apt to be bewildering." On the basis of these definitions he has to make the following comment upon 'poetry':

> "Poetry is an art, primarily connected with human experiences of universal character. Since they are enriched with imagination, they are capable of arousing emotion and the readers."

In his *Principles of Criticism* William Worsfold takes historical survey, as to which aspect of poetry was brought to light by a particular critic, as follows:

> "Plato pointed out the inter-dependence of art and morality. Aristotle identified creative literature with fine arts and traced both to the primitive tendency of imitation. It was Addison, who introduced the importance of imagination in literature and art. He has analysed how the faculty of imagination works in the poet's mind and appeals to the imagination of the reader. Lessing points out how the worldly material is modified by an artist or a poet so as to suit his artistic need. According to Meridith the art of pen consists in arousing the inward vision."

Conclusion

This survey of the definitions of poetry given by the Eastern and

Western critics makes it perfectly clear that giving a definition of *kāvya* is a very difficult task. This difficulty is inherent in the problem itself. Theoretically, a definition is expected to be very appropriate and accurate; but, in practice, it become as vague and loose as possible. Generally a chapter on 'the definition of poetry' closes not with a definition, but with an enumeration of all that poetry uses and expresses. Let us also close this discussion of the definition of *kāvya* on similar lines.

Poetry is an art, producing aesthetic delight. The poet feels an emotion and awakens its reflection in the mind of the readers. "By poetic imagination the poet invades the individual empires of the appreciative readers. Because of rich power of suggestion a good poet enables us to overhear his own emotions" as Dr. T.G. Mainkar[12] has put it. According to Hudson "The poet appeals directly to the poet in ourselves." That is why Dr. Mainkar says, "The dialogue of the two minds is the aim and fulfilment of all poetry and literature."

For this the poet uses the ordinary situations of practical life and endows them with charm by using various devices. He interprets the situations with his imagination and feelings. While using the material the poet dissociates it from individual connection. In other words he idealises the situation. This is what Mill called 'impassioned truth'. Sanskrit critics called it *sādhāraṇīkaraṇa*. It was Bhaṭṭanāyaka who used this concept, though he did not name it. Later Abhinavagupta formulated it as the theory of *śādhāraṇīkaraṇa*.

It is with all such devices that a poet gives us his 'creative literature'. Dr. K. Krishnamoorthy[13] points out that creative literature is an amalgam of the imaginative, emotional, intellectual and artistic elements.

References

1 *History of Sanskrit Literature (Classical Period)*, p. 42, S.N. Desgupta and S.K. De, University of Calcutta, 1964.

2. *Nāṭyaśāstra*, XXI.1.

3. *Kāvyālaṅkāra*, I.16.

4. *Kāvyādarśa*, I.10.

5. *Kāvyālaṅkārasūtravṛtti* — *Vṛtti on Sūtra*, I.1.1.

6. *Sāhitya-darpaṇa*, pp. 6-15, Nirnaya-sagara Press, Bombay, 1910.

7. *Introduction to the edition of the Sāhityadarpaṇa*, 1, II & X, p. 338, 1951.
8. *History of Sanskrit Poetics*, Calcutta, 1960. Volume II, p. 217.
9. *Essays in Sanskrit Criticism*, p. 223, Karnatak University, Dharwar, 1964.
10. *Introduction to the study of Literature.*
11. *The study of Poetry.*
12. Dr. Mainkar's paper in *The Proceedings of A Seminar on Indian Poetics*, University of Delhi.
13. *Essays in Sanskrit Literary Criticism*, p. 229.

3

The Goddess Sarasvatī in Sanskrit Literature

SARASVATĪ is honoured as the goddess of learning. In schools and centres of learning she is invoked at the beginning of functions. In some schools even the daily routine begins with her invocation:

> *yā kundendutuṣārahāradhavalā yā śubhravastrāvṛtā*
> *yā vīṇāvaradaṇḍamaṇḍitakarā yā śvetapadmāsanā,*
> *yā brahmācyutaśaṅkaraprabhṛtibhirdevaiḥ sadā vanditā*
> *sā mām pātu sarasvatī bhagavatī niḥśeṣajāḍyāpahā.*

It will be interesting to study the history of this goddess in Sanskrit Literature.

Sarasvatī in the *ṚV*

In the *ṚV,* Sarasvatī was a holy river, forming along with Dṛśadvatī, the boundaries of Brahmāvarta, the seat of ancient Indian culture. Rivers, like all other forces of nature, were deities for the *Vedic* Āryans. Among them Sarasvatī, on whose banks they held many a sacrificial session, and by whose margin they developed their Āryan culture, was particularly sacred to them. They call her *ambītamā* (the best of mothers), *nadītamā* (the best of rivers) etc. They invoked her in their hymns and sought her favours in all their undertakings. The *Sūtkas* sometimes invoke her as a deity, with a slight reference to her being a river, while on other occasions they are transparent enough to depict the river through their words. In *Nirukta*, II.23 Yāska says, *sarasvatī tyetasya nadīvaddevatāvacca nigamā bhavanti*. Sāyaṇa in his *Ṛgbhāṣya* very often remarks: *dvividhā hi sarasvatī vigrahavaddevatā nadīrūpa ca.*

As Dr. Muir[1] has said, "Once the river had acquired a divine character, it was quite natural that she should be regarded as the patroness of the ceremonies which were celebrated on the margin of her holy waters, and that her direction and blessing should be invoked as essential to their performance and success." Thus in the *ṚV*, Sarasvatī is a *nadīdevatā*. In the *Āprī*-hymns she is invoked along with Iḷā and Mahī or Bhāratī "Her position as *Vāk* finds no mention in the *ṚV*, but is recognised by the *Brāhmaṇas* and the *Mahābhārata*," says Mr. Dowson[2] in his *Hindu Classical Dictionary*. While Mr. Purani in his article on Sarasvatī holds the opinion that the word is used in the sense of abstract ideas like speech and not in the sense of physical river. Shri. Coomaraswamy[3] lays down that Sarasvatī is the mythical river of life, over which a bridge has been constructed by the *Pañcajanāḥ*, joining 'the dark world' with 'the light world'. According to Mr. Donald Mackenzie,[4] "Sarasvatī is the spirit of the river Sarasvatī, and was probably identified with Bhāratī, the goddess of the *Vedic* Bharata-tribe." Nature of Sarasvatī as a river is obvious in the *ṚV*. About her position as *Vāk*, it is true that she has never been invoked as the presiding deity of speech. Still it is worthnoting that even in the *ṚV* she has been intimately connected with speech and intellect, and has been invoked to stimulate good words of the seers and to guard their good thoughts and intellect, e.g.

I.13.11	*codayitrī sūnṛtānām cetantī sumatīnām*
II.3.8	*sarasvatī sādhayantī dhīyaṁ naḥ*
VI.61.4	*pra ṇo devī sarasvatī dhīnāmavitryavatu*
VII.35.11	*śam sarasvatī saha dhībhirastu*
X.65.13	*sarasvatī saha dhībhiḥ purandhyā*

Thus Sarasvatī's position as goddess of learning finds traces even in the *ṚV*. In the period of *Brāhmaṇas*, Sarasvatī was identified with *Vāk*, the deity of speech. *Nighaṇṭu* mentions Sarasvatī in *saptapañcāśat vāṅnāmani* as also in *saptaviṁśatiḥ nadīnāmāni*. Sāyaṇa, in his commentary, often calls her *Vāgdevatā* describing her as *sarvaviṣayagatā-vāk, mādhyamikā vāk* etc. In the *Brāhmaṇa* period she was identified with *Vāk*, the source of the universe, according to *ṚV*, X. 125. Dr. Muir[5] justifies Sarasvatī's connection with knowledge as follows:

> "The connection into which she was thus brought with sacred rites (as the patroness) may have led to the further step of imagining her to have an influence on the composition of the hymns, which have formed so important a part of the proceedings, and of identifying her with *Vāk*, the goddess of speech."

Professor A.B. Keith points out a brāhmaṇic legend as explaining Sarasvatī's connection with *Vāk* and learning. When Indra resorted to *Sautrāmaṇi* rite to be cured from the evil effects of drinking, Sarasvatī along with the Aśvins helped him. This scholar says,[6] "The fact that her instrument was speech, seems to have given rise to her identity with *Vāk*, as asserted by the *Brāhmaṇas*, as well as to her elevation to the rank of goddess of learning and culture". In fact intellectual progress and cultural advances are possible only in a settled society. For the wandering Āryans such a settlement was possible for the first time on the soil of Brahmāvarta. No wonder then, if they had given the credit of their cultural progress to this river, right from the beginning. Incidently it can be noted that the goddess Chalchiuhtlique (the goddess of jewelled water) of Pre-Columbian America was a goddess of waters, the Mother-goddess and culture-deity as well. However traces of *Vidyādevatā* are not very clearly seen in the Sarasvatī of the *ṚV*.

Sarasvatī as the Goddess of Learning in the Post-*Vedic* Literature

Once the *Brāhmaṇas* had identified Sarasvatī with *Vāgdevatā*, her identification with *Vidyādevatā* followed as a natural corollary.

Hence in the epics and *Purāṇas* her position as *Vidyādevatā* was firmly fixed and we find a detailed and poetic description of hers in these works. In *Bṛhaddharmapurāṇa,* Brahmā advises Sarasvatī to stay in his four mouths and in the mouths of the poets. She is described as staying in Vālmīki's mouth at the time of the *Krauñca*-incident. Pāṇini and Śākaṭāyana are described as wearing *Sarasvatīkavaca* while composing their works. An anec- dote is narrated that once Yājñavalkya lost his learning due to a curse. He then regained it by worshipping and glorifying Sarasvatī.

The *Purāṇas* give details about Sarasvatī-Pūjā. According to the *Devī-bhāgavata* this *pūjā* is performed on the fifth day of the bright half of *Māgha,* i.e., on the *Vasanta-pañcamī* day or at the beginning of a course. By the by it can be noted that the festival of the goddess Carmenta of Rome, who is credited with the invention of arts and sciences, is held five days after the spring-feast. In some provinces in India this *pūjā* is performed in the month of *Āśvina,* while in some other places on the first day of *Caitra.* The Jains worship books and writing material on the *Nāṇapañcamī* day, i.e., the fifth day of *Śrāvaṇa.* This too is a form of Sarasvatī-*pūjā.* Sārasvata, the son of Sarasvatī and the sage Dadhīca has been referred to in the *Mahābhārata* and the *Purāṇas* as having spread the *Vedic* learning. The *Brahmāṇḍa Purāṇa* gives a story that during a long-spread drought all sages were reduced to pathetic condition because of hunger, and hence study of the *Vedas* was neglected. Sārasvata sustained himself on fish and preserved the entire *Vedic* learning. Later he imparted it to all the *brāhmaṇas.*

This is found in the *Vanaparvan* of the *Mahābhārata* also. "This legend" says Professor Wilson,[7] "appears to indicate the revival or the introduction of the Hindu ritual by the race of *Brāhmaṇas,* or the people called *Sārasvatas,* who dwelt near the river Sarasvatī." In the Harṣacarita, Chapter I, Bāṇa has described Sarasvatī's union with the sage Dadhīca and then the birth of their son Sārasvata, who was a repository of *Vedic* lores. In classical Sanskrit literature Sarasvatī is the only goddess of learning and many verses of classical poets glorify her as such.

Description of Sarasvatī in the Post-*Vedic* Literature

Sarasvatī, the goddess of learning, wisdom and eloquence, the mother of the *Vedas* and the inventor of letters and script, has been described in details in Sanskrit literature. These details can be analysed as follows:

1. *Fair Complexion* — Sarasvatī is very fair in complexion. She is *kundendutuṣārahāradhavalā* (as fair as the *Kunda* flower, the moon and a necklace of frost). *Devībhāgavata-purāṇa* and *Bṛhaddharma-purāṇa* describe her as *suklavarṇā*. *Sāmba-purāṇa* calls her *Mahāśvetā*. This trait can be traced to the river Sarasvatī, whose bright white waters have been described in the *ṚV*, e.g., *Śuci* (VII 95, 2) *Vardha śukre* (VIII 95, 6).

2. *White Dress* — She is *śubhravastrāvṛtā* (clad in white garment). This too is in keeping with the bright white water of the river Sarasvatī.

3. *White Lotus Seat* — She is *śvetapadmāsanā* (sitting on a white-lotus). The white colour of the lotus indicates that this too is a trait of the white water of the river Sarasvatī. Further, lotus is very popular in India and in the Buddhist Mythology. It is the seat of Brahmā, Lakṣmī and Sarasvatī. In the Buddhist mythology it is closely associated with Gautama Buddha. Professor M. Williams[8] explains the symbolism of a lotus as: "Its constant use as an emblem seems to result from the wheel-like form of the flower, the petals taking the place of spokes, and thus typifying the doctrine of perpetual cycle of existence or from the idea that its expanded flower, reposing on a calm mirror-like lake is a fit emblem of *Nirvāṇa*."

4. *The Lute in Her Hand* — Sarasvatī is *vīṇāvaradaṇḍamaṇḍita-karā* (having her hand adorned by the staff of an excellent lute). In the *Devībhāgavata* also she is *vīṇāpustakadhāriṇī*. According to the *Bṛhaddharma-purāṇa* Sarasvatī laughed at Nārada when he committed mistakes in music. This seems to be an influence of Bāṇa's *Harṣacarita*, Chapter I. There the irritable sage Durvāsas commits mistakes in *Sāmagāna*. Sarasvatī, the young daughter of Brahmadeva laughs at him and consequently is cursed by him. Thus Sarasvatī, is supposed to be adept in the art of music, especially instrumental music. In Roman Mythology also, Athene, the goddess of wisdom and arts, has been described as

the inventor of Flute. Thus according to popular mythology knowledge and music seem to be intimately connected. One who is dedicated to the cause of knowledge is like a minstrel moving from door to door. That is why this *Vidyādevatā* is equipped with a lute. Sometimes, Sarasvatī is described as a *tapasvinī*, moving the *sphāṭikyākṣamālā*, the rosary of crystal beads.

5. *Sarasvatī's Vehicle* — The vehicle of Sarasvatī has not been described in the epics and the *Purāṇas*. Since a swan is the vehicle of Brahmadeva, Sarasvatī has been described as *haṁsavāhanā* in later *Stotra* literature. One wonders why the portraits and images of Sarasvatī depict her as riding a peacock. In Greek mythology Hera, the goddess of fertility is fond of cuckoo. Yet later paintings and images of Hera occasionally depict a peacock beside her. In Japanese mythology Sennin, the mountain-goddess is represented as riding a peacock. The connection between Sarasvatī and a peacock should be investigated further.

6. *Sarasvatī's enmity with Lakṣmī* — In popular concept Sarasvatī and Lakṣmī are inimical toward each other. Except for a few references in some later *Upapurāṇas*, this concept has no foundation. Some *Purāṇas* simply describe Lakṣmī and Sarasvatī or Bhāratī as Viṣṇu's *śaktis*. According to the *Devībhāgavata*, there once arose a quarrel among Viṣṇu's wives Lakṣmī, Sarasvatī, and Gaṅgā, during which each cursed the other two. In the *Bṛhaddharma-purāṇa*, Nārada sees Lakṣmī and Sarasvatī on two sides of Nārāyaṇa in Vaikuṇṭha. In classical Sanskrit literature their enmity is an established fact. This can be explained on the basis of common experience that wealth and learning very rarely go together. Kālidāsa refers to the enmity of Lakṣmī and Sarasvatī in *Raghuvaṁśa*, VI. 29 and *Vikramorvaśīya*, V. 24. Many other works like the *Kathāsaritsāgara* of Somadeva and *Rājataraṅgiṇī* of Kalhaṇa allude to this concept.

Metaphysical Aspect of Sarasvatī

During the spread of the cult of *Śakti* (Mother goddess) every goddess was elevated to the position of the Mother-goddess, i.e., the power of creation with feminine aspect. Like other female deities Sarasvatī also was identified with Durgā, the female counterpart of the creator of the world in the *Śākta-purāṇas.* The *Devīpurāṇa* identifies her with Durgā. Durgā, Lakṣmī, Sarasvatī and Rādhā are the forms of *parā-prakṛti* according to the *Bṛhaddharma-purāṇa.* In the *Bṛhadnāradīya-purāṇa,* Sarasvatī is Viṣṇu's *Śakti* and in the *Nāradīya-purāṇa* she is *aṁśāvatāra* of Rādhā. It is her identification with the Mother-goddess that justifies her description *yā brahmācyutaśaṅkara-prabhṛtibhirdevaiḥ sadā vanditā.*

Sarasvatī's Relation to Brahmā

While commenting upon *Kumārasambhava,* IV. 41. *abhilāṣamudīritendriyaḥ svasutāyāmakarot prajāpatiḥ,* Mallinatha says, *svasutāyāṁ sarasvatyām.*

This refers to an awkward incident of Brahmadeva's passion for his daughter Sarasvatī. In *Purāṇas* themselves, there seems to be a confusion about the exact relation of Sarasvatī with Brahmā. She has been described as his daughter in the *Māhābhārata,* XII, in *Matsya, Bhāgavata,* etc. while she is the wife of Brahmā according to *Brahmāṇḍa-purāṇa* and some *Upapurāṇas* like *Devībhāgavata.* According to Bāṇa she is his daughter. Professor M. Williams holds that Sarasvatī is really his daughter, his proper wife being Sāvitrī or Gāyatrī. The episode of Brahmadeva's intercourse with his daughter has been referred to in the *Purāṇas* very often, e.g., *Bhāgavata, Matsya, Kalikā,* etc., but the name of his daughter is given differently as Śatarūpā (*Bhāgavata*) Gāyatrī (*Matsya*), Sandhyā (*Kālikā*) etc. very rarely it is Sarasvatī. The origin of this episode is obviously the incident of *Prajāpati* entering into sexual intercourse with his daughter *Vāk,* as described in the *Śatapatha Brāhmaṇa,* I 7, 4 and *Aitareya Brāhmaṇa,* III.33. Some scholars trace the origin of this legend even to the *ṚV,* X 5, 61. Kumārilabhaṭṭa explains it on the basis of natural phenomenon as follows:

> *prajāpatistāvat prajāpālanādhikārādāditya evocyate. sa cāruṇavelāyamuṣasyudayanabhyeti. sā tadāgamanādevopajāyate iti tadduhitṛtvena vyapadiśyate. tasyām cāruṇakiraṇākhyabījanikṣepāt strīpuruṣasaṁyogavadupucārah.*

Thus according to him the legend is based upon the fact that the sun gives rise to the morning twilight and then spreads bright light through the twilight.

Mr. Dowson[9] explains the union of Brahmā and Sarasvatī as "Sarasvatī as wife of Brahmā and goddess of speech and wisdom, represents perhaps the union of power and intelligence, which was supposed to operate in the work of creation."

About the awkward incident of a god entering into intercourse with his own daughter or sister it must be pointed out that it is not peculiar to Indian mythology alone. A comparative study leads to the conclusion that it is common to many mythologies of the world. In Egyptian mythology Isis is wife and sister of the god Osiris. In Babylonian mythology Tammuz enters into union with his mother Ishtar. In Greek mythology Adonis enjoys with his daughter Aphoridite. Mr. Donald Mackenzie[10] offers the explanation for such legends. "The mother-goddesses were accompanied by shadowy male forms ere they became wives of strongly individualized gods, or by child-gods, their sons, who might be regarded as 'brothers' or 'husbands of their mothers' to use the paradoxical Egyptian term. Similarly great father-deities had vaguely defined wives."

Conclusion

In the *Ṛ*V, Sarasvatī was originally a river and then a river-deity. Soon she was regarded as 'the patroness of the ceremonies celebrated on the margin of her holy waters'. This led to the further step of imagining that she has an influence over the composition of the hymns recited at the sacrifices. Then her identification with *vāk*, the goddess of speech naturally followed. Though the hymns of the *ṚV* nowhere call her as *Vāgdevatā* there are sufficient traces of her intimate connection with *vāk* (speech) and *dhiḥ* (intellect). In the period of the *Brāhmaṇas*, she was identified with *vāk*, the origin of the universe according to *ṚV*, X.125.

As *vāk*, she became the mother of the *Vedas* and the goddess of learning. In the period of the epics and the *Purāṇas* her position as *Vidyādevatā* was an established fact. They even credited her son Sārasvata with the revival of the Vedic learning. These texts describe all details about Sarasvatī. She is fair in complexion, clad in white garment, sitting upon a lotus, having a swan as her vehicle, holding a lute in her hand, carrying books and moving a rosary of crystal-beads. Her association with a peacock as found in her portraits and images cannot be traced to any of these works. In the days of *Śakti*-worship she was identified with the Mother-goddess Durgā. Generally she is described as the daughter of Brahmā, only a few *Upapurāṇas* call her his wife. Many *Purāṇas* refer to Brahmā's intercourse with his daughter variously named as Śatarūpā, Sandhyā, Sāvitrī, *Vāk* and rarely as Sarasvatī.

A comparative study of the mythologies of the world shows that this absurd incident is found in many mythologies, because 'the mother deities are accompanied by shadowy male forms and great male deities have vaguely defined wives.' The *Prajāpati-vāk* legend which forms the origin of this legend in Indian mythology has been explained on the basis of natural phenomenon by Kumārilabhaṭṭa. According to Mr. Dowson it represents the union of power and intelligence.

References

1. *The Oriental Studies,* John Muir, p. 99, Ghosh and Brothers, Calcutta, 1878.
2. *Classical Dictionary of Hindu Mythology and Religion,* p. 284, Kegan Paul, Trench, TR. Buner & Co., London, 1903.
3. *The Ṛgveda as Land-Nāma-Bok,* pp. 9-12. Luzac and Co., London, 1935.
4. *Indian Myth and Legend,* p. 148, The Gresham Publishing Company, London, 1913.
5. *The Oriental Studies,* p. 99.
6. *The Mythology of All Races,* Vol. VI, p.93.
7. *Viṣṇu-Purāṇa,* p. 285, f.n. 9, John Murray, London, 1940.
8. *Buddhism,* Monier Monier-Williams, 1st Edition, 1889, 2nd Edition, p. 522, *Chowkhamba Sanskrit Studies,* Vol. XLV, 1964.
9. *Classical Dictionary,* p. 330.
10. *Indian Myth and Legend,* p. xxvi.

4

Sītā in Sanskrit Plays

MORE than twenty Sanskrit playwrights have drawn their inspiration from various episodes of the Rāmāyaṇa. While using the source-material, a Sanskrit dramatist moulds it as useful for his purpose, introducing a number of innovations and modifications. Very often the dramatic plot and the characters appear to be altogether different from the original. Now the story of the *R.* and the characters of Rāma and Sītā are too well-known to allow any glaring change. Had a dramatist tried any such thing his play would have been hooted out. Yet even in this limited scope dramatic genius and poetic insight of Sanskrit playwrights could work as many wonders as possible. Hence, a study of the character of Sītā as delineated by these dramatists is very interesting.

Views on Sītā's Birth

All *Rāmāyaṇa* plays glorify Sītā, as being born in a superhuman manner and call her *Dhariṇīsutā, Ayonijā,* etc. *MVC,* I.20. In this they are closely following the original. This incident of her birth can be traced even up to the *Ṛgveda,* IV. 57, where she appears as the deity of the field-furrow. In this capacity she has been referred to in many places in the *Vedic* literature, e.g., *AV,* XI.3; *TS,* V.2.4.6; *KS,* XX.3. In the *Adbhutādhyāya* of *Kauśikasūtra* Sītā as the genius of the ploughed field has been described as a woman of wonderful beauty and wife of Indra, i.e., the Rain-god. Curiousness about the birth of the deity of Agriculture is a feature found in other mythologies also, e.g., the Greek goddess

Athene, who is the presiding deity of many fine arts and handicrafts, is the deity of Agriculture also. She is said to have invented the plough. Her name has been explained by the modern Greek scholars as meaning, 'without mother's milk'. She has been born of Zeus without a mother. In the Attic mythology her outstanding characteristic, like that of Sītā, is the unimpeachable chasity.

The Sanskrit dramatists have dwelt upon this divine aspect of her birth very often, and have conveniently omitted all other Purāṇic versions referring to her previous births. In plays like the *URC* Sītā has been described as the daughter-in-law of Bhāgīrathī or Gaṅgā. This also suits well her nature as the ancient goddess of Fertility.

Sītā *Svayaṁvara*

The next important event in her life is the event of *svayaṁvara*. This is an episode, which is very favourite of Sanskrit playwrights. In the *R.* it is not a regular *svayaṁvara*-scene as in the case of Draupadī or Damayantī. It is a sort of challenge by Janaka — 'Whosoever is desirous of Sītā's hand must first perform the heroic feat of stringing the huge *Śivadhanu*". The test was not held on one particular day. While showing the big bow to Viśvāmitra, Janaka says, "Many brave kings have tried it till now, but none has succeeded." When the bow is split in two at Rāma's touch Janaka is highly delighted. He invites the bridegroom's party and then the four marriages take place.

The Sanskrit playwrights have joined together the scene of *dhanurbhaṅga* and the scene of *svayaṁvara*. They describe it on lines of Draupadī-*svayaṁvara*. The incident of Sīta-*svayaṁvara* forms the central topic of *Jānakī-haraṇa* of Rāmabhadra Dīkṣita. It has been described in Bhavabhūti's *MVC*, Act I; *URC*, Act I; Rājaśekhara's *Bālarāmāyaṇa*, Act I and Act III, Jayadeva's *Prasannarāghava*, Act I; Murāri's *Anargharāghava*, Act I and in many other places in Sanskrit plays. In the *Garbha-nāṭaka*, in Act III of *Bālarāmāyaṇa* Rājaśekhara has described it in imitation of Indumatī-*svayaṁvara* in Kālidāsa's *Raghuvaṁśa*, VI.

According to the *R.* at the time of marriage, Sītā was too young for amorous sentiment to peep in. But the Sanskrit dramatists are so much fond of describing love-scenes that they make Rāma and Sītā fall in love at first sight before the *Dhanurbhaṅga*. In the *Prasannarāghava*, Act II Sītā and her friends are moving about near the *Caṇḍikāyatana* in the Royal park. Rāma and Lakṣmaṇa see them and overhear their conversation. Rāma is enamoured of Sītā's charms and describes her glance as *sarvasvaṁ navayauvanasya, bhavanaṁ bhogasya, bhāgyaṃ dṛśam, rahasyaṁ śṛṅgārasya,* etc. Sītā notices Lakṣmaṇa first and observes that he is fit for Ūrmilā. Rāma and Sītā are being teased by Lakṣmaṇa and Sītā's friends respectively. Then throughout Act II and Act III, the marriage of Rāma and Sītā has been suggested. The *Anargharāghava* of Murāri has turned Sītā in a conventional *Nāyikā* of Sanskrit Love-Plays. She is possessed of the conventional feminine jealously also. In the course of Rāma's encounter with Paraśurāma, following the marriage, Murāri has described Sītā as casting a glance full of jealously with the thought *kanyā kācidihāpi karmaṇi paṇaḥ syāt*. When Paraśurāma challenges Rāma to string his *Vaiṣṇava-dhanu* she fears that the second *dhanurbhaṅga* might bring her a cowife. This conventional jealousy is ill-suited to an uncommon woman like Sītā.

In the *MVC* (Act I) also, Rāma and Sītā fall in love at first sight. Madness of the Sanskrit Playwrights for delineation of *śṛṅgāra* is carried to the extreme when they represent the villain Rāvaṇa also as an ardent and passionate lover of Sītā, e.g., in the *Bālarāmāyaṇa*, Act I Rāvaṇa describes Sītā's physical charms in the manner of a conventional lover: *sītāyāḥ purataśca hanta śikhināṁ barhāḥ sagarhā iva, nirmālyam nayanaśriyaḥ kuvalayaṁ vaktrasya dāsaḥ śaśī* etc. After his failure in stringing the bow, Rāvaṇa is shown in a loverlorn condition in Act II. In Act III he is being diverted by means of a *Garbhanāṭaka*, representing the scene of Sītā-*svayaṁvara*. During its performance he often bursts into emotion, forgetting that it is a *Prekṣaṇaka*. In Act V he is talking to a doll appearing as Sītā. In this Act, like a conventional separated lover, he goes on addressing all seasons, birds, etc. after the manner of Purūravas in the *Vikramorvaśīya,* Act IV.

This passion of Rāvaṇa for Sītā is connected to her previous life as Vedavatī in the *Uttarakāṇḍa* of the *R.* and in *Purāṇas* like *Kalikāpurāṇa, Devībhāgavata*. According to the *Ānandarāmāyaṇa*, Rāvaṇa collected five gems from the ashes of Padmākṣa's daughter, of whom he was enamoured. He handed over the box to Mandodarī. A girl was born from it and under instructions from astrologers she was left in a box at Mithilā. In the *Adhyātmarāmāyaṇa,* Sītā was actually a daughter of Mandodarī, who was left in a box near Mithilā for a similar reason. The Sanskrit dramatists refer to Rāvaṇa as a lover of Sītā and drop all these inconvenient references.

Preparing for *Vanavāsa*

After her marriage the next important event in Sītā's life is the occasion of starting for *vanavāsa* covering 14 years. Following the *R.*, where she says *vane nivatsyāmi yathā piturgṛhe tavaiva pādavupagṛhya sammatā,* all dramatists have depicted this faithful wife intent upon following Rāma, e.g., in Bhāsa's *Pratimā,* Act I she says, *tat* (*vanam*) *khalu me prasādaḥ* and is encouraged by Lakṣmaṇa, saying, *vrajatu vrajatu dharmam, bhartṛnāthā hi nāryaḥ.* In *Pratimā,* Act I Bhāsa makes her wear *valkalas* just out of jest and this serves as a suggestion of the impending *vanavāsa.* In Act VI of the *Bālarāmāyaṇa* Rājaśekhara gives a very touching picture of Sītā, as she starts for *vanavāsa.* She removes all ornaments excepting the *cūḍāmaṇi,* hands over a letter to Vāmadeva and bids farewell to the pet-birds like *cakora, mayūra, śuka,* etc. She even takes leave of the *krīḍāśaila, dolā, vilāsabhavana,* etc. saying, *eṣā vaḥ paricārikā vanabhuvaṁ rāmānugā gacchati.* After having walked three or four steps only, she inquires, *gantayamasti kiyat?* and forces tears from Rāma's eyes. In the *MVC,* Act IV Mantharā, who is Śūrpaṇakhā in disguise, brings the terrible message to Mithilā, saying that Lakṣmaṇa and Sītā have to follow Rāma in banishment. Thus, here the two have been deprived of the credit that they have always enjoyed.

Forest-Life in *Vanavāsa*

The forest-life was immensely enjoyable for Rāma and Sītā. A graphic picture of their happy life has been given in many dramas. In Act I of the *URC,* Rāma describes: *āraṇyakāśca gṛhiṇaśca ratāḥ svadharme sāṁsārikeṣu ca sukheṣu vayaṁ rasajñāḥ.* In Act III of the same play he says, *yatra drumā api mṛgā api bāndhavā me.* Sītā likes the life so much that in the *Āścarya-*

cūḍāmaṇi of Śaktibhadra she says, *āryaputra, yāvadaham jīvami tāvadihaiva vastum me buddhiḥ.* In the *BR,* Act VI, Kausalyā inquires how Sītā is faring as a house-wife. Vāmadeva describes how Sītā serves Rāma first, then Lakṣmaṇa and then sustains herself on whatever has been left over. Upon this Kausalyā remarks, *putrī sīte, mahārājarājajātayā bhūtvā kathaṁ tvayā nisargadāridragṛhinītvaṁ śikṣitam?* Even the very minor incident of the crow Dharādhara which played mischief with Sītā has been described in some places in Sanskrit plays, e.g., *BR,* Act VI, the *Anargharāghava,* Act V etc.

Sītā-haraṇa

Misfortune in the *vanavāsa* begins with the notorious Śūrpaṇakhā-incident. The Sanskrit playwrights have described it in a very interesting manner. In the *Ā.Cu.*, she appears as *lāvaṇyavatī sukumāragātrī sīmantinī.* In the course of this incident Śaktibhadra has put one remark in the mouth of Sītā, which makes her appear too timid and selfish. When Lakṣmaṇa is being tossed up by Śūrpaṇakhā, he calls for help. Sītā does not allow Rāma to go saying, *āryaputra ko mām rakṣati?*.

This leads to the most unfortunate event in their *vanavāsa,* viz., the abduction of Sītā. Vālmīki has described it graphically and the Sanskrit dramatists have elaborated it still further, e.g., *MVC,* Act IV, *Anargharāghava,* Act V; *Prasannarāghava,* Act V; *BR,* Act VI; *Ā.Cu,* Act II, *Mahānāṭaka,* Act III. It is the feminine greed for beautiful things on the part of Sītā which leads to this disaster. Most of the dramas have repeated this reason, e.g., in the *Ā.Cu.* Sītā says *āryaputra yasyodyāne'yam mṛgaḥ prativasati, tasya kimaparābhiḥ ṛddhibhiḥ?*. It is Bhāsa alone who has freed Sītā from this blemish. In Act V of his *Pratimā,* Rāvaṇa appears in the disguise of a brāhmaṇa, who has mastered several lores, *Śrāddhakalpa* being one of them. He informs Rāma, who is thinking of performing Daśaratha's annual *Śrāddha,* that on the mountain Himālaya there dwell deer of an extraordinary species, *Hiraṇyapārśva — taistarpitāḥ sutaphalaṁ pitaro labhante, hitvā jarām khamupayānti hi dīpyamānāḥ.* Rāma is desirous of going to Himālaya, when a *Hiraṇyapārśva* deer is seen outside the hut. Since Lakṣmaṇa has been sent elsewhere Rāma runs after the deer and Sītā is kidnapped by Rāvaṇa. This incident of *Sītā-haraṇa* is a very important landmark in the story of the *R.* As such it has received all poetic attention from the Sanskrit dramatists. In this regard Śaktibhadra has shown an exceptional originality. In Act II of the *Ā.Cu.*, when Rāma has gone after the *kāñcanamṛga,* Rāvaṇa and Śurpaṇakhā are seen driving in a chariot towards Rāma's hut.

A voice resembling that of Rāma calls for help and Sītā insists upon Lakṣmaṇa's going. After Lakṣmaṇa has departed there is a cry *sīte tvamapi māmupekṣase*. Sītā starts to go and now Rāvaṇa approaches her in the disguise of Rāma. Śūrpaṇakhā goes away in order to detain Rāma on the way, by assuming the disguise of Sītā. Rāvaṇa's charioteer now appears in the disguise of Lakṣmaṇa and approaches Sītā and Rāvaṇa with a chariot. He says, "Bharata is in the danger of foreign invasion. The sages have created this chariot out of their powers and have asked me to take you to Ayodhyā." None can now blame Sītā in getting into the chariot with Rāvaṇa, whom she saw as Rāma. Later in this Act we get a beautiful irony of situation when real Sītā sees real Rāma and feigned Sītā below; and real Rāma sees real Sītā and feigned Rāma above in the arieal car. Thus, Śaktibhadra has depicted the scene of *Sītā-haraṇa* in a more logical and more interesting manner. A dramatist named Bhāskara has brought in the separation of Rāma and Sītā without this incident of *Sītā-haraṇa* in his *Unmattarāghava.* This incident of *Sītā-haraṇa* has some parallels in other mythologies also, e.g., in Greek mythology Prosperine, the goddess of Vegetation, daughter of Ceres, the goddess of Agriculture, is kidnapped by Pluto, the king of the nether world. Professor A.B. Keith compares the incident of *Sitā-haraṇa* to the *Ṛgvedic* myth of theft of Indra's cows, i.e., water by Paṇis, the rain-clouds. He follows Professor Jacobi, who traces Rāma to Vedic Indra, Sītā to the Vedic deity of Agriculture and Rāvaṇa to *Vṛtra.* Professor A.B. Keith suggests that worship of Rāma and Sītā in India must have developed in a society which was mainly agricultural.

After *Sītā-haraṇa* Rāma lamented for her very piteously as described by Vālmīki. His lamentations have been graphically presented in the Sanskrit plays, *URC,* Act I and Act III; the *Kundamālā,* Act III, *Anargharāghava,* Act V; *Prasannarāghava,* Act

V; *Āścaryacūḍāmaṇi*, Act VI. In this regard Kālidāsa's description of the lemenations of *Purūravas* had become so popular that the dramatist Bhāskara has composed his *Unmattarāghava* specially for this description. In this play when Rāma goes after *kāñcanamṛga*, Sītā and her friend Madhukarikā are moving about collecting flowers. Sītā enters a grove and is lost to Madhukarikā's sight; but she finds there a beautiful fawn affectionately looking at her. On returning with the *kāñcanamṛga*, Rāma realises Sītā's loss and then he and Lakṣmaṇa carry on a mad search for Sītā. He follows her foot-prints, mistakes a *padminī* and a *latā* for her. He thinks *kokilālāpa* to be her sweet words and attacks the trees mistaking them for demons, robbing away Sītā. Finally Agastya comes there along with Sītā and explains that she had been transformed into a *hariṇi* by a curse of Durvāsas which affected every woman entering that particular grove.

Hanumat as a Messenger

As for Sītā her condition in Laṅkā is equally pathetic and it also has been described in details in the Sanskrit plays. According to the *R.* the reason why Rāvaṇa dared not touch her is a curse inflicted upon him by Rambhā; but the Sanskrit plays have attributed it to her *pātivratyamayaṁ jyotiḥ*. The incident of *Sītā-haraṇa* logically and psychologically leads to Rāma's friendship with Sugrīva, who is similarly placed. This friendship also has been described in Sanskrit plays, e.g., *Prasannarāghava*, Act V. This leads to Hanumat's visit to Laṅkā, a happy turn in the miserable life of Sītā. According to the *R.*, Hanumat introduces himself as Rāma's messenger and hands over Rāma's ring to her for recognition. Sītā feels very happy, gives her *cūḍāmaṇi* in return and also refers to some private incidents in their married life. All this has been used by the Sanskrit playwrights, adding touches of their dramatic genius and the elements of the miraculous, e.g., in the *Ā.Cu.* both the ring and the crest-jewel have miraculous powers. Their touch would reveal the demons in spite of the disguises assumed by them. In this play, in addition to the token of recognition, viz., the ring, Rāma sends a message referring to a private incident in their love-enjoyment. In Act VI, of the *Prasannarāghava,* when Hanumat arrives near the *Aśokavanikā,* Rāvaṇa is threatening Sītā, that if she does not yield to his desire he will cut off her head. He then says, "Let me have a *kapāla* to drink your blood" and he immediately gets in his hand the head of his son Akṣa, as it is cut off by Hanumat. Similarly Sītā desperately desires to catch hold of a piece of ember in her hand and finds there the ring of Rāma dropped down by Hanumat.

In the *R.,* Rāma gets the tidings of Sītā through Hanumt; but the Sanskrit playwrights have also used other interesting means for this purpose. In the *Prasannarāghava,* Act VI when Rāma and Lakṣmaṇa are moving in search of Sītā they overhear a conversation between two Vidyādharas Ratnaśekhara and Campakāpīḍa. Ratnaśekhara wants to demonstrate his magic-craft to his friend. He gives a magic show representing the events at Laṅkā. Everything from *Sītā-haraṇa* to *Laṅkādahana* is shown by him and Rāma and Lakṣmaṇa actually see all events themselves, giving a running commentary on the same. The play *Adbhuta-darpaṇa* of Madhādeva is based upon this topic only. There a magic-mirror shows the events from Aṅgada's mission to Rāma's coronation.

War Between Rāma and Rāvaṇa

The next important landmark in the history of Sītā is the unique type of battle fought between Rāma and Rāvaṇa. Throughout the war, Sītā is feeling very anxious. According to the *R.,* Rāvaṇa tries to intimidate her by showing an artificial head of Rāma and the same trick is played upon Rāma by showing *māyāmayī mṛtā sītā.* This description also has been incorporated by the Sanskrit dramatists in their dramas, e.g., in the *BR* also Rāma is shown Sītā's head, which is later on proved to be the head of *yantrasītā.*

Agnidivya of Sītā

The end of the war relieves Sītā of her agonies. Then follows an event which is well-known as the highest testimony to her exceptional chastity, viz., the event of her *Agniśuddhi.* At the end of the war Sītā is taken to Rāma by Hanumat. Unfortunately Rāma does not receive her. Sītā, clad in red garments, enters the fire and Agnideva appears bringing her in his lap. This fire-ordeal of Sītā has its miraculous element increased at the hands of Sanskrit dramatists, e.g., there is *puṣpavṛṣṭi* from the heaven as Sītā comes out safe from the fire according to the *BR* and the *Ā.Cu.* In the *Ā.Cu.*, Śaktibhadra gives a more convicting reason for the non-acceptance of Sītā by Rāma. When Sītā approaches Rāma she does not appear like a *virahiṇī*. Contrary to Rāma's expectation, she is richly adorned with a dress fit for *sambhoga-śṛṅgāra*. He expresses his doubt to Lakṣmaṇa, Hanumat and others. When Lakṣmaṇa reports that she is entering the fire, Rāma says that it is quite reasonable. After her *Agniśuddhi* he explains to her the reason for the non-acceptance and then she reminds him of a boon formerly conferred upon her by Anasūyā, viz., *vanavāsamalināyāstava bhartṛsamīpe sarvaṁ maṇḍanaṁ bhaviṣyati*.

This *Agnidivya* of Sītā can probably be a poetic interpretation of the baking of agriculutral land before monsoon, and can go back to the *Ṛgvedic* Sītā, the deity of Agriculture and Fertility. Sītā being handed over to Rāma by Agnideva is ingeniously connected by some *Purāṇas* to the incident of her kidnapping, e.g., according to the *Devībhāgavata* and the *Kūrmapurāṇa*, when Rāma and Sītā were staying in the forest, one day Agnideva came and took away the real Sītā with him, placing her replica as a substitute. Agnideva promised that he would return the real Sītā at the proper time.

Sītā's Separation from Rāma

After their return to Ayodhyā, Rāma and Sītā are leading a very happy life, but, unfortunately, another round of Sītā's sufferings begins. Sītā cheerfully expresses her pregnancy-desire to visit the forests on the bank of Gaṅgā once again, and fate fulfils her desire only through an irony. The subjects of Ayodhyā are not approving of Rāma's acceptance of Sītā. The king Rāma wants to set up an ideal example of behaviour before them and orders Lakṣmaṇa to leave Sītā in the forest. The king Rāma has done this but the husband Rāma suffers tremendous mental torture. Rāma's miserable plight has been vividly described in Bhavabhūti's *URC*, Acts II and III and in Diṅnāga's *Kundamālā*,

Act III. He rightly says in the *URC*, *duḥkhasaṁvedanāyaiva rāme caitanyamāhitam*. These two plays have also given a very touching picture of the agonies of Sītā during this second separation. Bhavabhūti describes her as *karuṇasya mūrtirathavā śarīriṇī virahavyatheva*. In the *URC* she has been separated from her sons also, for they are being brought up in the *Vālmīkyāśrama* while she is staying with Bhāgīrathī. This makes her picture all the more pathetic. In the *Kundamālā*, Act II she is in a desperate mood and is thinking of ending her life; but even at this stage she is full of affection for Rāma. He is not *parakīya* for her. Vedavatī points out that very soon she may have a cowife, for Rāma would require a *sahadharmacāriṇī* for his *yajña*. Even then this *pativratā* retorts, *āryaputrasya hṛdaye prabhavāmi, na haste*. However, this human heroine of the *Kundamālā* sometimes loses the balance of her mind and blames Rāma for his cruel action. In Act I she says, *āryaputra, na yuktaṁ tava niraparādham janam sapadi hṛdayāt nirvāsayitum, kiṁ punarviṣayāt*. Whenever Kuśa and Lava annoy her with their mischief she calls them *niranukrośasya putrau* but when she actually sees Rāma after 10 years her heart forgets all that and she is more than once tempted to reveal herself. In both these plays in Act III Rāma and Sītā are brought together after a long period, and Sītā remains invisible to Rāma. In the *URC* it is due to the favour of Gaṅgā and in the *Kundamālā* due to a boon of Vālmīki. The sight of Rāma after a long time arouses a mixture of feelings in Sītā's heart. *Dṛṣṭa iti paritoṣaḥ cirapravāsa iti manyuḥ, ciraparicita ityanurāgaḥ*. etc. Similar are the feelings expressed by Sītā in the *URC*, III. 23. In both the plays Rāma falls in a swoon and invisible Sītā revives him. In the *Kundamāla*, Rāma actually sees her reflection in water once, and snatches away her *uttarīya*, which was formerly *dyute paṇaḥ, praṇayakeliṣu kaṇṭhapāśaḥ, krīḍāpariśramaharaṁ vyajanaṁ vanānte* and *śayyā niśīthakalahe*. In both the plays the reunion of Rāma and Sītā and recognition of Kuśa and Lava take place gradually step by step. In the *URC* the fight between Lava and Candraketu forms the first step, while in the *Kundamālā* the garland of Jasmine-flowers offered by Sītā to Gaṅgā — that being her daily practice since the birth of Kuśa and Lava — forms the first step. In the *Kundamālā*, Vālmīki takes Rāma to task for having abandoned Sītā only because of *janāpavāda*. He says, *bho rājan, dhṛtasauhārda, samīkṣyakārin, kim yuktaṁ tava bhāvitaśudhim vibhāvasvā, duhitaram bhagavatyā viśvaṁbharāyāḥ janāpavāda-mātraśravaṇena nirākartum?*. In the *URC* Rāma has abandoned Sītā for *lokānuranjana*. Here also we feel that *loka* should not mean 'gossip-enjoying irresponsible people'. It must mean 'cultured responsible persons' or 'the well-established social standards'.

After the recognition of Kuśa and Lava in the *R.*, Rāma suggests that Sītā should declare her chastity on oath. Upon this Sītā addresses her touching prayer to Mother Earth as:

> *yathāham rāghavadanyam manasāpi na cintaye,*
> *tathā me mādhavī devī vivaraṁ dātumarhati.*

Dharaṇīdevī now appears with a brilliant throne, seats Sītā upon it and disappears with her. Rāma keeps on looking desperately.

Now in the *Kundamālā* and in the *URC* this tragic end has been changed to a happy one. Sītā is presented to Rāma by Bhāgīrathī in the *URC* and by *Pṛthivī* in the *Kundamālā*. This is in keeping with the conventions of a Sanskrit drama, according to which a *Nāṭaka* should represent the success of the hero in all fields. It is because of this happy end that Bhavabhūti and Diṅnāga had to introduce an innovation in their plays and to bring about a meeting of Rāma and Sītā and to make Sītā actually witness the pathetic condition of Rāma. For the final reunion such an assurance of Rāma's love for Sītā was absolutely essential. That is why Bhavabhūti brings Rāma to Pañcavaṭī by introducing the incident of Śambūka's penance; and Diṅnāga brings Rāma to Naimiṣāraṇya for the performance of *Aśvamedha yajña*.

Conclusion

Thus, from the simple innocent Sītā of Vālmīki the Sanskrit playwrights have produced a very appealing portrait of Sītā. While doing this they have been guided by the conventionalities of a Sanskrit *Nāṭaka*, viz., it must have *śṛṅgāra* or *vīra* as the principal sentiment, and must in addition depict all other *Rasas*. *Adbhutarasa* must be used especially towards the end. *Nāṭaka* must depict the prosperity of the hero in all fields.

In order to display their skill in the delineation of characters they have humanised Sītā as much as possible.

For the sake of having a good stage-effect they have introduced many marvelous scenes in the plays.

5

Poetic Conventions in Sanskrit Literature

apāre[1] *kāvyasaṁsāre kavirekaḥ prajāpatiḥ,*
yathāsmai rocate viśvam tathaitat parivartate.

THIS is true of all poets in all languages. In Sanskrit literature the poets have often created a world of their own and have set up some common matters, which cannot be found in the ordinary creation of Brahmā. These are technically known as *kavisamayas* or *kavisaṅketas.* A poet would use in his composition an idea, absolutely unknown to the world of reality. It might appeal to another poet, who repeats it. A critic who comes across the use of such an idea again and again would appreciate it and recommend its employment by other poets. That is how these conventions creep in literature. Sanskrit literature is very rich in these poetic conventions.

Origin and Development

As noted above, *kavisamayas* are first introduced by the poets and then regularised by the critics. The theory follows the practice. In Sanskrit literature it is Rājaśekhara *(Rā)* (9th cent.-10th cent. A.D.) who used the expression *kavisamaya* for the first time and dealt with the poetic conventions in details in his *Kāvyamīmāṁsā.* While introducing the topic he mentions a view of some predecessor-critics who take an objection to the use of such conventions in literature. It is thus obvious that before *Rā* some critics had already given some thought to this topic. The well-known critics preceding *Rā* like Bhāmaha, Daṇḍin, Vāmana, Rudraṭa, Udbhaṭa have not discussed this topic, but early poets had used the conventions in their works.

(1) Aśvaghoṣa has used the *kavisamaya* about *sarojas* blooming during day only and *kumudas* during night only, e.g., *Buddhacarita,* I.8. He refers to the Udayagiri in the Eastern quarter and the *Astācala* in the Western quarter. He describes the God of Love as *puṣpaśara* and *pañcabāṇa.* He refers to the *cakravāka* pair as a symbol of ardent passion, e.g., *Saundarānanda,* IV. 2.

(2) In the course of his 13 plays Bhāsa has used the following *kavisaṅketas* — *kumuda* blooming at night (*Avimāraka,* II), *Cakravāka* pair as a symbol of ardent love (*Svapna,* I) and their separation at night (*Svapna,* III), Malaya as the home of sandal (*Avimāraka,* IV). He describes glory as white and love as red and also refers to the Rising mountain and the Setting mountain.

(3) Kālidāsa is very much fond of these conventions. His works are full of them, e.g., the sun causing the day-lotuses to bloom and the moon the night-lotuses (*Śā,* V.28), *kalahaṁsas* going to the Manasa lake during the rainy season (*Megha,* II). *cakravākas* as symbol of sexual love and their separation at evening (*Śā,* IV, *Raghu,* III.24), *cātaka* begging of a cloud (*Raghu,* V.17), a female crane conceiving merely on hearing the thunder of the cloud (*Megha,* 9), a swan separating water from milk (*Śā,* VI), *Candrakāntamaṇi,* the Lunar gem oozing at the touch of the rays of the moon (*Megha,* 67) and *Sūryakāntamaṇi* burning when touched by the rays of the sun (*Śā,* II), a female cuckoo getting her eggs hatched by a female crow (*Śā,* V), *Gandhadvīpa* scaring away the elephants by means of the fragrance of its ichor (*Vi,* IV 18), an owl being afraid of the light of the sun (*Ku,* I.12), throbbing of the left eye in the case of women or the right eye in the case of men as an auspicious omen, (*Śā,* I and VII, *Megha,* 92). The use of common conventions like glory, smile and laughter being white, love and wrath being red etc., are naturally present in Kālidāsa's works. He has also used some interesting pregnancy-longings, *Dohadas* in connection with the *Aśoka* tree and the *Bakula* tree. The first desires to be kicked with the left foot of a beautiful woman (*Megha,* 75, *Mālavikā,* III) and the other

desires to be sprinkled over with a mouthful of wine by her (*Megha*, 75).

The two *Mahākāvyas* of Kālidāsa served as models for later writers of *Mahākāvyas.* Hence the things described by him were repeated by later poets. The *kavisaṅketas* used by Kālidāsa were also utilised in (4) Bhāravi's *Kirātārjunīya* (5) Māgha's *Śiśupāla-vadha* (6) The plays of Śrīharṣa and (7) *Kādambarī* and *Harṣacarita* of Bāṇabhaṭṭa.

Kāvyadoṣas and the Poetic Conventions

Now the use of *Kavisamayas* by the early poets like Aśvaghoṣa, Bhāsa and Kālidāsa was definitely known to the early critics like Bhāmaha and Daṇḍin; but as already observed they have not dealt with this topic. Though they have not discussed the *kavisamayas* they seem to have taken a note of these conventions in an indirect manner. This can be seen from their treatment of *kāvyadoṣas,* the defects of poetry.

(1) Bharata (about 3rd cent. A.D.) in his *Nāṭyaśāstra* has mentioned a defect *nyāyādapeta,* (illogical), which Abhinava-gupta divides in two types (i) *deśakālaviruddha* — That which involves contradiction of place or time, and (ii) *kalāśāstraviruddha* — That which involves contradiction of fine arts or technical sciences.

(2) Bhāmaha (7th cent. A.D.) in chapter I of his *Kāvyālaṅkāra* mentions a defect *ayuktimat* (that which does not stand the test of reason). In chapter IV he discusses *kāvyadoṣas* in detial. Here he mentions a defect *prasiddhiviruddha* (contrary to the established tradition). He divides it as (i) *kālaviruddha,* (ii) *deśa-viruddha,* (iii) *lokaviruddha,* (iv) *nyāyaviruddha,* and (v) *āgama-viruddha.*

He illustrates *deśaviruddha* by the mention of *Devadāru* trees on the mountain Malaya, implying that Malaya is the home of *candana.* His instance of *Kālaviruddha* describes the mango trees as blossoming in the rainy season. His instances of *lokaviruddha* are simply cases of excessive exaggeration.

(3) Daṇḍin (7th cent. A.D.) has discussed *kāvyadoṣas* in the fourth *pariccheda* of his *Kāvyādarśa.* Among the 10 defects he discusses *deśavirodha, kālavirodha, lokavirodha, nyāyavirodha* and

āgamavirodha. He illustrates *deśavirodha* with a verse describing Kāverī in *cola, candana* trees on the banks of Kāverī, camphor in, Malaya and elephants born in Kaliṅga. Coming to *kālavirodha* he illustrates it by the mention of *Padminī* blooming at evening and *kumudvatī* during day, *Nicula* trees blooming in the spring and there being *durdina* in *Grīṣma,* cackling of swans in the rainy season and peacock-dance in the autumn, clear sun-shine in *Hemantā* and use of sandal paste in winter.

(4) Vāmana (about 800 A.D.) discusses in his *Kāvyālaṅkāra-sūtrāṇi,* chap. II, the defect *lokaviruddha.* He explains *lokaviruddhāni* as *deśakālasvabhāvaviruddhāni.* He gives the mention of Madhura in Sauvira as an instance of *deśavirodha,* description of *Kadamba* flowers in spring as of *kālavirodha,* and the mention of *mañjarī* of *Saptacchada* as an instance of *svabhāvavirodha.*

These defects of poetry discussed by the ancient critics give sufficient warnings to a novice in the field of poetry about the things which should be scrupulously avoided from a good literary composition. By the time of Rājaśekhara it was already established that a good poet should avoid such things. This has led to the conventional description of everything like a mountain, a season, the sun-rise, the sun-set, the moonlight, etc. It is out of such prescriptions and prohibitions that the poetic conventions or *kavisamayas* have evolved, e.g., when the critics laid down that sandal should not be described as growing on any mountain other than Malaya or that *Devadāru* and other trees should not be described as growing on Malaya, obviously the convention that the mountain Malaya is the only abode of sandal gets formed. In the course of discussion of *kālavirodhadoṣa* Daṇḍin had already mentioned that description of blooming of *padminī* at evening or of *kumudvatī* during day is a defect. Similarly the description of peacock-dance during the autumn or of cackling of swans during the rainy season involves *kālavirodhadoṣa* according to him.

All these cases are covered by the *kavisamaya* of Sanskrit poets.

Now on the background of the poetic conventions used by Sanskrit poets and the *kāvyadoṣas* discussed by his predecessor critics, Rājaśekhara formulated his own synthetic theory of *kavisamaya.* At the end of chapter XVI, he frankly admits that he has not given anything new in this regard. He had just expressed in explicit terms the conventions which were left in an implied form by the poets:

> *so'yam kavīnam samayaḥ kāvye supta iva sthitaḥ,*
> *sa sāmpratamihāsmābhiryathābudhi vibodhitaḥ.*

Let us now look to the treatment of *kavisamaya* in Rājaśekhara's *Kāvyamīmāṁsā*. He aptly defines it as *aśāstrīyamalaukikaṁ ca paramparāgataṁ yamarthamupanibadhnanti kavayaḥ sa kavisamayaḥ.* "All such matter, which the poets use, as is not vouchsafed either by scientific knowledge or by the behaviour of the world, and which has just come down by tradition among the poets, constitutes *kavisamaya.*" He explains, "These are matters, which were actually experienced by the ancient scholars. In course of time they might have undergone a change. Still we poets do use them." However, he makes it perfectly clear that he approves of such poetic conventions only as have been established by ancient critics and discards all such matter, which is passed in the name of poetic convention by pseudo-poets. Then *Rā* divides them in 3 classes as: (i) heavenly, (ii) earthly, and (iii) nether-worldly. Further he divides the earthly conventions in 4 grammatical divisions of *jāti, dravya, guṇa* and *kriyā.*

Each is again divided threefold as (a) Employment of non-existing matter, (b) Non-employment of existing matter, and (c) Restriction.

It is this last classification which is of significance to us. Let us analyse *Ra*'s *kavisamaya* under these heads as follows:

(i) *Employment of non-existing matter:* Lotuses in any river, swans in any reservoir of water, gold and gems on any mountain, darkness as capable of being held in a fist or of being pierced with a needle, moonlight as capable of being carried in a pitcher, the separated *Cakravāka*-pair resorting to opposite banks of a river during night, *Cakoras* drinking in moonlight, whiteness of glory and smile, darkness of infamy and sin, redness of wrath and love, dwelling of a hare or a deer in the moon, the God of Love being bodiless or possessing a handsome form.

(ii) *Non-employment of existing matter*: *Mālatī* not blooming during spring, a sandal-tree not yielding flower and fruit, *Aśokā* tree not giving fruit, no moonlight in the dark-half of a month and no darkness in the bright-half of a month, no blooming of blue lotuses and no falling down of *Śephālikā* flowers during day, no red colour of *Kunda*-buds, no green colour of lotus-buds and no yellow colour of *Priyaṅgu* flowers.

(iii) *Restriction:* The crocodiles described as staying in the sea only, pearls found at the bottom of the river Tāmparaṇī only, sandal growing on the mountain Malaya only, Birch-trees (*Bhūrja*) growing on the mountain Himālaya only, the cooing of a cuckoo heard in the Spring only and the dance of the peacocks described in the rainy season only.

In the last two chapters of his *Kāvyamīmāṁsā Rā.* gives all detials as to which matters should be described in particular provinces and during particular seasons. This is an extension of the *deśavirodhadoṣa* and *kālavirodhadoṣa* as noted by his predecessors.

Comparative Views by Different Critics

A comparative study of *Rā*'s conventions and the defects as noted by the ancient critics will show that some of his poetic conventions can be easily converted into defects of poetry according to the earlier critics:

Deśavirodhadoṣa — *Candana* if described elsewhere than in Malaya, pearls if described as found in a river other than Tāmraparṇī, etc.

Kālavirodhadoṣa — *Mālatī* blooming in *Vasanta,* blooming of blue lotuses or falling of *Śephālikā* flowers during day, description of the notes of a cuckoo in a season other than the Spring, description of peacock-dance in a season other than the rainy season, description of darkness during the bright half and of moonlight during the dark half of a month, etc.

But many of the *kavisaṅketas* of *Rā* are actually involving the defect *lokavirodha. Rā* does not deny it. His definition of *kavisamaya* as *aśāstrīya* and *alaukika* makes sufficient allowance for the same. In chapter XVIII, he is discussing as to how the breeze in the rainy season should be described. He notes down that according to the poets *varṣāsu pūrvo vāyuḥ* while the ancient teachers say, *varṣāsu pāścātyo vāyuḥ, paurastyastu varṣāyāḥ pratihantā*. Then *Rā* clearly gives his opinion that the Eastern breeze must be described during the rainy season, for the poetic tradition is more important than the fact to a poet, *vastuvṛttiratantram, kavisamayaḥ pramāṇam iti yāyāvarīyaḥ*.

A few of *Rā's* successor-critics were highly enamoured of this topic of *kavisamaya* and have discussed it in details. In his *Kāvyānuśāsana*, Hemacandra (12th cent. A.D.) has reproduced all these *kavisamayas* of *Ra* while commenting upon *Sūtra*, I.10 — *sato'pyanibandhosato'pinibandho niyamaschā yādyupajīvanādayaḥ śikṣāḥ*. Viśvanātha (14th cent. A.D.), the author of *Sāhityadarpaṇa* has discussed *kāvyadoṣa* in the seventh chapter. In the course of his discussion he says that *nirhetutā* (being without a reason) ceases to be a fault in the case of well-known matters like the separation of *cakravāka* at evening. Then coming to the defect *khyāta- viruddhatā* (contradiction of well-established matters) he says clearly, *kavīnāṁ samaye khyāte guṇaḥ khyātaviruddhatā*, (In the case of poetic conventions it turns out to be a merit). Then he gives a long list of the *kavisamayas* in verses 23 to 25. To the list given by *Rā*, he adds for the first time, the two *vṛkṣadohadas* as *pādāghātādaśokaṁ vikasati bakulaṁ yositāmāsyamadyaiḥ*. Similarly he gives in explicit terms the *kavisamaya* about the flowery arrows of cupid, and says, *bhinnaṁ syādasya bāṇairyuvajanahṛdayaṁ strīkaṭākṣeṇa tadvat*. This topic of *kavisamaya* was extremely popular with the poet-critics belonging to the *kaviśikṣā*-school. In his *Alaṅkāracintāmaṇi* Ajitasena repeats all these conventions adding a few of his own as — *nirebhādyam khagaṅgāyām* (water-elephants in the *Ākāśagaṅgā*), *ramāyāḥ padmavāsitam* (Lakṣmī staying in a lotus), *samudramathanaṁ tatra surendraśrīsamudbhavaḥ* (The churning of the ocean and the origin of the glory of Indra from there). In addition to the redness of love and anger he mentions it as belonging to *Bimba*-fruit, *Bandhūka*-flower and the disc of the sun.

Kāvyakalpalatā of Amarasiṁha and *Kavikalpalatā* of Devendra repeat the *kavisamayas* of *Rā*. In enlisting the things which are conventionally white Devendra adds *chatra* (a parasol), *ambhas* (water) and *vāsas* (a garment).

In the senventh chapter of his *Sāhityakaumudī*, Vidyābhūṣaṇa describes all the *kavisamayas* of *Rā*, adding that about the *Aśokadohada* as *pādāghaṭena padminyāḥ syādaśokastu puṣpitaḥ*.

Keśavamiśra (16th cent A.D.) gives a detailed treatment of *kavisamaya* in the 15th *Marīci* of his *Alaṅkāraśekhara.* In the list of things which are non-existent he adds — *pratāpe raktatoṣṇatve.* In case of the colour conventionally attributed to various things he enlarges the list as follows:

White-colour — *dhvaja* (a banner), *cāmara* (a chowry), *haṁsa* (a swan), *hāra* (a necklace of pearls), *baka* (a crane) and *bhasma* (ashes).

Black colour — a mountain, a tree, a creeper, a cloud, the sea, a *Bhilla,* an *Asura,* smoke, mud, and hair.

Red colour — a mineral, a ruby, a *Japā*-flower, a gem, the sun, a *Padma*-lotus, sprouts, *Bandhūka*-flower, pomogranate, and nails.

Yellow colour — a rice plant, a frog, a bark-garment, and pollen-dust.

In addition to the *Aśokadohada* he mentions *Bakuladohada* as *kesarāśokayoḥ satstrīgaṇḍūṣāt pādāghātato māsāntare'pi puṣpāṇi.*

In connection with the *vṛkṣadohada,* Mallinātha, while commenting upon *Meghadūta,* 75 has quoted the following verse, enumerating very interesting and romantic pregnancy-longings on the part of various trees:

> *strīṇāṁ sparśāt priyaṅgurvikasati bakulaḥ sīdhugaṇḍū-ṣasekāt*
> *pādāghātadaśokastilakakurabakau vīkṣaṇāliṅganābhyāṁ,*
> *mandāro narmavākyāt paṭumṛduhasanāccampako vaktravātā-*
> *ccūto gītānnamerurvikasati ca puro nartanāt karṇikāraḥ*

I have not come accross the use of these *dohadas* excepting *Asokadohada* and *Bakuladohada* in Sanskrit literature, nor could I trace this stanza to its source.

A survey of these *kavisaṅketas* in Sanskrit literature can easily point out that many of them are based upon just a matter of common sense and general observation. It is quite natural to look upon glory and smile as white or anger and love as red just as it is natural to look upon knowledge as light and ignorance as darkness. Similarly, the restrictive conventions like the notes of a cuckoo being heard in the spring only or the peacock-dance witnessed in the rainy season only, are matters of general observation. These conventions are found not only in Sanskrit literature but even in literature of other languages like English. The convention about the cupid piercing the hearts of young folk with his flowery bow and arrows also is one such common convention.

Conclusion

The poetic conventions of Sanskrit critics, which we can really describe as *asato'pi nibandhanam* or *vastugatyā yanna bhavati tasya nibandhanam* are the following cases only:

(1) Separation of the *Cakravāka* birds during night.

(2) *Cakora* birds drinking in the moonlight.

(3) The swans going to the Mānasa lake during the rainy season.

(4) *Aśoka* and the *Bakula* trees having pregnancy-longings.

(5) A hare or a deer staying in the moon.

In addition to these conventions noted by Sanskrit critics there are some such cases, which have not been noted by them, but which have been freely used by the poets like Kālidāsa, e.g.:

(1) A female crane conceiving simply on hearing the thundering of the clouds.

(2) A swan being able to separate water from milk.

(3) A female cuckoo getting her eggs hatched by a female crow.

(4) *Candrakānta*-gem oozing at the touch of the rays of the moon and *Sūryakānta*-gem burning at the touch of the rays of the sun.

(5) A *Gandhadvīpa* scaring away other elephants merely by means of the fragrance of its ichor.

(6) The *Kalpavṛkṣa* (the Desire-yielding tree), the *Kāmadhenu* (the Desire-yielding cow) and the *Cintāmaṇi* (the Desire-yielding gem) fulfilling all desires.

(7) Throbbing of the left eye in the case of women and that of the right eye in the case of men as auspicious omens.

Such matters are really *aśāstrīyā*, *alaukika* and *paramparāgata*. These are nothing but the flights of imagination of Sanskrit poets.

Reference

1. *Dhvanyāloka of Ānandavardhana*, III 42 *Vṛtti*.

6

Samudra in the *Ṛgveda*

THE word *Samudra* has been used in various meanings in the *ṚV*. It occurs more than 150 times, about 60 times in Books I and X together, about 40 times in Book IX, and about 60 times in the rest of the *Ṛgveda.*

Differental Meanings According to the Eastern and the Western Scholars

The various meanings of the word are as follows:

> (a) the ocean, or the sea, (b) the firmament, (c) a cloud, (d) water, (e) the *soma*-juice, (f) a vat of *soma,* (g) *Vasatī-varī* water in which the juice flows and (h) the sun.

Sporadically it has been used to denote Agni, Indra, Varuṇa, etc., or has been used as an adjective of various deities.

According to Sāyaṇa the word means the ocean 77·times, the firmament 37 times, *soma* or its adjective 6 times, a *soma*-vat 5 times, a cloud 3 times, water or its adjective 2 times, the sun 2 times, and in a few pḷaces it is an adjective qualifying some deity.

Very often Sāyaṇa himself is not sure about its exact meaning and he has to remark:

> *"samudro'ntarikṣaṃ vā" "samudro megho vā"*
> *"samudraḥ kalaśoantarikṣam vā"*, etc.

Sometimes Sāyaṇa offers two or three different explanations of the word, e.g.:

mama yoniraspsvantaḥsamudre. (X. 125.7)

Sāyaṇa explains:

(1) *samudravantyasmād bhūtānīti samudraḥ paramātmā.*

(2) *yadvā samudre jaladhau.*

(3) *yadvā samudre'ntarikṣe.*
samudre antaḥ kavayo vi cakṣate. (X.177.1)

Sāyaṇa remarks:

(a) *samudravantyasmādraśmaya iti samudram surya-maṇḍalam.*

(b) *yadvā samudravantyasmād bhūtajātanīti samudraḥ paramātmā.*

The statistical analysis of the meaning of the word given above shall perhaps have to be revised in the light of the fact that Sāyaṇa's interpretations themselves very often need revision.

Yāska in his *Nirukta* gives five derivations of the term *samudra.* When it means 'the firmament', Yāska derives it as *Samudravantasmādapaḥ.*

Waters flow from it. When it means 'the ocean' the following derivations are given:

(a) *samabhidravantyenamapaḥ* — Waters flows in it.

(b) *sammodante asmin bhūtāni* — Creatures like fish find delight in it.

(c) *samudako bhavati* — Water is accumulated in it.

(d) *samunatti iti vā* — It makes the earth wet.

Out of the various meanings of the word, as noted above the meaning No. (a) is important for our consideration, since there has been a lot of controversy about it. Scholars are divided in two groups on the problem whether the ocean or the sea was known to the *Ṛgvedic* Āryans. Eminent scholars like Hopkins,

Ragozin, Keith and Zimmer held the opinion that the sea was not known in the days of the *Ṛgveda* and that the word *Samudra* in the *ṚV* means the gushing and expansive stream of the lower course of the river Sindhu or Indus, after it had received water from the rivers of Punjab. Later Prof. Macdonell has strongly refuted this opinion in the *Vedic Index,* vol.II (p. 432). He remarks, "Knowledge of the ocean was inevitable to the people who knew Indus."

Prof. Max-Müller points out that in many passages of the *ṚV* the word *samudra* means the ocean. With reference to VII.95.2:

> *ekācetat sarasvatī nadīnām*
> *śuciryatī giribhya ā samudrāt.*

Max-Müller feels that it is a proof of the fact that the Āryans had followed the river Sarasvatī as far as the Indian Ocean. He further remarks that the river must have changed its course, as early as the composition of the *Sūtras* and that the place where it disappeared underground was called the *Vinaśana,* 'the Loss'.

Taking a clue from this scholar Shri A.C. Das[1] says that the *Ṛgvedic* Āryans definitely knew the ocean and that in those days the river Sarasvatī flowed into the sea, which then existed to the immediate east of Punjab. He feels that later the river disappeared probably because of a marine transgression. Among other proofs he points out the legend of Agastya as supporting his theory.

This topic has been discussed further by Shri Amiya Kumar Chakravarty in his article[2] on "*Samudra* in the *Ṛgveda*". He claims that the Vedic Āryans knew not only the western Arabian Sea but also the eastern Bay of Bengal. He does not accept Mr. Das's theory about the existence of the sea to the east of Punjab. According to him, Sarasvatī flowed into the Arabian Sea only and later the silting up of the river was caused due to inability of the current to wash off the sand from its course. Charkravarty concludes, "Therefore, the term *samudra* in the *Ṛgveda,* except perhaps in some particular cases, where a big river has been meant — the truth of which again is open to considerable doubt — always means the ocean or the sea."

In this chapter an attempt has been made to go through all occurrences of word *samudra* in the *Ṛgveda* and to study its meaning in every case. At the end an attempt is made to show how the different meanings of this word might have developed.

Special-attention has been given to the point whether *samudra* means the sea or a big river, and additional proof to support the opinion of scholars like Shri C.V.Vaidya, Shri A.K. Chakravarty has been put forth.

(a) The theory that *samudra* denotes only the lower course of Indus can be refuted on the basis of the evidence of the *ṚV* itself, e.g.:

> *yat sindhau yadasiknyāṁ yat samudreṣu marutaḥ*
> *subarhiṣaḥ, yat parvateṣu bheṣajam.* (VIII. 20.25)

Samudra has been mentioned along with the rivers Sindhu (Indus) and Asiknī (Chenāb).

In *samudraḥ sindhu rajo antarikṣamaja ekapattanayitnu-rarṇavaḥ.* (X. 66.11)

Samudra has been mentioned along with Sindhu. Such references clearly prove that the *Ṛgvedic* Āryans knew the *Samudra*, which was distinct from Sindhu.

In VII. 92.2 the river Sarasvatī has been described as flowing from the mountains up to the *samudra.* Here *samudra* can never mean the river Sindhu, because Sarasvatī was never a tributary of the Sindhu.

> *sahasraśṛṅgo vṛṣabho yaḥ samudrādudācarat.* (VII. 55.7)

The sun has been described as coming out of *samudra,* and

> *yaddevā yatayo yathā bhuvanānyapinvata,*
> *atrā samudra ā gulhamā sūryamajabhartana.* (X. 72.7)

The gods are said to have called the sun, that was hidden in *samudra*. This is a clear reference to the sun-rise, when the sun seems to come out of the ocean. Here it may be argued that this *samudra* can be the ocean of the firmament; but to my mind the description suits the terrestrial ocean with greater propriety.

The references like the above-mentioned *ṛks* categorically rule out the possibility of *samudra* meaning the river Sindhu.

(b) There are many other passages which can be explained in a better and more reasonable way by taking *Samudra* as the ocean rather than river Sindhu, e.g.:

> *ádha yádeṣāṁ niyútaḥ paramāḥ*
>
> *samudrásya ciddhanáyanta pāré.* (I. 167.2)

The Maruts are described as carrying things accross the *samudra*. Sometimes they are described as urging the clouds across *samudra*.

> *ná kṣóṇībhyāṁ paribháve ta indriyám*
>
> *ná samudraíḥ párvatairindra te ráthaḥ.* (II. 16.3)

Indra's chariot has been described as unimpeded by *samudras* and *parvatas*.

In I.71.7 all oblations ae described as going to Agni like the seven rivers going to *samudra*. In I.30.3 *Soma* is described as stored in Indra's belly like *samudra*. In VII.49 waters have been described as *samudrajyeṣṭhāḥ* and *samudrārthāḥ*. The surging of *samudra* has been referred to in many places. e.g.:

> *yáḥ kukṣíḥ somapā́tamaḥ samudráiva pínvate.* (I.8.7)
>
> *ayáṁ sahásramṛ́ṣibhiḥ saháskṛtaḥ samudráiva paprathe.* (VIII.3.4)
>
> *imáṁ juṣasva girvaṇaḥ samudráiva pinvate.* (VIII.12.5)

This obviously refers to the tide of the ocean. Sāyaṇa takes it as such explaining it as:

> *samudro yathā candrodayam prāpya pinvate vardhate tāthā.*

The well-known and oft-repeated simile *samudrámiva síndhavaḥ* or *samudrā́yeva síndhavaḥ* sounds better when *samudra* denotes the ocean rather than the river Sindhu.

In cosmological and cosmogonical hymns as:

> *yásyéme himávanto mahitvā́ yásya*
>
> *samudráṁ rasáyā sahāhuḥ.* (X. 121.4)
>
> and
>
> *táto rā́tryajāyata tátaḥ samudrá arṇaváḥ.* (X.190)

samudra means the ocean only. On X. 190.1 Sāyaṇa remarks that *arṇava* is mentioned in addition so that *samudra* should not be misunderstood as the firmament. In many mythologies of the world the ocean or water is the first creation.

Following Sāyaṇa's interpretation, the meaning of this word statistically, next to the ocean, is the firmament. Obviously it is the poetic imagery of the Vedic poets that sees the firmament as a big ocean. It is however worthnoting that the poets knew the ocean as different from the firmament. The two are distinguished from each other as *avarasamudraḥ* and *parasamudraḥ* in VII.6.7 or *ayaṁ samudraḥ* and *uttaraḥ samudraḥ* in X.98.6.

Knowledge of 'The Sea' to the Āryans

Thus it is clear that the word *samudra* primarily denotes the sea or ocean in the *ṚV*.

Scholars have advanced other arguments also to prove that the *Ṛgvedic* Āryans had knowledge of the sea and many other things associated with it:

> *ubhaú samudrā́vakṣeti yáśca pū́rva utā́paraḥ.* (X.136.5)

speaks of the sun as going to the eastern and the western ocean. As noted above, Shri Chakravarti points out that here the Bay of Bengal and the Arabian Sea are meant.

The four oceans form the four boundaries of the earth according to the post-*Ṛgvedic* literature. Even these four oceans are known to the *Ṛgvedic* poets.

rāyaḥ samudrāṁścaturo'smabhyaṁ soma viśvataḥ ā pavasva sahasriṇaḥ. (IX. 33.6)

and

catuḥsamudraṁ dharuṇaṁ rayīṇām. (X. 47.2)

there is a very clear reference to the four oceans.

In the classical Sanskrit literature the ocean is called *Ratnākara,* repository of gems. The *Ṛgvedic* poets also have spoken about the treasures of the ocean very often, e.g.:

rayim samudrāduta vā divasparyasme dhattaṁ puruspṛham. (I. 47.6)

svadasvendrāya pavamāna indo rayim ca na ā pavasvā samudrāt. (IX. 97.44)

In X.5.1. Agni is called *samudra* being 'the holder of the treasures'. In VI.69.6 Indra and Viṣṇu are called *samudrau* and are requested to bring wealth.

Navigation by sea has been referred to in many places, e.g.:

veda nāvaḥ samudriyaḥ. (I. 25.7)

samudraṁ na sañcaraṇe saniṣyavaḥ. (I. 56.2)

ā yadruhāva varuṇaśca nāvam pra yat samudramīrayāva madhyam. (VII. 88.3)

Among the exploits of Aśvins the help that they rendered to Bhujyu, who had fallen amidst the ocean is well-known; and the *ṚV* refers to it time and again, e.g.:

yuvaṁ bhujyumarṇaso niḥ samudrādvibhirūhathur ṛjrebhiraśvaiḥ. (I. 117.14)

According to Shri C.V.Vaidya[3], this is a proof that even Āryan king like Bhujyu went on sea, no wonder if the simile *samudraṁ ná sañcáraṇe saniṣyávaḥ* or *samudré ná śravasyávaḥ* is very popular with *Ṛgvedic* poets.

Thus the *Ṛgvedic* Āryans definitely knew the Arabian sea and at a later stage even the Bay of Bengal.

Knowledge of 'The Submarine Fire'

If one accepts Sāyaṇa's interpretation the *Ṛgvedic* poets knew not only the ocean but even 'the submarine fire'. In I.95.3 Agni's three births are referred to. There Sāyaṇa remarks *samudrebdhau vaḍavānalarūpeṇa*. Moreover, in VIII.102.4. *aurvabhṛguvácchucimapnavānávadā huve, agníṁ samudrávāsasam* there is clear reference to the submarine fire. Sāyaṇa explains *samudravāsasam* as *samudramadhyavartinam vāḍavam.*

It is worthnoting that in later mythology the submarine fire is called Aurva, the son of Bhṛgu.

In *yadákrandaḥ prathámaṁ jāyamāna*
udyántsamudrāduta vā purīṣāt. (I.163.1)

The horse is described as coming out of the *samudra.* Here Sāyaṇa explains *samudra* as 'the firmament' or 'the sun'. But I feel that the terrestrial ocean is meant here. Prof. Geldner translates *samudra* as 'the sea' here and he thinks that this is the first trace of the horse *Uccaiḥśravas,* which is one of the 14 gems churned out of the ocean according to the later mythology.

Development of the Meanings of the Word *Samudra*

It can be clearly seen that the word *samudra* has been used in the *Ṛgveda* in various meanings. It is interesting to find out as to which meaning is the earliest and how it was extended to other cases (i) In Vedic India, Mr. Ragozin says that the accumulation of atmospheric moisture in the shape of rain-cloud is the earliest meaning of this word. To my mind the original meaning of the word is the terrestrial sea. As noted above, it is in this meaning that the word has been most frequently used in the *ṚV*: (ii) Next in frequency comes the meaning 'the firmament', the vault of the heaven. It is the terrestrial ocean actually on the earth that must have suggested the imagery of this aerial ocean to the Vedic poets. In later mythology *samudra* as the firmament also was of common occurrence, e.g., according to Prof. Adalbert Kuhn, *samudra* in the legend of the *samudra-manthana* is the firmament only. (iii) *Samudra* meaning a cloud is nothing but an extension of this. (iv) *Samudra* as water is nothing but a marginal meaning of the ocean only. (v) When *soma*-sacrifice occupied an important place in the life of the Vedic Āryans, the word *samudra* came to be applied to the *soma*-juice, which used to flow in streams during the sacrifice. *Samudra* meaning (vi) a vat of *soma* and (vii) the *Vasatīvarī* waters in which the juice is mixed, are nothing but extension of (v). (viii) The sun was allegorically called *samudra* because the rays of light were looked upon as allegorical streams of water. That is why Sāyaṇa explains this meaning as *samudravantyasmādraśmaya iti.* (ix) The purpose of using *samudra* as an adjective of various deities like Agni, Varuṇa, Indra, etc., is to glorify them by bringing out the vastness of their power.

References

1. *Ṛgvedic Culture,* pp. 3-4.
2. *Indian Historical Quarterly,* Vol. VII, pp. 353-57, June 1932.
3. *History of Sanskrit Literature,* pp. 36, 101-2.

7

The Moon in the Vedic Literature

THE problem of the identity of the moon with *Soma* has attracted attention of the scholars since long. In this chapter an attempt has been made to collect together all possible details about the moon from the Vedic literature to analyse them, and then to study the various aspects of the moon critically and comparatively. The information has been collected from the *Saṁhitās* of the four *Vedas,* the *Brāhmaṇas,* the *Āraṇyakas* and the principal *Upaniṣads.*

The Moon in the *ṚV*

(a) The words for the moon — The most common word is *candramāḥ*. The word *candra* occurs mostly as an adjective, meaning 'bright', which Sāyaṇa renders as 'delighting'. In some places, as a noun, it means 'gold'. The authors of the *Vedic Index* have said that *candra* in the sense of the moon has been used for the first time in the *AV*; but even in the *ṚV*, the word can better be interpreted as the moon in a few places, e.g., II.2.4 *candramiva surucam hvāra ā dadhuḥ.* Though Sāyaṇa takes it to mean gold, Griffith translates it as the moon. Similarly in X.106.8, Aśvins have been addressed as *patareva cacarā candranirṇik.* Here Sāyaṇa gives both the meanings 'the moon' and 'gold'. Wilson follows the former in his translation. In cases like these *candra* clearly means the moon; in a few more cases *candra* as the moon would yield a better meaning. The word *indu* mostly occurs in the sense of *Soma* and very rarely in the sense of the moon. Grassmann in his *Wörterbuch zum Ṛgveda* gives 'the shining drop' as the meaning and applies it to *Soma* alone. The word *candramāḥ* means the moon only. It is derived from the root *mā* to measure. The word *Soma* is rarely used in the sense of the moon in books IX and X.

(b) Information about the moon — (i) The phases of the moon *navonavo bhavati jāyamāḥah* (X.85.19). (ii) The regularity of appearance, following the laws of Varuṇa (I.24.10). (iii) The measure of time, the banner of the day (X. 85.19). (iv) The maker of the seasons (X. 85.5; X. 85.18, etc.). (v) The prolonger of life (X.85.19). (vi) The sun and the moon as companions entering upon an agreement (X.85.18) and as two forms of *Agni* (I.95.1). (vii) The lustre of the moon borrowed from the sun (I.84.15 — according to Sāyaṇa and Griffith). (viii) The moon as an eagle running through the aerial waters (I.105.1). (ix) As lying in the lap of the stars (X.85.2). (x) As a suitor of Sūryā — when identified with *Soma* (X.85). Born from the mind of the Cosmic Being (X.90.13).

(c) *Candra-Soma* identity — This aspect of the moon has been studied by a number of scholars. Hillebrandt[1] claimed that throughout the *ṚV*, *Soma* primarily means the moon and only secondarily as the juice. The opinion is rejected by Griffith,[2] though he does not deny such identification in the later portions of the *ṚV*, as is clear from his introduction to book IX. Griswold[3] contradicts this view and maintains that the moon was identified with *Soma* in the post-Vedic literature. Bergaigne[4] contends that *Soma* was not accepted as the moon in the *ṚV*, but more definitely was identified with the Sun. Macdonell[5] feels that in the whole of the *ṚV* there is no single distinct and explicit instance either of the identification or of the conception that the moon is the food of the gods. Yet in the *Vedic Index* the foot-note to the word *candra* is "The identification is closely found in the later portions of the *ṚV*." The same opinion is expressed by Eggeling[6]. Akshay Kumari Devi[7] remarks, "The *Soma*-drink, the *Soma*-plant and *Soma* as the moon, though entirely separate, have been, in later Vedic times, confused into a religious ritual and mysticism".

In the light of these various opinions we can study the references to *Soma* and *Indu* critically and try to review the problem once again. It is clear that the word *candra* or *candramas* has never been used in the sense of the *Soma*-juice. The word *Indu,* on the other hand almost always means 'the juice' and very rarely as in VI.39. 3 'the moon'. As far as *Soma* is concerned, the word is clearly used in the sense of the moon and the identity of the two is clearly intended in some passages e.g.:

> *trayaḥ pavayo madhuvāhane rathe somasya venāmanu viśva isadviduḥ.* (I.34.2)
>
> *tvaṁ soma pitṛbhiḥ saṁvidāno'nu dyāvāpṛthivī ā tatantha.* (VIII. 48.13)
>
> *ati trī soma rocanā rohanna bhrājase divam.* (IX. 17.5)
>
> *eṣa sūryeṇa hāsate pavamāno adhi dyavi.* (IX. 27.5)
>
> *adhi dyāmasthadyṛṣabho vicakṣaṇo. ruruadvi divo rocanā kaviḥ,*
>
> *rājā pavitramatyeti roruvaddivaḥ pīyūṣam duhate nṛcakṣasaḥ.* (IX. 85.9)
>
> *divā harirdadṛśe naktamṛjraḥ.* (IX. 97.9)
>
> *somam yam brahmāṇo vidurna tasyāśnāti kaścana.* (X. 85.3)

Though it is so, the two are often mentioned together separately, e.g.:

> *ayaṁ sa yo varimāṇam pṛthivyā varṣmāṇam divo akṛṇodayaṁ saḥ,*
>
> *ayaṁ pīyūṣam tisṛṣu pravatsu somo dādhārorvantarikṣam.* (VI. 47.4)
>
> *yo apsu candramāiva somaścamūṣu dadṛśe.* (VIII. 82.8)

There are some places where *Soma, drapsa,* etc. have been interpreted as 'the moon' by the scholars like Griffith; but where, they can be better understood as the juice, e.g.,

ava drapso aṁśumatimatiṣṭhadīyānaḥ kṛṣṇo daśabhiḥ
sahásraiḥ. (VIII. 96.13)

IX.15.5 where *patiḥ sindhūnām bhavan* suits the juice better. So also in X. 30.2 *aruṇáḥ suparṇaḥ* can be better taken as the juice.

Thus *candra-soma* identity was just taking its shape in the *ṚV* and was not yet fixed in the minds of the Vedic seers. It should be noted that the *Haoma* had no connection with the moon in the *Avestā*. It is clear that the moon was always super-human for the *Ṛgvedic* seers, while *Soma* in the beginning was just a bevearage, dear to gods and men. As the next step it was first identified with 'the Drink of Immortality' and then only it was elevated to the rank of a deity. Now the flowing juice has a shining glow. It was often referred to as *candrāsa indavaḥ*, thus reminding the poets of the bright moon. Further the moon was looked upon as the storehouse of nectar in other mythologies like the Teutonic also. Hence the invigorating *Soma*-juice, the Drink of Immortality, easily offered itself for identification with the moon. The detailed process in this regard has been clearly described by Griswold.[8]

(d) A few remarks about *RV*, I. 84.15:

atrāha goramanvata nāma tvaṣṭurapīcyam,
itthā candramaso gṛhe.

According to Sāyaṇa the *ṛk* means: The rays of the sun found their concealed lustre in this orb of the moving moon. Wilson construes *goh* with *Tvaṣṭuḥ* and understands that the rays of the sun found the bull of *Tvaṣṭṛ* concealed in the mansion of the moon. Griffith takes 'The people' as the subject of *amanvata* and refers *Tvaṣṭṛ's* Bull to the sun. In the foot-note to the *ṛk* he takes it as explaining the fact that the light of the moon is borrowed from the sun. However, Geldner understands it quite differently. He translates it as: There, in the house of the moon, they (i.e., the gods or the seers) reminded themselves of the secret name of the cow of *Tvaṣṭr*. In the detailed foot-note to this stanza he connects the triplet 13-15 with III.48.2-4 and explains that this cow of *Tvaṣṭṛ* is the *Soma*-plant, which was kept concealed by him on the *Śaryaṇavat*. Though it is not possible for us to discuss the whole of that interesting foot-note here, it clearly points out the identity of *Soma* with the moon. Further I feel that the clear reference to the house of the moon' can be taken as the first indistinct hint at the moon being an abode of the departed souls. I.164.30 refers to a place *madhya ā pastyānām,* where a soul lives on *svadhā*. May this also not refer to the moon, amidst the aerial waters?

The Moon in other *Saṁhitās*

(A) The ideas about the moon, as seen in the *ṚV* are now developed further.

(a) The phases of the moon, hence the moon as the measurer of time and prolonger of life (*AV*, VII.81.2; IX.10.9; X.7.33; X.8.25; *YV* (*Vāj. Mādhy S.*) XII.9.10 and 45, 46, (*Kāṇ. S*) XXV.3.7; XXV.9.2; *TS*, VII.4, 8, 12). Repeating the *Brahmodaya:*

> *kaḥ svidekākī carati ka u svijjāyate punaḥ,*
> *kiṁ sviddhimasya bheṣajam kiṁvāvapanam mahat.* (9)
> *sūryo ekākī carati candramā jāyate punaḥ,*
> *agnirhimasya bheṣajam bhumirāvapanam mahat.* (10)
> *Vā. Mādhya Su. YV Saṁhitā,* XXIII. 9

(b) The moon as the creator of seasons (*AV*, VIII.8.23; XIII.3). It is in this connection that the moon is described as staying with Anumati, the 14th night and Rākā, the Full-moon night. (*YV*, *Kāṭh. S.*, XII.8; *Mai. S.*, IV.3, 5).

(c) Birth of the moon from the mind of the Cosmic Being and her intimate connection with the mind (*AV*, XIX.6.7; *YV*, *Vāj Madhy. S.*, XXXI.12.)

(d) The sun and the moon as playing children and companions performing different functions (*AV*, VII.81.1).

(e) *Candra-Soma* identity has been fully accepted in the other *Saṁhitās*. The moon is called the lord of the planets as well as of the plants. (*AV*, VI.21.2; XIV.1.1-3; XIX.6.11; XX.143.1, *YV Kāṭh. S.*, XI.3, XI.5; *Mai. S*, II.1.5; III.2.11; IV.4.12; *TS*, 4, 4, 20; *Vāj. Mādhy. S.*, XXXIII.90).

(f) Many of the *Saṁhitās* repeat *ṚV*, I.84.15 *Atrāha goramanvata*, discussed above. (*AV*, XX.42.3; *YV Mai. S*, II.13.6; *SV Pūrvārcika*, II.4.3; *Uttarārcika*, III.8.3).

(B) In addition to this, some interesting points about the moon have been added by these *Saṁhitās*.

(i) *AV*, VIII. 2 calls the sun and the moon as the sons of Aditi. *AV*, XVII describes them as the right and the left eyes of the Supreme Being, *Vrātya*, while *AV*, X.7.33 refers to the moon as the eye of Brahmā; so also *Mai. S.*, IV.6.3 *Mai. S.*, IV.2 calls the moon as the eye of *Pitṛs*, while IV.7.1 calls the sun and the moon as eyes of Prajāpati.

(ii) *AV*, VIII.8.23 poetically calls the moon 'the driver of the car of the year'.

(iii) The effect of the moon upon the vegetation and the medicinal herbs is referred to very often in this *Saṁhitā*. VI.21 calls the moon as the best of the medicines.

(iv) The moon is intimately connected with the well-being of progeny and cattle. In the *AV* the deities Anumati and Rākā, so also Sinīvālī and Kuhu (*Amāvasyā*) are often invoked for the welfare of the children and of the pregnant woman.

(v) The *Saṁhitās* refer to the fact that the light of the moon is borrowed from the sun and further look upon the moon as a *Gandharva*, the stars being the nymphs *susumṇaḥ, sūryaraśmiś-candramā gandharvastasya nakṣatrāṇyapsaraso* (be) *kurayo nāma*. (*YV Vāj. Kāṇ. S.*, XX.2.3; *Kāṭh. S.*, XVIII.14; *Kap. S.*, XXIX.3; *Mai S.*, II.12.2). Similarly *Mai S.*, II.13.15 addresses the Goddess of Planets as *Nakṣatrāṇi* and says *sā candramasi garbhamadhatthāḥ*.

(vi) In this connection *Kath. S.*, XI.3 gives an interesting account.

> *prajāpatirvai somāya rājñe duhitṛradadānnakṣatrāṇi. sa rohiṇyāmevavasat. tasminnanṛte yakṣmo'gṛhṇāt. candramā vai somo rājā. yadrājānaṁ yakṣmo'gṛhṇāttadrājaya-kṣmasya janma.*

Prajāpati offered his daughters, the Nakṣatras to King Soma, the moon. He stayed with Rohiṇī alone. Hence the other daughters complained to the father, who warned the son-in-law to behave properly. He agreed but failed to keep the promise. The father-in-law cursed him and the moon was caught hold of by Tuberculosis on consumption. This is how the waning of the moon is interpreted.

(vii) *Kap. S.*, XXXVIII.2, XLV.2 calls the moon as Vṛtra and looks upon the moon's disappearance on the New Moon night as Vṛtra being killed by Indra.

(viii) *T.S.*, V.2.33 interprets the black spot on the body of the moon as a worthy offering made by the Earth into the Heaven. This is the first attempt to interpret the spot; through the eye of a priest.

(ix) *YV Vā. Madhya. S.*, XXIV.35; XXV.7.5 and *Mai. S.*, III.14.16 give an interesting detail. In the list of the animals to be offered to the various deities we read *puruṣamṛgaścandramasaḥ*. Is this not an early hint at the spot on the moon being looked upon as a deer?

(x) *AV*, XIX.9.10 refers to the *grahāścāndramāsāḥ* (The demons that seize the moon).

The Moon in the *Brāhmaṇas*

(A) What the *Saṁhitās* have said about the moon is repeated and developed further.

(a) The phases of the moon — the riddle referring to *candramā jāyate punaḥ* is repeated, e.g., *T. Br.*, III.9.5.

The moon as the measurer of time — *Ś. Br.*, V.7.1, 19 remarks that the year is linked up to the moon by means of the seasons. *G. Br. Pūrvabhāga*, II.8 looks upon the two fortnights as the wings of the bird — the moon.

(b) The moon as the creator of days, nights and seasons, (*T. Br.*, III.1.6; *J. Br.*, 314; *Ś Br.*, 1.6.4, 5 *Ṣaḍ. Br.*, II.4, II.10). In this connection the moon is looked upon as having intercourse with Anumati and Rākā (*G. Br., Uttarabhāga*, I.10; *Ṣaḍ. Br.*, IV.6). Similarly the moon and the stars are described as forming a loving couple. *G. Br., Pūrvabhāga*, I.33 remarks:

> *yatra hyeva candramāstatra nakṣatrāṇi. Yatra vai nakṣatrāṇi tataścandramā ityete dve yonī ekam mithunam.*

(c) Similarly the statement of the *Saṁhitās* — *suṣmnaḥ*

sūryaraśmiścandramāḥ tasya . . . bekurayo nāma is repeated in the *Brāhmaṇas,* e.g. *Ś.B.,* IX.4.19 obviously accepting the fact that the light of the moon really comes from the sun. *T. Br.,* III.11, I says that the stars are established in the moon, and the moon in the sun. Similarly while explaining the derivation of the word *Āditya* *Ś. Br.,* XI.8, 3, 1 remarks that *Āditya* takes away the lustre of the moon.

(d) *Candra-Soma* identity has been totally accepted now. *G.Br., Pūrvabhāga,* V.14 says that *Soma* becomes the moon and visits the whole universe. *J. Br.,* III.50 records that *Soma* once disappeared from the gods. When they searched for it *tebhya etena rūpeṇādṛśyata yaccandramasaḥ.* Similarly in the *Ai. Br.,* VII.10; *Ś. Br.,* XI.1.53 and in many other places the identity has been clearly expressed.

(e) The sun and the moon dividing their function as *ahareva nāvanyatarobhijayet, rātrimanyataraḥ.* (*J.Br.,* II.98)

(f) The intimate connection of the moon with the mind has been alluded to in a number of places, e.g., *Ś. Br.,* XIV.5.5, 7; XIV. 6. 2, 13; *G. Br., Pūrvabhāga,* II.12. The moon is identified with the mind in *Ś.Br.,* XIV.4.1, 17; XIV.6.1, 7; *J. Br.,* II.54.

(g) The sun and the moon are looked upon as the eyes of Prajāpati (*Ś.Br.,* VII. 1, 2, 7) and the eyes of Svāhā, the daughter of Brahmā (*Ṣaḍ. Br.,* IV.7).

(h) The moon is connected with the well-being of the cattle (*Ś.Br.,* XI.1, 5, 6); *Ś. Br.,* VI.2.2, 16 remarks *candro vai devānām paśustaṁ devāḥ pauranamāsyāmālabhāte.*

Eggeling adds a foot-note that here the moon has been identified with *Vrtra.*

(i) As in the *T.S.* the *Ai. Br.,* IV. 27 calls the black spot on the moon as the *devayajana* established by the Earth in the Heaven.

(B) Further the *Brāhmanas* have added some new ideas about the moon.

(i) The waning of the moon is looked upon as the moon being eaten by the gods (*Ai. Br.,* IV.4; VII.10; *Ś. Br.,* VII.3.1.46; XI.1.3.3; XIV. 9.1. 10) (*Ś. Br.,* XI. 1.5.3) says that *Candra-Soma* is pressed by gods on the Full-Moon night and in the remaining fortnight the moon enters waters, plants and cattle and then returns after a fortnight. (ii) If the *ṚV* had faintly suggested the moon's connection with the departed souls (Section 1, above); the idea is now fully developed in the *Brāhmaṇas* (*Ś. Br.*, XIV.9.1.10). *Ś. Br.*, IX.1.2.39 says that whenever a sacrifice is completed the essence goes to the moon. *Ś.Br.*, IX.4.4.1 describes the moon as one of the six doors, leading to *Brāhmaṇ J. Br.*, III.341 remarks, 'One who performs *Agnihotra* goes to *Ādityaloka*, then mounts the chariot of the sun-beams and goes to the moon.' (iii) *T. Br.*, II.2.10, and *J. Br.*, III.368 give an interesting derivation of the word *candramāḥ*. Prajāpati's son Indra cried for the moon *candram me āhara*. The father brought the lustre from the heaven. The text remarks, *sa yaccandram me ityabravīttasmāccandramāḥ*. (iv) *Ai. Br.*, symbolitically interprets the passing of rain into the moon, and the disappearance of the moon on the *Amāvasyā* as death of these two. (v) *Ś. Br.*, XI.1.5.1-2 describes the moon as a watch-dog eager to seize the cattle of the sacrificer and suggests that the black spot on the moon is a hare. *J. Br.*, III.341 clearly identifies the departed performer of *Agnihotra* with the hare, *eṣa vai śaśo ya eṣontaścandramasi*.

The Moon in the *Āraṇyakas*

(a) *Candra-Soma* identity is very often repeated e.g., *Śāṅkh. Ār.*, IV.9.

(b) The sun and the moon as forms of one lustre, *Śaṅkh. Ār.*, IV.12.

(c) The moon as abode of the manes and the waxing and the waning of the moon being dependent upon the manes. *Sāṅkh. Ār.*, III.2 *teṣām prānaiḥ purvapakṣa āpyāyate. tānaparapakṣeṇa prajanayati.* Being an abode of *Pitṛs* the moon is called *svargasya dvāram* in *Tai. Ar.*, X.64.1.

(d) Intimate connection of the moon with the mind. The birth of the moon from the mind of the Cosmic Being *abhitaptasya hṛdayaṁ nirabhidyata hṛdayānmano manasaścandramāḥ.* and the remark *candramā mano bhūtvā hṛdayaṁ prāviśat* (*Ai. Ar.*, II.1.7), Again *Ai. Ār.*, II.4.3. The identity is repeated in *Ai. Ār.*, II.1.5, *Śānkh. Ār.*, IV.8; X. 4; XI.6. *Śāṅkh. Ār.*, XI.1 says that Prajāpati elevated the human being and placed the various deities in him and says, *manasi candramasam. Tai. Ar.*, refers to *Paramātman* as moving in the moon through the mind.

(e) The moon's favour is looked upon as essential for the

progeny and the cattle.

The Moon in the *Upaniṣads*

(a) The well established identity of the moon with *Soma* forms a common topic, e.g., *Ch. Up.*, I.6.4; II.9.1; III.13.2; *Bṛ. Up.*, II.1.3 (where, following the *Ś. Br.*, the moon is called *bṛhtāṇḍaravāsāḥ somo rājā*). *Kau. Up.*, II.9. *Mai. Up.* calls the moon's sprout of nectar'.

(b) The most favourite reference to the moon is as the abode of the departed souls, in the description of the *Dhūmādimārga*. *Ch. Up.*, IV.15.3; V.10.2; V.4; *Bṛ. Up.*, V.16; *Pr. Up.*, I.9; *Kau. Up.*, I.2 (where the moon is called *svargadvāram*).

(c) The intimate connection of the moon with the mind is also a very common topic, e.g., *Ch. Up.*, I.3.16; II.5.7; III.2.6; II.2.13; *Ai. Up.*, I.4.

(d) In the *Pañcāgnividyā* the moon's connection with the rain also is suggested (*Bṛ. Up.*, VI.2.10).

A Few Similar Ideas in Other Mythologies of the World

Thus the various aspects of the moon have attracted attention of the Vedic Āryans, as was the case with other primitive people also. Mr. Fallaize[9] has rightly said, "The moon occupies a prominent place in the primitive folk-lore, for which her periodical growth, diminution and disappearance, phases more marked than those of the sun, may, not unreasonably be held to be responsible". Many of the ideas about the moon as found in the Vedic literature are met with in other[10] mythologies also.

(a) As in the Vedic literature so also in the Teutonic mythology 'the Elixir of Life', issuing from Mimmer's well is kept by Odin in the moon.

(b) The waxing and waning of the moon have been variously interpreted in different mythologies, e.g., in the Eddic mythology the God Mane steers the course of the moon for this purpose.

(c) The notion of the eclipses of the sun and the moon being caused by a demon or demons is traced to Svarbhanu in the *ṚV*, V.40. It is repeated in other places in the Vedic literature also. This has its parallels in other[11] mythologies like the Teutonic, Sibarian, etc.

(d) The spot on the moon has been variously interpreted in the different mythologies. Mongolians and Altais believe that a hare dwells in the moon. The Chinese believe that the rabbit *Pu* sits there pounding the drugs of the elixir. According to a Mexican myth once the sun angrily threw a rabbit on the face of the moon, which darkened the moon's face. In a number of myths a hare is associated with the moon.

(e) If the Vedic Āryans look upon the moon as an eye of the creator, the moon has been described as springing from the creator's eye in the Japanese and Indonesian mythologies, reminding us of the Purāṇic myth about the birth of the moon from Atri's eye.

(f) The moon's effect upon vegetation and fertility is recognised in the Celtic and Armenian mythologies.

(g) The moon's intimate connection with the mind also is noted in other mythologies, e.g., the Armenians call epilepsy as 'the moon disease'.

The sun and the moon have been looked upon as forming a couple, the moon being mostly the female, in many mythologies. It is, however, worthnothing that this idea is totally absent in the Vedic literature.

Many of the beautiful fancies about the moon, which later became favourite with the classical Sanskrit poets can be traced to the Vedic literature.

References

1. *Vedishe Mythologie.*
2. *Hymns of the Atharvaveda,* XIV. 3 fn.
3. *The Religion of the Ṛgveda.*
4. *Vedic Religion,* A. Bergaigne, translated into English by Dr. V.G. Paranjpe, Pt. I.
5. *Vedic Mythology,* p. 113.
6. Translation of the *Śatapatha Brāhmaṇa,* I.6.4.5 f.n.
7. *Evolution of the Ṛgvedic Pantheon,* p. 145, Vijaya Krishna Brothers, Calcutta, 1938.
8. *The Religion of the Ṛgveda,* p. 237.
9. *Encyclopaedia of Religion and Ethics,* Vol. II, p. 63.
10. *Mythology of All Races,* Volumes I to XII.
11. Cf., chapter 12, 'The Rāhu-Ketu Myth'.

Dreaming-sleep and Deep-sleep in Vedic Literature

THE *Upaniṣads* which are the most ancient treasures of philosophical information, are also very rich in psychological material. They deal with mind and its various aspects in details. They give a detailed analysis of the three mundane states of the mind. Their analytical distinction between the dreaming condition and the deep-sleep condition of the mind is superb. One would like to find out if the earlier Vedic literature, viz., the *Saṁhitās* and the *Brāhmaṇas* had already attempted a psychological study of these two conditions of the mind. Here is an attempt to note down the ideas about the dreaming-sleep and deep-sleep in the Vedic literature and to trace their development up to the principal *Upaniṣads*.

Saṁhitās of the *Veda*

(1) The *Ṛgveda:* In the *Ṛgveda* the word *nidrā* occurs only once, in VIII.48.14 *mā no nidrā īśata mota jalpiḥ* Sāyaṇa explains this as *svapnā asmān bādhitumīśvarā mā bhuvan.* Thus here the word denotes troublesome sleep. The word *svapna* occurs several times in the sense of something harmful. In II.15.19 Indra is said to have overpowered Cumuri and Dhuni with *svapna,* 'beguiling sleep' in order to destroy them. X.162, 6 supposes that some evil-minded person might beguile a woman — probably a pregnant woman — by means of *svapna* or *tamas* (darkness).

Svapna is often called *duḥsvapna,* evil dream and various deities are invoked to avert it. In VIII.47.15 the Dawns are requested to consign all *dḥsvapna* to Trita Āptya. In X.86.21 Vṛṣākapi is addressed as *svapna-naṁśana,* destroyer of dreams. VII.55 is a hymn consisting of 8 stanzas. According to the *Anukramaṇī* the deity of the first stanza is Vāstoṣpati and of the rest Indra. Modern commentators like Prof. Wilson and Professor Griffith call this hymn 'a sleep-song'. In stanzas 2 and 3 the dog is asked to sleep *ni ṣu svapa.* In the 5th, a wish is expressed that the mother, the father, the dog, and the lord of the locality, all kinsmen and all people around should sleep. In the 6th the poet says, "We will close the eyes of each one, as one shuts a mansion." In the 7th he says, "We will lull people to sleep through the thousand-horned bull." While introducing this hymn Sāyaṇa gives an account from the *Bṛhaddevatā,* VI. 11-13 according to which Vasiṣṭha, entering Varuṇa's house at night is prevented by a barking dog. Vasiṣṭha recites stanzas 2 and 3 to lull it to sleep. Sāyaṇa also notes another tradition as *kathāsu parikalpyate.* According to Prof. Wilson it is from the *Nītimañjarī.* Vasiṣṭha could not get anything to eat for three days. On the fourth night he wanted to steal away some eatables from Varuṇa's store-house. He recited the 7 stanzas in order to lull to sleep the watch-dog and other people in the house. Thus this hymn is meant to induce sleep, may be, deep-sleep; but even here the reciter wants others to be asleep so that he may accomplish his selfish purpose. Thus even this hymn does not refer to deep-sleep for repose. Same is the case with *Khila,* II.14 where *svapna* is requested that all people should be lulled to sleep and the singer alone should keep awake. X.164 which is known as *Duḥsvapnaghna* has been addressed to Manasaspati, who has been asked to go away. By *manas* evil thought seems to be meant. The hymn seems to hint at the psychological cause of a dream when it says: *bahudhā jīvato manaḥ.* Thus *svapna* is understood as something bad and *duḥsvapna* is abhorred the most. Whenever forms from the root *svap* are used, they denote sleep, as a waste of time or as laziness. V.44.13 clearly says:

> *anubruvāṇo adheyti na svapan.*

> "One who recites the text daily can learn it and not one who sleeps."

(2) The *Yajurveda* also supposes *svapna* to be something bad. Sleep is associated with committing of mistakes. In VII.2 Soma is called Jagṛvi ever watchful, implying that one who sleeps is negligent of his duties. In XXX.7 says *jāgaraṇaṁ bhūtyai, svapnamārtyai.* 'Waking is for prosperity, sleep for affliction'. In XXXIV.55 the five sense-organs and the incoming and outgoing breaths are called *saptarṣis,* ever staying in the body without *svapna* or negligence. The seven are described as coming to the heart of the embodied being during sleep. *Prāṇa* and *apāna* are called *asvapnajau,* 'not born of *svapna*', i.e., entirely devoid of laziness. In this sense only are the forms of the root *svap* used in the *Taittirīya* and the *Kapiṣṭhala-saṁhitās.* Since this *Veda* is purely of sacredotal nature, it looks upon sleep from the point of view of the sacrifice only. According to the *TS,* VI.1.4 the sacrificer, who has been initiated for sacrifice, is not to sleep. In VI.1.5 *Agni* is requested to be a watchful guardian of the sacrifice. So also in the *KS,* I.15 *agne tvan su jāgṛhi vayam su mandiṣāmahe.*

These *Saṁhitās* interpret certain ritualistic actions in the language of sleep, symbolically. When the fire is getting dim and requires to be stirred *TS,* V.2.2.6 calls this awakening of the sleeping *Agni. KS,* V.4.10.5 lays down that too many sticks should not be piled upon the fire, the fire being now called a sleeping lion. *KS,* V.8 narrates a myth about the origin of night. According to this myth, earlier there existed day only and there was no light. When Yama died, his sister Yamī could not control her grief and went on crying ceaselessly. The gods created night in order to give her some consolation.

(3) The *Sāmaveda:* The *Saṁhitās* of this *Veda* do not contain any peculiar notion about dream or sleep. As in the *Yajurveda,* here also, sleeping is looked upon as a negligence in one's duty. The light which the worshippers of Indra see is called *jāgṛvi* 'watchful' implying that sleeping is negligence.

(4) The *Atharvaveda:* Sleep and dream have an important place in the magic and incantations of this *Veda.* IV.5 is called *Svapanam* a sleep charm. Part of it is repetition of VII.55 from the *Ṛgveda.* The first stanza (*ṚV,* VII.55.7) says, "we will lull people to sleep through the thousand-horned bull." The meaning seems to be that the same sun, who inspires people to work, puts them

to sleep when it sets. According to Prof. Aufrecht this hymn is intended to lull the whole household to sleep, while a young maiden is expecting a secret visit from her lover; but Prof. Lanman feels that the use of many forms of the plural does not warrant this interpretation. There are many hymns called *duḥsvapnanāśana* 'averting of evil dreams'. IV.46 is addressed to *svapna*. The god Svapna is described as neither living nor dead. Varuṇānī is mentioned as his mother, and Yama as the father. He is called as the son of the sister (the wives according to XIX.59) of gods. The Dream-god is then requested to protect the singers from all evil dreams and to transport these to their enemies. Similar are the contents of XVI.5. There *duḥsvapna* is called the son of destruction (*nirṛti*) misery (*abhūti*), disappearance (*nirbhūti*) and defeat (*parābhūti).* In IV.46 *svapna* is addressed as *ántakó'si mṛtyúrasi.* The sleeping condition, when all organs stop working outwardly, comes close to the condition of death. No wonder if the poet calls *svapna* as death. Even Homer calls sleep and death as 'feathered twins' in his *Iliad*. Shelly and Tennyson also call sleep and death as twin-brothers.

Duḥsvapna being transported to rivals is a very common idea in this *Veda* and recurs at several places. In XIX.56 the Ādityas are said to have transported the whole evil dream to Trita Āptya, at the behest of Varuṇa. Trita Āptya was already associated with evil dream in the *Ṛgveda*, VIII.47.15.XIX.59 refers to *svapna* as born in *asurasya yoniḥ*. This god is described as moving alone in a chariot and his nature is incomprehensible —

> *naínam viduḥ pitáro nóta devā́,*
> *yéṣāṁ jāliścáratyantaré'nam.*

Neither the manes nor the gods can know him, though their talk is often about him. XVI.6 even makes a distinction between *jāgrad duḥsvapna* (evil dream while awake) and *svapne duḥsvapna* (evil dream while in sleep). XIX.56.5 clearly says *yásya krūrámabhajanta duṣkṛtós svapnenas sukṛtaḥ puṇyamayuḥ.*

"Evil-doers have the cruel consequences of bad dream. By not having *svapana* the performers of good deeds enjoy a holy life."

Thus throughout the *Atharvaveda* also, *svapna* or sleep is looked upon as something bad and there is no allusion to sound sleep.

The *Brāhmaṇas*

In the *Brāhmaṇas Yajña* has become the centre of all thoughts. Hence sleep and dream also are thought of in connection with sacrifice only. They know that negligence in the performance of sacrifice can be committed during sleep also. Hence they request the deities to remove all such sin, that they might have committed while awake or while asleep (*Taittirīya Br.*, II.6.6.1; *Tāṇḍya Br.*, I.6, etc.) Following the sacerdotal *Yajurveda* the *Brāhmaṇas* also emphasise the rule that a sacrificer, who is initiated should not sleep during some prescribed periods, e.g., *Tāṇḍya Br.*, X.4.3 warns that he sould not sleep when the two *Atirātra yāgas* are going on. Before sleeping the sacrificer has to hand over the sacrifice to the charge of the deity Agni. (*Śatapatha Brāhmaṇa*, III.2.2.22 and 23). The *Chāndogya Brāhmaṇa*, 69, 27 advises a *Brahmacārin* not to sleep during day. The *G. Br.*, I.2.2, says that if the *Brahmacārin* can control his sleep at the proper time, then it is not transferred to a boa. When he is sleeping they say *svapitu mainam bobudhyatha.* "Let him sleep. Do not awaken him." In the *Jaiminīya Br., Upaniṣad*, IV.1.1.2-6 Varuṇa is invoked to protect a sleeping sacrificer with an armour prepared out of various hard metals. In the *Jaiminīya Brāhmaṇa*, IV.5.2 *Soma* is described as entering human beings in sleep. In general the *Brāhmaṇas* also teach that keeping awake leads to prosperity, sleeping to misery, e.g., (*T. Br.*, I.4.14.1 *bhūtyai jāgaraṇam.* I.4.14, 2 *abhūtyai svāpam. Śāṅkh Br.*, XVII.9 also remarks *jyotirvai jagarpitam. tamaḥ pāpmā rātriḥ.*

In the *Tāṇḍya Br.*, XII.5.18 there is a *Sāman* called Tvaṣṭṛ Sāman. It can be called a sleep charm, because the daughters of Tvaṣṭṛ lulled Indra to sleep with this *Sāman.*

Following the *Yajurveda* the *Brāhmaṇas* also interpret some ritualistic actions in terms of sleep. In the *Śāṅkh Br.*, I.4 the act of covering fire with a piece of hide is looked upon as lulling Agni to sleep and removing the piece as awakening Agni. So also the *Śa. Br.*, III.2.2.21. In *Śa. Br.*, I.6.3.41 Agni-*somīya* offerings are looked upon as the eyes of the sacrifice. In X.5.2.11 and 12 the two persons in the eyes are described as forming a couple. The reason why a sleeping person should not be awakened is given as 'thereby these deities are likely to be disturbed'.

A psychological analysis of dream and sleep is, for the first time, attempted in the *Brāhmaṇas.* The fact that all other organs merge in *prāṇa* during sleep is given in the *J. Br.,* III.I.1.4. *Jaiminīya Br.,* III.1.2.5-8 explains the same by saying that *prāṇa* temporarily devours other organs. The same fact that all organs merge in *prāṇa* during sleep and come back when a person is awake is vividly explained in the *Śa. Br.,* X.3.36. This *Brāhmaṇa* also gives the etymology of the words *svapiti* and *svapna* in X.5.2.14 as follows:

> *tasyaite prāṇāḥ svāḥ. sa yadā svapityathainamete prāṇāḥ svā apiyanti. tasmāt svapyayaḥ. svapyayo hi vai tam svapna ityācakṣate.*
>
> These organs are his (*prāṇa's*) own. When he sleeps, these organs, his own, merge in him. Hence it is going back of one's own. This going back of one's own is what they call as sleep.

So far there was no reference to deep-sleep. It is *Śa. Br.,* that thinks of deep-sleep for the first time. In X.5.2.11 it speaks of the two persons in the eyes forming a couple and remarks: *tau hṛdayasyākāśam pratyavetya mithunībhavataḥ. tau yadā mithunasyantaḥ gacchato'tha haitat puruṣaḥ svapiti; tadyathā hedam mānuṣasya mithunasyantaṁ gatvāsaṁvida iva bhavatyevaṁ haivedamasaṁvida, iva bhavati. daivam hyetad mithunaṁ. paramo hyeṣa ānandaḥ.* "During this sleep the two are described as if losing consciousness of everything else (*asaṁvida*). This reminds us of the description of *suṣupti* in *Bṛhadāraṇyakopaniṣad,* IV.3.21. Though here the word *suṣupti* has not been used, it is obviously the condition of *suṣupti.*"

The *Āraṇyakas*

The *Āraṇyakas* simply add a few more examples of the ritualistic actions being symbolically interpreted in the frame-work of sleep. Like the *Brāhmaṇas* they preach that the sacrificers and the priests must be ever vigilent and never negligent, e.g., *Tai. Ār.*, I.27 *uttisthata mā svapta*. The *Ait. Ār.*, II.4.3 just mentions three abodes of the soul, which, according to Śaṅkarācārya are the three states of mind.

The Principal *Upaniṣads*

The principal *Upaniṣads* have made a remarkable advance in the ideas about dream and deep-sleep. They give a very interesting and psychologically scientific analysis of dream, e.g., *Bṛhadāraṇyaka*, II.1.17 — *yatraiṣa etatsupto'bhudya eṣa vijñānamayaḥ puruṣastadeṣāṁ prāṇānāṁ vijñānena vijñānamādāya ya eṣ'ontarhṛdaya ākāsastasminchete . . . gṛhītaṁ manaḥ.* "The intelligence is located in the small space within the heart and the power of all other organs is seized by intelligence alone." *Praśnopaniṣad* describes this as: *tat sarvam pare deve manasyekībhavati.* "All other organs are unified in the great deity, the Mind." The fire in the form of the vital breaths alone is keeping awake now *Bṛ Up.*, II.i.18 describes that the *vijñānamaya puruṣa* becomes a sovereign (*mahārāja*), and moves all over the body, taking the senses with him, just as a sovereign would move all over his territory, along with his retinue. *Bṛ Up.*, IV.3.9 calls dream, *sandhyam sthānam* an intermediary locality, joining this world and the next'. The well-known fact that the objects in the dream are all illusory, created by the mind, is given in *Bṛ. Up.*, IV.3.10 as follows:

> *na tatra rathā na rathayogā na panthāno bhavantyatha rathān rathayogān pathaḥ sṛjate.*

The analysis of dream-creation is given very vividly in *Br. Up.*, IV.3.9 as follows:

> *sa yadā svapityasya lokasya sarvāvato mātrāmapādāya, svayaṁ vihatya, svayam nirmāya, svena bhāsā svena jyotiṣā prasvapiti.*

The experience is collected from the waking condition only (*asya lokasya sarvāvato mātrāmapādāya*) and yet the context or the juxtaposition is different *svayaṁ nirmāya.* In the ancient verses quoted by this *Upaniṣad* in support of its statement, the dreaming soul is called *eka haṁsaḥ,* a swan, going out of its nest (the body), and going wherever it pleases him, and enjoying whatever experience he desires. The *Praśnopaniṣad,* IV.5 calls him *deva,* 'god', enjoying great majesty. This passage makes it very clear that the dream-experience is entirely based upon that of the waking world. *Dṛṣṭam dṛṣṭamanupaśyati śrutaṁ śrutamevārtha-manuśṛṇoti . . .,* etc. The passage also explains that though the experience of the dreamer is based upon his own actual experience, in the dream it gets mixed up with imagination . . . *dṛṣṭaṁ cādṛṣṭaṁ ca śrutam cāśrutaṁ cānubhūtaṁ cānanubhūtaṁ ca saccasacca.*

The condition of *suṣupti* deep-sleep also is vividly analysed in various *Upaniṣads. Br. Up.,* IV. 3.19-34 gives a detailed analysis of the same. Section 19 describes it saying that in this state, to which the soul resorts, being weary, it does not entertain any desire. Nor does it witness any dream. Section 21 describes it as follows:

> *tadyathā priyayā striyā sampariṣvakto na bāhyam kiñcana veda nāntaramevamevayam puruṣaḥ prājñenātamanā sampariṣvakto na bābyam kiñcana veda nāntaraṁ tadvā tasyaitadāptakāmamātmakāmamakamām rūpam śokāntam.*
>
> It is intelligence alone that is awake. The soul, closely embraced by it, is oblivious of everything else within or without, the experience being similar to that of a lover in close embrace of his beloved. He has no desire, no grief.

According to *Bṛ. Up.,* II.19 during *suṣupti* the soul is resting in the pericardium of the heart, after moving through 72000 *nāḍīs,* veins. *Chāndogya Up.,* VIII.2.2 describes the soul as resting in the heart and gives the etymology of the word *hṛdayam,* as *hṛdi ayam. Chāndogya Up.,* VI.8.I uses the root *svap* in connection with *suṣupti* also and gives the same etymology as found in the *Śatapatha,* X.5.2.14. *Chāndogya Up.,* VIII.3.4 calls the soul in deep- sleep as *samprasāda* (the serene one) and describes it as resting in the highest light and as appearing in its own form. According to *Praśna*, IV.6 the soul now overpowered by brilliance, sees no dream and that is the state of happiness. The *Kauṣītakī* (III.3 and IV.19) describes the same fact.

The *Maitrāyaṇī*, VII.11.18 enumerates these three conditions and even mentions the fourth one, greater than all these. It is the *Māṇḍūkya* which teaches about this forth and supreme condition for the first time. When it describes the soul in the dream condition as *antaḥprājña* (having intelligence inwardly) and *praviviktabhuk* (enjoying subtle objects). It is summarising what the earlier *Upaniṣads* like the *Bṛ* have already said. Its description of the soul in the deep-sleep condition as *ekībhūtaḥ*, *ānandamayaḥ* and *ānandabhuk* also is based upon that of the earlier *Upaniṣads*.

Thus the distinction between the dreaming sleep and deep-sleep is quite unknown to the period of the *Saṁhitās*, the word *suṣupti* being entirely absent. In the *Ṛgveda* the word *Svapna* and the forms of the root *svap* have been used to denote disturbed or harmful sleep, bad dreams being looked upon as the most harmful. In the liturgical *Saṁhitās* of the *Yajurveda* and the *Sāmaveda* sleep is looked at from liturgical point of view only. Sleep is looked upon as a negligence in the performance of rituals and the sacrificer is prohibited from sleeping on some particular ritualistic occasions. Certain ritualistic actions like the stirring of the fire have been symbolically interpreted in the language of sleep. Dream and sleep play an important role in the magic and incantations of the *Atharvaveda*. Dreams are hated as something bad. There are many hymns for averting the evil effects of dream. While the singers of the *Ṛgveda* request the deities only to remove evil dream, the singers of the *Atharvaveda* request them further to transport these dream to their enemies.

As in the liturgical *Saṁhitās*, in the *Brāhmaṇas* also sleep can be thought of in the context of the sacrifice only. In several places the sacrificers and the priests are warned against sleep. Symbolic interpretation of ritualistic actions to suit the frame-work of sleep is more common in the *Brāhmaṇas* than in the liturgical *Saṁhitās*. However the first attempt at the psychological study of dreams is met with in the *Brāhmaṇas* for the first time. Without using the term *suṣupti* the *Śatapatha*

Brāhmaṇa has, for the first time, described the state of deep-sleep.

The *Āraṇyakas* merely add a few more instances of symbolic interpretation of ritualistic actions in the context of sleep.

The *Upaniṣads* show a clear advance in this regard. Various passages from the principal *Upaniṣads* like the *Bṛhadāraṇyaka,* the *Chāndogya,* the *Praśna,* etc., give a sound analysis of dreaming-sleep and deep-sleep. The distinction between the two is very clearly pointed out. The relation between the waking condition and the dream condition is very scientifically explained on a psychological basis.

Finally a late *Upaniṣad* among these principal *Upaniṣads,* viz., the *Māṇḍūkya* goes beyond these three conditions and explains about the fourth supramundane condition also.

One feels wonderstruck with the study of the various conditions of the mind, that the *Upaniṣadic* thinkers had advanced in that ancient period.

9

Uśijaḥ in the *Ṛgveda*

THE word *uśij* in its various grammatical forms occurs 31 times in the *ṚV*. Sāyaṇa mostly derives it from the root *vas* 'to desire' and explains it as *kamayamāna,* i.e., 'desiring, desireful, zealous.' Sometimes he understands it as *medhāvin* 'intelligent'. The Western scholars like Langlois, Wilson, Ludwig, Grassmann and Griffith follow him. It is Bergaigne,[1] who for the first time, suggests that it could be taken as a proper noun. Oldenberg[2] supports him in his notes on *ṚV,* II. 31.6. Geldner,[3] in his German translation of the *ṚV,* takes *uśij* as a proper noun in 23 places. In 2 more places he translates it as a common noun, but in the footnotes he suggests that it can be taken as a proper noun. Prof. H.D. Velankar's[4] English translation of *Maṇḍalas* II, III and VII has been published. In the course of this portion the word *uśij* has occurred 14 times. He understands it as 'an ancient priest'. Prof. Renou[5] has translated some select portions from the *ṚV* into French. He always translates it as 'a model priest'. Hence it is interesting to investigate as to what this word signifies in the *ṚV*.

Sāyaṇa's Explanation of the Word *uśij*

I have attempted to understood the word individually in every occurrence. Sāyaṇa's explanation of the word is not acceptable for various reasons. Since the scholars coming after Geldner have not accepted it, it is unnecessary to discuss it in details. Yet one can point out a few instances where Sāyaṇa has to strive hard to remain consistent to his explanation. He is often not sure as to which is the substantive qualified by this adjective, e.g.:

asyá śā́surubháyāsaḥ sacante haviṣmanta uśíjo ye ca martā́ḥ. (I. 60.2)

First he says:

uśijaḥ kāmayamāna devāḥ

and then,

yadvā uśija iti medhāvināma medhāvinaḥ stotāraḥ. III.27.10.

He is not sure whether *uśij* is to be taken in active or in passive sense. He says, *puroḍāśadihaviḥ kāmayamāno'gniḥ* 'Agni, desirous of oblations, like *puroḍāśa* or *kāmārthibhiḥ kāmyamānaḥ* 'longed for by desireful sacrificers'.

Whenever this word occurs in a clause giving a comparison with *na* as the *upamāvācaka,* Sāyaṇa takes *na* in a quite different manner and faces a difficulty in explaining the clause, e.g., II.4.5, *uśígbhyo nāmimīta várṇam.* Sāyaṇa explains: *asmadīyaṁ rūpam kāmayamānebhya ṛtvigbhaḥ svasadṛśam rūpaṁ nirmimīte.* 'Agni reveals to the priests his form as they would like it'. Here he understands *na* as 'and' *naśabdaścārthe.*

In VII.10.2 he explains *yajñám tanvānā́ uśíjo ná mánma* as *yajñam vistāryantā ṛtvijo mananīyāni stotrāṇi paṭhantīti śeṣaḥ.* He has to add the word *paṭhanti.* 'The priests carrying forward the sacrifice (are singing) songs of praise.' He understand *na* as 'now' *neti sampratyarthe.*

Often his explanation of *uśij* as *kāmayamana* sounds very unreasonable, e.g., III.15.3 *kṛdhī no rāyé uśíjo yaviṣṭha.* Here he explains it as *asmān dhanaṁ kāmayamānān kuru.* 'Make us long for wealth.' As we know the Vedic seers are ever eager for wealth. Agni need not create that longing in them. Sāyaṇa has, therefore, to explain this somehow as *abhilaṣitadhanapradānena prāptakāmān kuru.* 'Fulfil our desire by giving us the desired wealth.' While explaining IV.6.11 *hótāramagníṁ mánuṣo ní ṣedurnamasyántā uśíjaḥ śáṁsamāyóḥ.* He says, *āyormanuṣyasya śaṁsanīyam hotāram tvāṁ pūjayantaḥ paśvādilakṣaṇam dhanaṁ kāmayamānā manuṣyā ṛtvija upāviśan.* 'The men, i.e., priests, desiring wealth in the form of cattle, etc. have sat near you honouring you, the praiseworthy invoking priest of the mortals." When the same line recurs in V.3.4 with *daśasyantaḥ* for *namasyantaḥ*, Sāyaṇa takes *uśijaḥ* as a form of Gen. sg. qualifying *āyoḥ* and explains: "The priests, offering oblations, attend upon you, O Agni, for the sake of the mortal sacrificer, desiring covetable fruit."

He has to explain some portions somehow in order to understand *uśij* as *kāmayamāna*, e.g.:

> *mandram hotāramuśijo namobhiḥ prāñcam yajñam netāramadhvarāṇām.*
> *viśāmakṛṇvannaratim pāvakaṁ havyavāham dadhato mānuṣeṣu.* (X.46.4)

He explains: *uśijaḥ kāmayamānā ṛtvijo manuṣyeṣu madhye hotāramagniṁ dadhānā viśām yajamānānāmarthāya stutibhiḥ (suprītam) kṛtavantaḥ.*

The desireful priests, placing the invoking priest Agni amidst the mortals, rendered him (agreeable) with praises for the sake of the people, i. e., sacrificers. He has to take *aratim* as *arthāya* and *viśām* as *yajamānānām*. Then he attempts alternative explanation as follows:

> *yadvā viśām prajānamaratimaryam svāminaṁ kṛtavantaḥ* 'They made Agni the lord of the people' now explaining *arati* as 'the lord'.

There are at least 5 places where Sāyaṇa has to add the substantive. Aṅgirasaḥ as qualified by *uśijaḥ*, III.34.4 *indraḥ . . . jigāyośigbhiḥ pṛtanā abhiṣṭhiḥ* is explained by him as — *yuddhaṁ kāmayamānairaṅgirobhiḥ saha indraḥ parakīyāḥ senā jigāya*. Indra conquered the inimical forces in company of Aṅgirasas, who were desirous of battle'. In IV.1.15 *te vrajaṁ gomantamuśijo vi vavṛḥ*, *uśijaḥ* is explained as 'desiring Agni' and the pronoun(te) is taken as standing for Aṅgirasaḥ — when the same line recurs in IV.16. 6, Sāyaṇa explains *uśijaḥ* with *marutaḥ* as 'the desireful *Maruts* enveloped the cowpen (belonging to Aṅgirasas)'. In VII.90.4 *gavyam cidurvamuśijo vi vavṛḥ* his explanation is — "The desireful Aṅgirasas obtained the wealth in the form of cattle." In X.104.4 he takes *usijaḥ* with Aṅgirasaḥ and explains it as 'Aṅgirasas, desiring you, O Indra'. In some places *uśijaḥ* and *icchamānāḥ* stand together. Hence Sāyaṇa has difficulty in explaining the term, e.g.:

> *tvā́yā sahá drávinamicchámānā vrajáṁ gómanta muśíjo ví vavṛḥ.* (X.45.11)

Here in connection with the same clause *vrajáṁ gómatamuśíjo ví vavṛḥ* he takes the gods as the subject of *vi vavṛḥ* and explains *uśijaḥ* as *medhāvinaḥ*, intelligent.

Similarly, in X.46.2 *gúhā cátantamuśíjo námobhiricchánto dhīrā bhŕ̥gavo'vindan* — he construes *usijaḥ* with *Bhṛgavaḥ* and explains it as *kāmayamānāḥ* 'longing' and then he has to add *ātmanaḥ* before *icchantaḥ*. 'The wise longing Bhṛgus found out Agni, moving secretly in waters, since they desired to have him (as their own).'

Thus the possibility of taking *uśij* as an adjective meaning 'desireful' is completely ruled out. Now, before discussing as to what the word signifies, let us put together what the *ṚV* says about *uśijaḥ*: The mortal *uśijs* obey the precepts of Agni (I.60.2). Agni is *uśij*, i.e., a representative of *uśij*s (I.60.4). Indra protects *uśijs*, who desire friendship with him (I.131.5). In ancient times when Agni was polished, i.e., decorated by the *uśijs* he became agreeable to them (I.189.7). Agni had formerly revealed his real form to the *uśijs* (II.4.5). The *uśijs* found their way through sacrifce (II.21.5). The *uśijs*, in ancient times, offered excellent praise to Agni. The singers, now, desire to offer similar praise (II.31.6). The immortal *uśijs*, i.e., the ancient ancestors of the present *uśijs*, ordained three fuel sticks in the fire. One of these was for the mortals, the other two for the neighbouring worlds or the sister-worlds (III.2.9). The ancient *uśijs* were favoured with excellent wealth by Agni. Hence the present singer says, "For the winning of treasures make us *uśijs*" (III.15.3). Indra conquered the inimical forces and won light with the help of the *uśijs* (III.34.4). The poet Viśvāmitra Gāthina tells the Ṛbhus that his ancestors, the *uśijs*, have come to know about the miraculous powers, with the help of which the Ṛbhus have obtained a share in the sacrifice. This they could know through a lot of thinking, through family-ties and through the knowledge of the *Sagas* (III.60.I). With their divine speech the *uśijs* have thrown open the cowpen of the cows — Vala myth — (IV.1.15; IV.16.6; X.4.5. II). After that the waters flowed in ancient times (VII.90.4). The *uśijs*, the men, have sat beside Agni, the invoking priest (IV.6.11; V.3.4) Agni has carried forward the sacrifice just as the *uśijs* extend their thought, i.e., their thoughtful songs (VII.10.2). The *uśijs*, the clans, invoke Agni in the sacrifice (VII.10.5). The *uśijs* caught hold of fire first (IX.86.30). The *uśijs*, the Bhṛgus, have found out Agni, hiding in the waters (X.46.4). The *uśijs*, the connoisseurs of the right ways, praising Indra, stayed in the house of Manu (X.104.4).

Uśijs as a Clan

In the light of the above description of *uśijs* I feel certain that *uśij* is the name of an ancient family or a small clan well-known for its religious inclinations, for its priestly efficiency and for its mystical powers. *Uśijaḥ* and *manuṣaḥ* are mentioned in apposition in IV.6.11; V.3.4 and *uśijaḥ* and *viśaḥ* are mentioned together in VII.10.5. This proves that the present *uśijs* form a well-known family or clan among the mortals. They seem to form a branch of Aṅgirasas, especially of the Pajra-Aṅgirasas (*ṚV*, I.116, 7). As seen above, even Sāyaṇa, who takes *uśij* as an adjective, has to bring in the Aṅgirasa, in connection with the *uśijs* in 5 places. Prof. Velankar, who translates *uśijaḥ* as ancient priests has referred *uśijaḥ* to Aṅgirasas in his foot-notes on III.2.9, III.34.4 and VII.90.4. In X.46.2. *uśijaḥ* and *Bhṛgavaḥ* are standing in apposition. In III.2.4 Agni has been described as *bhṛgūṇām rātiḥ* 'a gift of the Bhṛgus.' It has been accepted by all scholars that Bhṛgus and Aṅgirasas form an ancient priestly clan. Sāyaṇa always explains the phrase *pūrve ṛṣayaḥ* as *bhṛgvāṅgirasa-prabhṛtayaḥ*. From very ancient times Bhṛgus and Aṅgirasas have been intimately connected with the cult of fire. Dr. Rahurkar[6] says, "This can only mean that the illustrious priestly family of the Bhṛgus claimed that their ancestors taught men to produce fire by friction and also initiated them into the proper fire-cult."

Similarly, the prestigious position of the Aṅgirasas in this regard has been clearly brought out by Dr. Shende[7] in the following words, "The Aṅgirasas thus form the ancient family of the priests of Agni. They found out Agni, churned him and employed him for the sacrificial purpose. Agni is Aṅgirasa or Aṅgirasa is from *aṅgāra*, the burning ember. They must have first started the worship of Agni. This is acknowledged by all seers of the *ṚV* and the *Brāhmaṇas*." In the same article Dr. Shende points out that according to B.G. Tilak Aṅgirasas must have been the ancient sacrificers of the whole Indo-European race.

Following this history of the Bhṛgus and the Aṅgirasas I feel that *uśijs* formed a small clan belonging to this illustrious priestly clan. Geldner has already explained 25 occurrences of this word, taking *uśij* as a proper noun. I feel the remaining 6 occurrences also can be explained in that light as follows: (1) I.60.4 Agni has been installed in the human clans as the chosen priest among the mortals. He is *uśij*, i.e., a representative of *uśijs*, a purifier and a Vasu. (2) I.189.7: Agni, at the evening time, be aggreeable to us just as you become agreeable to the *uśijs* when they polished, i.e., decorated Agni (in ancient times). (3) III.3.7: Agni, you are *uśij* among the gods, very intelligent of the singers. The implication is that Agni is representative of the *uśijs* among the gods. Similarly (4) III.3.8: Agni is *uśij* among the singers. (5) III.11.2 Agni is immortal *uśij*, implying that Agni is *uśij*; but he is immortal whereas the present *uśijs* are mortal. (6) X.92.12 the poet Śaryāta Mānava requests Ahirbudhnya 'to listen, even from a distance, to the praise that the *uśijs* are offering to you.' Here the exact relation between Śaryāta and *uśijs* cannot be explained. Perhaps *iva* is to be added after *uśijām*.

The fact that *uśij* was the name of an ancient family or a clan is further corroborated by the presence of its secondary derivative *auśija* in the *ṚV*. It has occurred 10 times in the *ṚV*. All scholars have explained it as a proper noun. Only in 3 places Sāyaṇa has somehow explained it as a common noun. In IV.21.6 and 7 he explains it as 'a sacrificer' and in V.4.6 as "the Sun'. Kakṣīvat, the poet of a few hymns in the *ṚV*, is *auśija* (I.18.1). The merchant Dīrghaśravas is *auśija* (I.112.1). The king *Ṛjiśvan* in the Pipru myth is *Auśija* (X.99.11).

Different Views About *Auśija*

Sāyaṇa,[8] on the evidence of *Anukramaṇī*, explains *auśija* as a matronymic in the case of Kakṣīvat. According to him Kakṣīvat's father is Dīrghatamas and his mother is a Śūdra maid servant of the queen of Aṅga. He takes *uśij* as the name of that Śūdra woman. On I.112.11 Sāyaṇa[9] says about Dīrghaśravas that *uśij* is the name of the wife of Dīrghatamas and her son, the sage Dīrghaśravas worked as a merchant during the course of a drought. Because of this Auśija has been understood as a matronym by later scholars; but it can be definitely explained as a patronym. In the *ṚV* the seers are rarely designated by their matronyms alone. Kakṣīvat is Auśija because he is a son or a descendant of *uśij*. The evidence provided by Pargiter[10] is very helpful in this regard. It is true that he has mostly depended upon the evidence of the *Purāṇas*. Yet, he has ably corroborated it with the evidence from the Vedic literature. Since Ṛjiśvan also is called Auśija in *ṚV*, X.99.11 Pargiter points out that Auśija must be taken as a patronym. Ṛjiśvan was a son of Bharadvāja Vidathin and had no connection whatsoever with the śūdra woman. He points out that *uśij*, an ancient member of Aṅgirasa family, had three sons Ucathya, Bṛhaspati and Saṁvarta. Dīrghatamas was a son of Ucathya and as such he was an Auśija. Kakṣīvat, therefore, is naturally an Auśija. According to Pargiter[11] "A man had various patronymics from different ancestors and the choice in poetry was often governed by the metre." He feels that this can explain why Kakṣīvat is called Auśija and not Dairghatamasa or Aucathya. Pargiter has further pointed out that the name of the śūdra woman was Auśīnarī according to the *Mahābhārata*, II.20. While discussing the genealogy of Bharadvājas, Rahurkar[12] mentions that Bharadvāja Vidathin was a son of Bṛhaspati and grandson of Aṅgirasa according to the Sarvānukramaṇī. Then with the evidence of the *Purāṇas* he gives a table according to which Uśij, a descendant of Aṅgirasa family, had three sons Ucathya, Bṛhaspati and Saṁvarta. Bṛhaspati had two sons Dīrghatamas and Bharadvāja. Kakṣīvat was a son of Māmateya and a grandson of Dīrghatamas, while Ṛjiśvan was a son of Vidathin, and a grandson of Bharadvāja. Thus both Kakṣīvat and Ṛjiśvan are Auśijas.

According to Pargiter, Auśija is one of the 15 branches of Aṅgirasa-family in the genealogies given by the *Purāṇas*. He, therefore, is of the opinion[13] that "Uśij — (as śūdra mother of Kakṣīvat) — seems to have been invented to explain Auśija through the lack of the historical sense."

All this leads to the proof that the *Ṛgvedic* seer Kakṣīvat was a descendant of the Uśij family, forming a part of the Pajra-Aṅgirasa clan. In *ṚV*, I.116.7 he is called Pajrīya and Sāyaṇa there says, *Pajrā vā Aṅgirasaḥ*.

Uśij as Uiskhsh Part of a Trio in the Avestā

It is interesting to note that the word *uśij* is found in the Avestā also in a slightly different form as Usikhsh. In his paper on 'An *Avestā*-amulet for contracting friendship' Jivanji Jamshetji Modi[14] has provided very intersting information in this regard. He refers to the following portion from the *Gāthās:* "O Mazda, I ask this. The Daevas who fight according to their wishes and through whom the Karapans and the Usikhshs have entrusted the cattle to Aeshma Daeva, and through whom the Kavis grew in power, have they ever been good rulers? They did not procure for these (cattle) water or pasture through piety."

Here the Karapana, the Usikhshs and the Kavis form a trio of wicked persons. According to Modi, it corresponds to a similar trio in the *Avestā*-amulet and a similar one in Ahur Mazda Khodae prayers. He gives the following table:

Avesta-amulet	Kura	Tarvaṇi	Karapan
Gathas	Kavi	Usikhsh	Karapan
Ahur Mazda Khodae Prayer	Kikan	Shastaran	Karapan

Thus Usikhshs of the *Gāthā* are the same as *Tarvaṇis* of the *Avestā*-amulet and Shastaran (Sg. Shastar) of the Ahur Mazda prayer. Jivanji Modi further points out that according to Zad Sparam[15] Usikhshs and Karapans were two families that were related to Zoroaster, but were opposed to his new religion. According to Zad Sparam XV, five Karap brothers and their first cousins Usikhshs have descended from the demon Wrath and a sister of the king Manuskihar. The three family names in the above trios signify moral vices. Kavi means 'mentally blind', i.e., 'unmindful of moral truth'. Karapan or Karafan means 'mentally deaf', i.e., 'unmindful of moral instructions'. Usikhsh or Shastar means 'oppressive, cruel'.

Dr. Shende[16] has already said, "The Aṅgirasas seem to be the champions of Deva-worshippers and hence Zarathushtra turned them into archdemons, leading the Daevas." The Uśijs or the Usikhshs, forming a branch of the same family naturally became the enemies of Zoroaster.

Conclusion

Thus the word *uśij*, which has been explained as an adjective by Sāyaṇa and the earlier Western scholars, is definitely a proper noun. It can be so explained in all 31 places where it occurs in the *Ṛgveda*. From the references to the Uśijs in the *ṚV* it can be said that Uśij was the name of an ancient family or a small clan, belonging to the Pajra branch of the Aṅgirasas. They are expert priests possessing mystic powers. They are intimately connected with the cult of fire. The presence of the secondary derivative from this word, viz., *Auśija*, provides strong evidence in this regard. Sāyaṇa's explanation of the term as a matronymic of Kakṣīvat, on the basis of the story of the śūdra woman Uśij, occurring in the *Sarvānukramaṇī*, is not at all convincing. The word is a patronymic. This fact finds support from the evidence given by Pargiter in his *Ancient Indian Historical Tradition* and by V.G. Rahurkar in his *The Seers of the Ṛgveda*. The presence of an ancient family called Uśij in the period of the *Ṛgveda* is further corroborated by the evidence from the *Avestā*. Usikhshs have been mentioned in the *Avestā* and the *Gāthās* as being inimical to Zarathushtra.

References

1. *Vedic Religion*, Vol. I, French (1877), Translation into English by V.G. Paranjpe, pp. 57-59. Arya Saṁskṛti Prakāśana, Poona, 1969.
2. *Ṛgveda*, pp. 212-13. Textkritische und Exegetische Notem, Buchhandlung, Berlin, 1909.
3. *Der Ṛgveda*, Vol. I, Göttingen, 1923, *H.O.S.* Volumes 33 to 35 Leipzig, 1951.
4. *Hymns from the Ṛgveda Maṇḍala* VII, B.V.B. 1963, *Maṇḍala* II, University of Bombay, 1986, *Maṇḍala* III, University of Bombay 1968.
5. *Etudes Védiques et Panineénnes*, Editions E De Boccard, Paris, 1960-66.

6. *The seers of the Ṛgveda*, Dr. V.G. Rahurkar, p. 218, University of Poona, 1964.
7. *Aṅgirasas in the Vedic Literature.* Dr. N.J. Shende, p. 121, *ABORI*, XXXI. 1951.
8. *Vedārthadīpikā* on I.116, V.S.M. p. 712.
9. *Ibid.*, p. 680.
10. *Ancient Indian Historical Tradition*, pp. 160-61, F.E. Pargiter, Ist edition, 1922, Reprint Motilal Banarsidass, 1962.
11. *Ibid.*, p. 140.
12. *The Seers of the Ṛgveda*, pp. 100-01.
13. *Ancient Indian Historical Tradition*, p. 161.
14. *Anthropological Papers*, Anthropological Society of Bombay, 1911.
15. *S.B.E.*, Volume XLVII, p. 143.
16. *ABORI*, XXXI, p. 129.

10

Ṛgvedic *Ṛṣi* Nābhānediṣṭha

AUTHORSHIP of the *Sūktas* 61 and 62 of *Maṇḍala* X of the *Ṛgveda* has been attributed to Nābhānediṣṭha. The *Aitareya Brāhmaṇa*, V.14 has given the following story about him: While Nābhānediṣṭha was staying away as a student, his brothers divided the father's property among themselves, depriving him of his share. They told him that they had given the father himself to him. The father directed Nābhā to go to the Aṅgirasas, whose sacrifice was stuck upon the sixth day. Nābhā helped them in accomplishing the ritual of the sixth day and received from them 1000 (cows) as a reward. When he was collecting his share a man wearing black garments appeared there from the North and said that whatever was left at the place of the sacrifice belonged to him. Nābhā's father explained to him that the person was Rudra and that he had a rightful claim over whatever was left at the place of the sacrifice. Then Nābhā gave over everything to Rudra and Rudra, being pleased with his truth-speaking, returned the whole to him. This story also occurs in *Taittirīya Saṁhitā*, III.1.9.4 to 6, *Śāṅkhyāyana Brāhmaṇa*, XXVIII.4, XXX.4, *Śāṅkhyayana Śrauta Sūtra*, XXVI.11, 28 to 30, etc. The hymn X.62 has been mentioned in the Vedic literature at several places, e.g., *Aitareya Brāhmaṇa*, VI.30.31, *Pañcaviṁśati Brāhmaṇa*, XX.9.4, *Kauṣītakī Brāhmaṇa*, XXX.4, etc.

Later on the *Purāṇas* like *Padma*, *Bhāgavata*, *Viṣṇu*, *Vāyu* and the *Mahābhārata* have transferred this story of Nābhānediṣṭha to a sage named *Nabhāga* or *Nābhāga*. They have sometimes elaborated it with their usual details.

Nābhānediṣṭhạ — A *Mānava*

One would like to know about Nābhānediṣṭha from his two hymns; but they do not offer much help in this regard. We know that he is *mānava*, i.e., a son or a descendant of Manu. The hymn 61 mentions a king, who is a *vipra* (stz.16). The sacrificer is Vaitaraṇa, who is *dvibandhu* (stz.17). According to Oldenberg[1] this implies that he has priestly as well as royal relatives or that he claims relationship with Yadus and Turvaśas both. The poet of this hymn, i.e., Nābhānediṣṭha is a descendant of this king and he is conscious of this privilege (stz. 18). As such he wants to be recognised as a *dvija* (stz. 19). In the hymn 62 Nābhā is requesting the Aṅgirasas to accept him *prati gṛbhṇīta mānavaṁ sumedhasaḥ*. (stzs. 1 to 4). Oldenberg explains that Nābhā is a descendant of Manu Sāvarṇi, who, as a *grāmaṇī* (stz. 11), was a vaiśya and he wants to be recognised as a brāhmaṇa. According to Oldenberg the story of Nābhā in the *Aitareya Brāhmaṇa* has been freely invented by combining the elements from these two hymns.

According to Geldner[2] hymn 61 has very little to do with the story of Nābhānediṣṭha. The poet Vaitaraṇa, son of Vitaraṇa, calls himself *dvibandhu*. Geldner suggests that Vitaraṇa is the poet's real father and Aśvaghna (stz. 21) his adopted father. According to Geldner Turvayāṇa in stz. 2 and Nābhānediṣṭha in stz. 18 are simply mythical figures. About hymn 62 Geldner feels that it has some connection with the story of Nābhānediṣṭha. About Manu Sāvarṇi presenting in thousands (stza. 9 and 11) Geldner discusses whether he is a contemporary of Yadu and Turvaśa (stz. 10) or is the same as Manu Vaivasvata, Vaivasvata being his patronym and Sāvarṇi or Sāvarṇya his matronym. Geldner feels that probably he is a contemporary of Yadu and Turvaśa, Manu Sāvarṇi being his assumed name. As already seen this king is *grāmaṇī*. According to Geldner *grāmaṇī* need not necessarily be a *vaiśya* in the ancient period; because even *Śaryāta Mānava*, a kṣatriya, has been described as wandering with his *grāma* (clan) in the *Śatapatha Brāhmaṇa*, IV.1.5.2. Nābhānediṣṭha is a descendant of this king.

Relationship Between Nābhānediṣṭha and Nabanazdista

Long ago Colbrooke[3] had pointed out the resemblance of 'nabansazdista' occurring in the Yasna of *Avestā* with Nābhānediṣṭha in the *Veda*. Taking a hint from it Eugene Burnouf[4] has discussed in details the phonetic relationship between the two words in his commentary in French language on Yasna I. 39. Burnouf accepts the interpretation of the adjective nabanazdista as '(the men) of new posterity, the nearest' as given by Neriosengh and discards the meaning 'the near ones, the parents' as given by Anqetil. According to him it means 'the nearest among the moderns'. According to the *Avestā* they are the new men opposed to the ancestors, who were called 'the men of premier law'. These new men are contemporary of him, who addresses this Yasna. Thus Burnouf comes to the conclusion: "The relation of these two terms must be regarded as furnishing one of the most explicit proofs of the high antiquity of the events, which have separated the Āryan people in two great branches, one which has remained in Bactrian Arie and the other which has gone to establish itself in Brahmanic Arie." Burnouf feels that nabanazdistas are the famous Pichadadians celebrated in the Persian literature and that they are the common ancestors of the Ariens of Bactria and the Āryans of India. Prof. Néve[5] says that Nābhānediṣṭha is probably the youngest son of Manu. According to him Bactria and Mdso-Persian nations have applied the name of a celebrated descendant of Manu to the class of new men, opposed to the men of premier law, though they have forgotten the name of Manu himself. On the basis of the story in the *Aitareya Brāhmaṇa* Néve thinks that Nābhānediṣṭha must have preserved excellent science of sacrifice and must have secured all good of the sacrifice while working as a priest. He asks, "Would Nābhānediṣṭha and his people have taken part in the migration, which the first Āryans penetrated in India?" Prof. Lassen[6] also sees 'a reminiscence of an Indo-Iranian split' in the legend of Nābhānediṣṭha. Prof. Roth[7] disagrees. Though Prof. Weber[8] admits that it is not a case of borrowal on either side yet he remarks that in the *Avestā* the term has kept its original sense of 'the nearest relation' while in the *Ṛgveda* it has became a proper noun. Sanskrit commentators explain the name as *nābhau nediṣṭha*, 'nearest in birth', 'nearest relation'. Dr. K.R. Potdar[9] understands it as 'a person moving in the vicinity of the altar.' He suggests that Nābhānediṣṭha may be a secret name assumed in order to have the desired mystical effect for the purpose of sacrifice. According to him it suggests the poet's constant association with the sacrifice, which qualifies him for the technical discussion of sacrifice, which he is undertaking in these hymns, viz., X.61.62. The editors[10] of the *Vedic Index* have remarked — "Nābhānediṣṭha is etymologically connected in all probability with *nabanazdista* in the *Avestā*, which refers to the Fravaṣi of Paoriyo-tkaesha and Fravaṣi of Nabanazdista."

Thus the phonetically close relationship between Nābhānediṣṭha and *nabanazdista* seems to be acceptable in general. In the light of all this one can surmise about Nābhānediṣṭha as follows:

In the *Avestā* nabanazdistas were 'men of new law', followers of zoroaster, as opposed to the men of premier law. Similarly towards the last stage of compilation of the hymns in *Maṇḍala* X there might have come up a group of young reformists, who wanted to introduce some convenient reforms in the technique of sacrifice. These reformists, probably, were not brāhmaṇas; but they had studied the technique of sacrifice thoroughly well. They claimed that though they wanted to introduce some reforms in the sacrifice, they were not opposed to that institution. In fact they came quite close 'nediṣṭha' to the orthodox sacrificers. They might have assumed the name 'Navanediṣṭhas' which, in course of time, might have been changed to 'Nābhānediṣṭhas'. When there were so many words like *jñāti, bandhu, āpi, jāmi*, etc. meaning 'a relation' in the Vedic language a new word like 'nābhānediṣṭha was, otherwise, not necessary.

Conclusion

We know that whenever new reforms are suggested, these are always resisted by the orthodox section in the society. When the Ṛbhu-group suggested some reforms in the sacrifice these were strongly protested by the orthodox Tvaṣṭṛ-group. But later on these reforms were accepted and the Ṛbhus got their share in the sacrifice. Similarly, the reforms of these Nābhanediṣṭhas must have been strongly protested against. After some time those at the head of the institution might have realised that these new reforms were really convenient. Hence they might have assimilated these new techniques and then the Nābhānediṣṭhas must have been invited to participate in the sacrifice. As a reminiscence of this, the authorship of these two *Sūktas* might have been attributed to a *ṛṣi* named Nābhānediṣṭha.

The fact that these Nābhānediṣṭhas were not allowed a share in the sacrifice earlier seems to be reflected in the story of the *Aitareya Brāhmaṇa,* where Nābhānediṣṭha has been deprived of his share in the father's property.

These reformists could secure the right to participate in the sacrifice on the merit of their expert knowledge of sacrifice. Similarly, in the story of the *Aitareya Brāhmaṇa*, Nābhānediṣṭha could secure 1000 cows by means of his skill in performing the ritual of the sixth day.

From the prayer of Nābhānediṣṭha to the Aṅgirasas in hymn 62 we know that he aspires to be recognised as a *brāhmaṇa*. His illustrious ancestor Manu Sāvarṇi, as we have already seen, was a *vaiśya* or a *kṣatriya*. In the story of the *Aitareya Brāhmaṇa*, Nābhānediṣṭha is honourably invited by the Aṅgirasas to perform the sacrifice. All this can be traced to the belated admission of the Nābhānediṣṭhas to the sacrifice.

The incident of the Nābhānediṣṭhas securing their right to sacrifice, which they were denied for quite some time, seems to be quite important. Hence later the *Purāṇas* have transferred the story of Nābhānediṣṭha to a sage actually named Nabhāga or Nābhāga.

References

1. *Ṛgveda Noten*, Vol. II, pp. 261-69, Weidmansche Buchhandlung, Berlin, 1912.
2. *Der Ṛgveda*, pp. 225-26, *HOS*, Vol. 35.
3. *Miscellaneous Essays*, Vol. I, p.25.
4. *Commentaire sur Yasna*, Vol. I pp. 563-69, Royal Printing Press, Paris, 1883.
5. *Essai sur le mythe des Ribhavas*, Paris 1847, English Translation by Miss G.V. Davane, p. 65, Notes 18, 19 pp. 90, 91. Ajanta Publications, Delhi, 1985.
6. *Vedic Index*, Vol. 1, p. 442, fn. 5. Macdonell and Keith, Motilal Banarsidass, 1958.

7. *Op. cit.*, fn. 6.
8. *Op. cit.*, fn. 7.
9. *Sacrifice in the Ṛgveda*, p. 220. Bharatiya Vidya Bhavan, Bombay, 1953.
10. *Op. cit.*, p. 442.

11

The Fourteen Gems in the Legend of *Samudra-Manthana*

THE legend of *Samudra-manthana* occurs in the *MB (critical edition, Ādi Parva,* Chapters 15-17; *SR, Ādi,* 12-14; *NR, Ādi Parva,* Chapters 17-19); *Rāmāyaṇa* (Gujarati Press, *Bālakāṇḍa* 45; Bengali, *Ādi Kāṇḍa* 46; *NWR, Bālakāṇḍa* 41) and in a number of *Purāṇas* like *Viṣṇu,* IX; *Padma, Sṛṣṭikhaṇḍa,* IV; *Brahma Khaṇḍa,* IV; *Matsya,* 249-251; *Skanda,* IX and *Bhāgavata,* VIII.6. It has been frequently referred to by Classical Sanskrit Poets like Kālidāsa, Bāṇa, Bhavabhūti and Prakrit Poets like Guṇacandra. All details in the story are very interesting; but here the author is confining herself only to the concluding part of the legend. This legend ends with the acquisition of *Amṛta* along with some other gems. The list of these gems varies with every account.

(a) *MB Critical edition* — 7 gems:

Soma, the Moon; Śrī or Lakṣmī; *Surā;* wine; the speedy horse Uccaihśravas; Kaustubha gem; Dhanvantari, carrying a pot of *Amṛta.*

(b) *MBNR* — 9 gems:

Soma; Śrī; *Surā;* Uccaiḥśravas; Kaustubha; Dhanvantari, *Amṛta,* the white elephant Airāvata; *Kālakūṭa,* the deadly poison.

(c) *MBSR* — 12 gems:

Poison; Jyeṣṭhā (elder sister of Lakṣmī); *Soma; Śrī; Surā;* Uccaiḥśravas; Kaustubha; Pārijāta tree; the desire-yielding cow or Surabhi; Airāvata; Dhanvantari and *Amṛta.*

(d) *R* (Gujarati Press) — 7 gems:

Poison; Dhanvantari; 60 crores of nymphs; *Vāruṇī* (wine);

Uccaiḥśravas; Kaustubha and *Amṛta*.

(e) *Padma Purāṇa, Brahma Khaṇḍa* — 12 gems:

Kālakūṭa; Alakṣmī; Airvāvata; Uccaiḥśravas; Dhanvantari; Pārijāta; Surabhi; *Apsarasaḥ;* Lakṣmī; *Candra; Sudhā* and Tulasī.

(f) *Padma Purāṇa, Sṛṣṭikhaṇḍa* — 11 gems:

Alakṣmī and *Tulasī* omitted. *Amṛta* added.

(g) *Matsya Purāṇa* — 14 gems:

Vāruṇi; Soma; Śrī; *Surā;* Uccaiḥśravas; Kaustubha, Pārijāta; Kālakūṭa; Dhanvantari; *Madirā; Amṛta;* Surabhi; *Chatra* and *Kuṇḍala*.

(h) *Bhāgavata Purāṇa* — 11 gems:

Poison; Kāmadhenu; Uccaiḥśravas; Airāvata; Kaustubha; Pārijātaka; Nymphs; Lakṣmī; *Vāruṇī;* Dhanvantari; *Amṛta*.

(i) *Viṣṇu Purāṇa* — 9 gems:

Surabhi; *Vāruṇī;* Pārijāta; Nymphs; the Moon; Poison; Dhanvantari; *Amṛta* and Śrī.

(j) *Skanda Purāṇa* — 13 gems:

Poison; the Moon; Kāmadhenu; Airāvata; Pārijāta; Kaustubha; Nymphs; *Surā;* the Śārṅga bow; the Pāñcajanya conch; Śrī; Dhanvantari and *Amṛta*.

Later on traditionally the gems were taken to be 14 in number as enlisted in the *Subhāṣita*:

lakṣmīḥ kaustubhapārijātakasurā dhanvantariścandramā
gāvaḥ kāmadughaḥ sureśvaragajo rambhādidevāganāḥ,
aśvaḥ saptamukho viṣam haridhanuḥ śaṅkhāmṛtaṁ cāmbu-
dhe ratnanīha caturdaśa pratidinam kuryurdvayor-
maṅgalam.

Various accounts of this legend describe, in a very interesting manner, all details about these gems, and the reaction of their appearance on gods and demons. It will be interesting to study each of these gems critically.

(I) *Lakṣmī*: Sāyaṇa explains Lakṣmī as *Lakṣaṇavatī* quoting the etymology given by Yāska as: *lakṣmirlābhādvā lakṣaṇādvā.*

St. Petersburg dictionary derives the word as follows: *lag* (to stick) — *Lakṣma,* Lakṣmī; meaning, gaining, prosperity, auspicious thing, grace, etc. Curiously enough Lakṣmī has not been reckoned among gems in the *R*. In all other accounts she has been described as wearing a white garment, having a golden complexion, standing in a lotus; carrying a lotus in hand, etc. In *ṚV, Khilasūkta* (II.6, i.e., Śrīsukta) many of these details have been mentioned. Lakṣmī is taken by Viṣṇu. The *Purāṇas* give an interesting description of Lakṣmī-*svayaṁvara*. *MB (SR)* and some of the *Purāṇas* mention Alakṣmī as appearing earlier to Lakṣmī. She has been wedded to Kālakūṭa and then is advised to go to bad persons.

According to *MB(SR)* and almost all the *Purāṇas* loss of Lakṣmī led to *samudra-manthana*. According to those accounts the world becomes devoid of glory, i.e., Lakṣmī due to a curse addressed to Indra by Durvāsas.

According to Sorensen's *Index of Proper names in the MB,* she is one of the 10 wives of Dharma, daughter of Brahmā and sister of Dhātṛ and Vidhātṛ. Sky-raging horses are her spiritual sons. Draupadī is an incarnation of hers.

Professor Shembavanekar[1] has rightly pointed it out that the *Śrī-Sūkta* in the *ṚV* supports his theory, viz., that in Lakṣmī we find a metamorphosis of the *Vedic Uṣas.* At the same time the *Sūkta*[2] shows Lakṣmī as prosperity, or glory in general in requesting her to drive away Alakṣmī and describing her as inexhaustibly rich in cattle and men.

Professor Adalbert Kuhn[3] also holds that Lakṣmī represents morning ruddiness. He has pointed out how she resembles the Greek deity Aphrodite.

Thus Lakṣmī[4] meaning the morning ruddiness or prosperity in general can be traced right up to the *ṚV,* Vaiṣṇavism has played a great part in elevating Lakṣmī to the highest position. In *Purāṇas* like *Kūrma,* she appears as representing the Primeval creative power. Lakṣmī as wealth has been popularly described by classical Sanskrit poets as fickle-minded, and in this capacity she has been referred to as being a rival to 'Sarasvatī', the goddess of Learning. Throughout Sanskrit Literature Lakṣmī indicates grace in general, e.g., *Vanalakṣmī, Gṛhalakṣmī, Vasanta-lakṣmī,* etc.

Originally 'Lakṣmī' may be referring to the grace in general and when *Samudra,* conveyed 'the firmament' and the terrestrial ocean, Lakṣmī was associated with her residence in both places. Hence in the legend of *samudra-manthana* she is described as coming out of the ocean. Lotus, that always grows in water, which is supposed to be the birthplace of Brahmā, was now naturally associated with her. It is worthnoting that even in the *Śrī-Śukta,* she is described as arising out of a lotus and having the complexion of a golden lotus. This explains why in classical Sanskrit literature Lakṣmī is closely associated with a lotus and is called "Kamalā".

(2) *Kaustubha*: The etymology of this word can be given as — *kau nāma pṛthvyām stubhyaḥ,* meaning 'praiseworthy on the earth'. It is one of the gems churned out of the ocean according to all accounts except in the *Padma Purāṇa* and *Viṣṇu Purāṇa.* It is described as being very resplendent and belonging to the class of *Padmarāga.* It is coveted for by all gods and demons, but Viṣṇu gets it and wears it on his chest. In classical Sanskrit literature whenever Viṣṇu is described his Kaustubhamaṇi is invariably mentioned. In point of brilliance it resembles another jewel associated with Kṛṣṇa and known as Syamantakamaṇi.

According to Kuhn, Kaustubha is representation of the Sun, as it is made to belong to Viṣṇu, a solar deity. This also proves that the *samudra* in the legend originally means "the firmament".

(3) *Pārijātaka*: This is reckoned among gems in the *SR* of the *MB* and in all the *Purāṇas.* In classical literature, it is one of the five heavenly trees; and Kṛṣṇa is given the credit of bringing it down on the earth for the sake of his wife. In the *MB,* nectar-giving saps are described as flowing from the burning trees on the Mandara. 'This', says Professor Kuhn, 'explains why *Purāṇas* have included Pārijātaka in the gems. Kuhn further connects it with the Ash-tree in the Indo-Germanic fire-myths. Greeks and Germans derive their origin from Prometheus, the Fire-bringer and from the Ash-tree. This according to Professor Kuhn may be responsible for the inclusion of Pārijātaka and of the trees on Mandara in this legend. It is clear, however, that Pārijātaka has been included in the gems at a late time by the *Purāṇas.* Its inclusion here is purely sectarian. *Purāṇas* later on included in this list whatever is associated with Viṣṇu or Kṛṣṇa, e.g., *Padma Purāṇa* includes *Tulasī* plant, *Matsya Purāṇa* includes *Chatra* and *Kuṇḍala* and *Skanda Purāṇa* includes *Śārṅga dhanuḥ* and *Pāñcajanya śaṅkha* also.

(4) *Surā*: All versions of the legend excepting that in the *Padma*

Purāṇa Brahma Khaṇḍa mention *Surā* or *Vāruṇī* as one of the gems. *MB* describes how it went to gods, following the path of the sun. *R.* here gives a wrong etymology of *Sura* and *Asura* saying that gods became *Suras* as they accepted the wine. Intoxicating effect of wine has been described in all the *Purāṇas*. They describe *Surā* variously as — *madaghūrṇitalocanā; ekavastrā; muktakeśī; raktāntastabdha-locanā; āyatākṣī; lokacittapramāthinī; sarvamādaka-devatā*, etc. *Matsya Purāṇa* mentions *Surā, Vāruṇī* and *Madirā* as three distinct gems, obviously out of oversight. Dr. Gai in his paper on "Wine in the Orient and its Prohibition" has said that wine existed since the very dawn of civilization. He says "It appears that for some time ancestors of the Gothic and Vedic races had an identical rite of extracting juice from a fresh plant, conserving it and drinking the same as sacramental wine." Mr. Slater (*Dravidian Element in Indian Culture*) traces *Amṛta* to the Egyptian beer or fermented juice of date-palm. This can be connected with *Surā* which can definitely be traced to the *Somarasa* of the *Vedas*, which was later divided in three aspects. Its invigorating aspect became *Amṛta*, intoxicating part became *Surā* and the divine aspect became *Candramāḥ*.

Professor Kuhn connects this *Surā*, as an aspect of *Soma*, with the Ash-Tree which in itself combines the two Indo-Germanic legends, viz., 'winning of the heavenly fire as lighting', and 'the birth of human beings from a tree.' Linguistically *Surā* and*Sūrya* have affinity. (St. Petersberg dictionary derives *Surā* from the root *su* to press and explains it as brandy, god's drink, etc. that is full of vigour). Thus it can be traced to the heavenly fire.

(5) Dhanvantari has been mentioned as a gem in all available accounts of the legend. He brings the pot of *Amṛta* and is the master of *Āyurveda*. *R.* calls him "The king of Physicians". He is described in the *Purāṇas* as having white complexion and clad in white garment.

St. Petersburg dictionary explains the name as Dhanvanā taratīti (one who moves in the manner of a bow). Kuhn points out his close resemblances with the deity Asklopios. (Guardians of Asklopios are equipped with bows). *Dhanvan* a part of his name refers to the rainbow. *Amṛta* that he bring signifies healthiness, which has been bestowed upon *Sūrya* ever since the days of the *ṚV*. He has a staff in his hand. All this according to

Prof. Kuhn proves that he represents the lightning aspect of fire; but the lightning has not got the soothing effect that is expected of a *Vaidyarāja*. I think he can better be a representation of the sun, taking into account the following facts:

(i) He has got a white complexion and is clad in white.
(ii) He is *Āyurvedamaya*. The sun is an embodiment of vigour.
(iii) The Etymology 'Dhanvanātarati' proves the same.

(6) *Candramāḥ*: Except for *R.* and *Bhāgavata Purāṇa* the moon has been mentioned as one of the gems. *Soma* is its synonym. *Candra* is described as having cool rays and being a brother of Lakṣmī. This can be traced to the divine or agreeable aspect of *Soma* which Kuhn has already connected with the fire-legend. When *samudra* referred to the ocean, and the firmament the moon that was already in the sky was to be brought out by churning. Intimate relation of the moon with the ocean is a matter of our experience also.

(7) *Gāvaḥ Kāmadughaḥ*: *SR* of *MB* and all *Purāṇas* mention this gem. Surabhi is referred to in various places in the *MB*. She has ben described as staying in the Pātāla. Kṣīrasāgara is a lake prepared with her milk. According to Kuhn it represents lightning, the sole bearer of heavenly waters. As the *Kṣīrodadhi* was thought of as the firmament also, the cow may represent the rays of the sun, that have a wholesome effect. The rays have been often referred to as cows even in the *ṚV* (cf. *ṚV*, II. 2.24). Further if the ocean is called *Kṣīrodadhi* its connection with cows is natural.

(8) *Sureśvara-gajaḥ*: This has not been included in gems by the critical edition of *MBR*, *Matsya* and *Bhāgavata*. It is called Airāvata or Airāvaṇa. It is white in colour and has four tusks. In Indian mythology it belongs to Indra. Kuhn traces this to the lightning aspect of fire, pointing out how Airāvaṇī is a synonym for the lightning. If Indra is the Rain-god this should naturally be a white cloud or lightning. This again leads us to look upon the *samudra* as being the sky in this legend.

(9) *Rambhādi-devāṅganāḥ*: Except for the *MB* and the *Matsya Purāṇa* the nymphs have been reckoned among the gems by all versions of the legend. St. Petersburg dictionary gives three

different etymologies of the word, according to which the word would mean 'moving in water', 'shapeless', 'having beautiful cheeks'. *R.* gives a fourth one as 'arising from the sap in water, as the water was churned'. They are residents of the heaven, possessing the power to have any form at their will, and are fond of the game of dice. They are often referred to in the *ṚV, AV, MB,* and *R. Vājasanejī Saṁhitā* gives many names of the nymphs. *R.* suggests their connection with courtesans saying how they were not accepted either by gods or demons. *Padma Purāṇa, Brahmakhaṇḍa* also repeats the same.

Kuhn holds that they represent the lightning. These may as well represent the rays of the Sun moving in the ocean of firmament.

(10) *Aśvaḥ saptamukhaḥ*: It has been reckoned among gems by all except *Viṣṇu* and *Skanda Purāṇas.* It is white in colour and is as speedy as the mind. Gods get it. It is Uccaiḥśravas 'Roaring loudly'. According to the *Bhāgavata,* it was given by Viṣṇu to Indra in preference to Bali. Dr. Ghatage, in his scholarly note on *samudra-manthana* had pointed out how Prof. Geldner[5] believes that *ṚV,* I.163, I refers to the origin of this horse, and how *R,* X[6].72 seems to suggest the birth of the sun, along with that of other gods out of the ocean.

The name of the horse is not mentioned in the *ṚV,* but occurs in the *AV.* It is known to the *VS* also. The horse reminds us of *Indrāyudha* in the *Kādambarī.*

According to Kuhn this horse represents the lightning or more accurately the thunderstorm as is evident from its name; but to the author it seems to be a representation of the sun, for the following reasons:

> (i) It is white in colour. (ii) It is described as going to the Gods, following the course of the sun. (iii) In later mythology, the Sun's chariot is described as having 7 horses. (iv) The two hymns in the *ṚV,* as referred to above seem to suggest that.

(11) *Kālakūṭa*: Except for the critical edition of the *MB* all other versions reckon this among the gems and describe how Śiva was kind enough to swallow it. Poison is not a desirable thing. Hence

it ought not to have been included in the list. Probably it was included here in order to bring out the greatness of God Śiva. Its inclusion here is very convenient for the various philosophical interpretations put upon the legend. According to Kuhn it stands for the disastrous flash of lightning and thus can be connected with fire. It is associated with two notions (i) terrible heat and (ii) disastrous effect. Kuhn connects the first aspect with fermentation of *Soma*, and the second with consuming power of the fire.

(12) *Haridhanuḥ or the Śārṅga-bow:* is mentioned by *Skanda Purāṇa* only. Its inclusion is purely sectarian. It might have been suggested by the rainbow. Due to its resemblance with the rainbow and from the fact that it is given to Viṣṇu, a solar deity, it can easily be looked upon as representing the sun.

(13) *Śaṅkha*: Like the earlier gem it is mentioned only in the *Skanda* on sectarian basis. While speaking of the ocean one is naturally reminded of the conches and shells that lie at its bottom. It is white in colour and hence extending Prof. Kuhn's theory, we can look upon this as a representation of the sun.

(14) *Amṛta*: is the object of *samudra-manthana* according to almost all versions of the legend. (We have already seen how according to some *Purāṇas* the object of *samudra-manthana* was regaining Śrī). The word appears in the *Vedas* under different grammatical forms like *Amṛtaḥ, Amṛtam, Amṛtāni, Amṛtebhiḥ*, etc. St. Petersburg dictionary mentions different meanings of the word as 'not dead', 'immortal', 'the state of immortality', etc.

According to the epics and the *Purāṇas* it comes out of the churning of the Milky Ocean and gods alone can taste it. It is the drink of immortality. It has been stored in the moon. According to Paul Thieme[7] the word primarily means 'the vital energy' and 'that which gives vital energy', 'a drink giving immortality' is a later development of its meaning. According to Dumezil it may be beer extracted from barley, belonging to Indo-European period. According to Slater it is Egyptian beer or juice of date-palm. Donald Mackenzie[8] traces it to the meal of Odin in Teutonic mythology. Though *Amṛta* and *Soma* are both mentioned in the *Veda* side by side, one represents the invigorating aspect and the other exhilarating one. As *Soma* is later identified with the moon, this also should represent some luminary in the sky, like the moon or more probably the sun.

Thus a critical study of all these gems leads us to the conclusion that the ocean in the legend of *samudra-manthana* primarily means the firmament. We can further see that through some of the gems can be traced to the Vedic or Pre-Vedic period the legend as such is of epic origin. The list of the gems went on growing following the idea — *jātau jātau yadutkṛṣṭaṁ tadratna-mityabhidhīyate.*

References

1. *The Metamorphosis of the Uṣas.*
2. Recently Dr. (Kum.) Usha Bhise has suggested a new interpretation of the hymn in *Journal of BORI,* Vol. LIII, 1973.
3. *Der Herabkunft des Göttertranks.*
4. A paper on this topic was read by Prof. V.S. Patil at the 27th Session of the *AIOC* held at Kurukshetra in December 1974.
5. *Der Ṛgveda, HOS,* Vol. 33.
6. *Ibid., HOS,* Vol. 35.
7. *Studien Zur Indogermanishen Wortkunde und Religion-Geschichte.*
8. *Indian Myth and Legend.*

12

The Rāhu-Ketu Myth

THE Rāhu-Ketu incident forms a part of the interesting myth of the *samudra-manthana*. It appears in the *Mahābhārata* (Critical ed., *Ādi Parva*, XVII.4-8; Northern Recension, *Ādi*, XIX.4-9, Southern Recension, *Ādi*, XIV.5-9) and in various *Purāṇas* like the *Padma* (*Brahmakhaṇḍa*), *Matsya* and *Bhāgavata*.

Rāhu-Ketu in the *Mahābhārata*

Following is the version of the story as it occurs in the *Mahābhārata*:

> *tataḥ pibatsu tatkālaṁ deveṣvamṛtamīpsitam,*
> *rāhurvibudharūpeṇa dānavaḥ prāpibattadā.*
> *tasya kaṇṭhamanuprāpte dānavasyāmṛte tadā,*
> *ākhyataṁ candrasūryabhyām surāṇāṁ hitakāmayā*
> *tato bhagavatā tasya śiraścinnamalaṅkṛtam,*
> *cakrāyudhena cakreṇa pibato'mṛtamojasā.*
> *tacchailaśṛgapratimaṁ dānavasya śiro mahat,*
> *cakreṇotkṛttamapataccalayadvasudhātalam.*
> *tato vairavinirbandhaḥ kṛto rāhumukhena vai,*
> *śasvataścandrasūryābhyāṁ grasatyādyapi caiva tau.*

When Dhanvantari, with a pot of *amṛta* in his hand, appeared on the surface of the Milky Ocean, the demons started shouting for *amṛta*. When the demons took possession of the pot Viṣṇu used his miraculous power to infatuate them. He appeared as a beautiful woman, Mohinī and went amongst the demons. Being enamoured of Mohinī's charms the demons handed over the pot of nectar to her. Viṣṇu stealthily came back to the gods and then all the gods together happily drank the nectar. When the gods were enjoying this feast of nectar Rāhu, a demon, secretly sat amongst them in the disguise of a god. Scarcely had the nectar reached his throat when the moon and the sun detected this mischief and exposed it to Viṣṇu out of their desire for the well-being of the gods. Viṣṇu then used his discus *sudarśana* and severed the head of this mischievous demon. The demon's head, which was as big as the summit of a mountain fell down and the whole earth trembled at that moment. Viṣṇu now cast off his feminine garb and had a furious fight against the demons. After defeating the demons completely the gods celebrated their acquisition of *amṛta*.

This incident gave rise to unflinching enmity of Ṛāhu against the moon and the sun, and even to this day Rāhu devours them.

A similar account of the incident is found in the Northern and the Southern recensions of the *MB*.

Rāhu-Ketu in the *Purāṇas*

The various *Purāṇas* amplify and enlarge the same story adding details of their own:

The incident has been described in the *Bhāgavata Purāṇa* as follows:

devaliṅgapraticchannaḥ svarbhānurdevasaṁsadi,
praviṣṭaḥ somamapibattaccandrārkābhyaṁ ca sūcitaḥ.
cakreṇa kṣuradhāreṇa jaghāna pibataḥ śiraḥ,
haristasya kabandhastu sudhayāplavito'patat.
śirastvamaratāṁ nītamajogrāhamacīkṛpat,
yastu parvaṇi candrārkavabhidhāvati vairadhiḥ.

This *Purāṇa* adds:

> The trunk of the demon's body fell down on the earth, but the head had become immortal due to the nectar, and hence it ever persues the moon and the sun on eclipse-days.

The *Matsya Purāṇa* gives the account exactly as it is found in the *MB*.

The *Padma Purāṇa* goes a step further and calls the fallen trunk of the demon's body as 'Ketu.

This interesting episode has not been referred to in the *Rāmāyaṇa* and in a few *Purāṇas* like the *Viṣṇu Purāṇa*. In his edition of the *Viṣṇu Purāṇa*, Prof. Wilson takes a stock of the various versions of the story and adds the following foot-note:

> (In the *VP*) No notice is taken of the story told in the *MB* and some of the *Purāṇas,* of the *Daitya* Rāhu insinuating himself among the gods and obtaining a portion of the *amṛta*. Being beheaded for this, by Viṣṇu, the head becomes immortal, in consequence of the *amṛta* having reached the throat, and was transferred as a constellation to the skies; and as the sun and the moon detected his presence amongst the gods, Rāhu persues them with implicable hatred, and his efforts to seize them are the causes of eclipses, Rāhu typifying the ascending and descending nodes. This seems to be the simplest and the oldest form of the legend. The equal immortality of the body, under the name Ketu, and his being the cause of meteorical phenomena, seems to have been an after-thought. In the *Padma Purāna* and the *Bhāgavata Purāṇa* Rāhu and Ketu are the sons of Siṁhikā, the wife of *Dānava* Vipraciti.

Views of Different Scholars

In his dictionary Prof. Monier Monier-Williams understands Rāhu as 'the Seizer', deriving the word from the root *rabh* or *grabh* 'to seize'. He notes the meaning of the word Rāhu as — "A demon who is supposed to seize the sun and the moon, and thus cause eclipse." Prof. Williams also adds the following lines about Rāhu:

> He is fabled as a son of Vipraciti and Siṁhikā, and

> as having a dragon's tail; when the gods had churned the ocean for the *amṛta* or nectar of immortality, he disguised himself as one of them and drank a portion; but the sun and the moon revealed the fraud to Viṣṇu, who cut off Rāhu's head, which thereupon became fixed in the stellar sphere, and having become immortal through drinking the *amṛta,* has ever since wrecked its vengeance on the sun and the moon by occasionally swallowing them; while at the same time the tail of the demon became Ketu and gave birth to a numerous progeny of comets and meteors; in astronomy Rāhu is variously regarded as a dragon's head, as the ascending node of the moon (or the point where the moon intersects the ecliptic in passing northwards), as one of the planets and as the regent of the South-West quarter; among Buddhists many demons are called Rāhu. Rāhu denotes the eclipse itself, or rather the moment of the beginning of an occulation or obscuration.

Prof. Dowson,[1] gives similar notes on Ketu and Rāhu. He gives the following additional information about them — "Rāhu had four arms and his lower part ended in a tail." According to the *Viṣṇu Purāṇa* eight black horses draw the dusky chariot of Rāhu, and once harnessed are attached to it forever. The eight horses of the chariot of Ketu, swift as mind are of dusky and red colour of the lac or of smoke of burning straw.

Donald Mackenzie,[2] on a comparative study of this myth says, "One of the terrible *Asuras* is Rāhu, who causes eclipses by swallowing the sun and the moon, like the Chinese dragon, the wolf Managaram of Teutonic mythology, and the Grecian demons who devour Helena, the sun-maiden, the sister of the twin Dioscuri. In the Vedic period Rāhu was represented by the demon Svarbhānu. *Daityas* and *Dānavas* are the demons of the ocean. In Teutonic mythology the mead is snatched away by Odin from the giants of the under-world, and is concealed in the moon, which is ever persued by the demonwolf Mangaram, who seeks to devour it.

In his *Purāṇa-Index,* Shri Dikshitar records that Rāhu and Ketu are two out of 100 sons of Vipraciti and Siṁhikā. According to this *Index,* Ketu has been described as a planet, with a chariot, to which have been yoked 8 green horses. In size it is one-fourth of Bṛhaspati and he iṣ the first among the *Dhūmaketus.*

Shri Sorensen in his *Index to the names in the Mahābhārata* records numerous references to Rāhu, the mischief played by him at the churning of the ocean, the punishment he receives, his grudge against the sun and the moon, his being a cause of eclipses, etc. As recorded here the *MB* gives 12000 *yojanas* as the diameter and 42000 *yojanas* as the circumference of the globular planet Rāhu. Ketu was originally the tail or the body of Rāhu. The sight of either of the two has been described as an ill-omen.

According to the *Vedic Index of Names and Subjects,* edited by Macdonell and Keith Svarbhānu *Asura,* which is the older form of Rāhu, has been referred to in the *ṚV,* V.40, and later in the *T.S.,* II.i.22.1, *Pañc. Br.,* IV.5.2; 6-13; VI.8.1; *Ś.Br.,* V.3.2.2, *Kau.Br.,* XXIV.3. This demon is supposed to have eclipsed the sun with darkness, while Atri does the work of rescuing him.

According to Prof. Ludwig *ṚV,* I.110.2; mentions the indication of the ecliptic with the equator and axis of the earth.

In his *Orion*[3] Shri B.G. Tilak has referred to *ṚV,* V.40 which according to him shows "that an eclipse of the sun was then first observed with any pretensions to accuracy by the sage Atri." According to Shri Tilak this observation of the solar eclipse is noticed in the *Śaṅkhyāyana Brāhmaṇa* and in the *Tāṇḍya Brāhmaṇa* also.

The earliest clear version of this Rāhu-Ketu myth is found in the *MB* though references to an eclipse caused by the demon Svarbhānu can be noted even in the *ṚV.*

It is clear that right from the beginning of this myth it has been ever connected with the natural phenomena of lunar and solar eclipses. Hence a critical study of the myth requires a study of the notion of eclipse in mythologies other than Indian.

Eclipse-Myth According to Other Mythologies

A comparative study of Mythology of various races points out that the idea of an eclipse being caused by a demon or an evil spirit is common to most of these. In all mythologies the sun and the moon are looked upon as the storehouses of vitality and vigour. Even in the *ṚV* the sun has been referred to as the very soul of all things, movable and immovable. (*ṚV*, I.115.1) *sūrya ātmā jagatastasthu ṣaśca.*

This is but natural, since the bright sun-light does give us vigour. Similarly the moon has always been looked upon as the treasure of *amṛta* or *soma* in Indian mythology. The moon is also the lord of the herbs and plants. In the Chinese and Japanese mythology the moon-water has been described as nourishing plants and trees. This moon-water and the dew of immortality in the Jade-cup appear to be identical with the Indian *soma* and the *amṛta* or nectar of the classical gods. In the Teutonic mythology Odin has been described as keeping the mead of gods in the moon. It is needless to multiply instances. One thing is clear from all this that we always love the bright sunshine and the pleasant moon light.

In Indian mythology *amṛta* was identified with *soma,* and later *soma* with the moon. Hence the moon was looked upon as the store-house of nectar. Naturally her waning was looked upon as the feasting by the gods of the nectar, contained within her.

In the Egyptian mythology Set, the black pig, is supposed to eat up the waning moon, which happens to be the left eye of god Horus. According to the Yakuts of Sibaria the waning of the moon is caused by wolves and bears. In this context one can quote Shri Tilak's remark in his *Orion*:[4] "According to my explanations, our common Indo-European ancestors believed that the sun or the day-light, which was personified under the image of various animals, was everyday killed in the evening and yet re-appeared almost unhurt the next morning."

If it is so, no wonder that all races look upon the eclipse with a still greater awe.

(i) As referred to by Prof. Livy, Egyptians[5] follow the custom of making a din during an eclipse of the moon, presumably to frighten away the beast, that is devouring her. Tacitus also refers to a similar custom.

(ii) In Teutonic[6] mythology, the sun and the moon are ever in fight and are persued by two fierce wolves. The wolf 'Skoll' (the adherer) chases the sun, and 'Hati' or 'Mangaram' is after the moon. "Again and again at dreaded eclipses would these giant-wolves have swallowed now the sun and now the moon, had not their evil designs been thwarted by the spells which were wrought against them and by the clamour of affrighted people" (Mackenzie).

(iii) According to the Chinese the eclipses of the moon and the sun are caused by a furious dragon or a terrific beast, that follows them.

The people beat gongs to frighten away the demon.

(iv) The Todes fire off guns and send up rockets to frighten away the snake that is trying to eat the hare in the moon.

(v) Some of the Maori people said that the sun and the moon were swallowed by a god, whom the celestial bodies had offended through neglect.

Similar beliefs were prevalent amongst the natives of the North Queensland and the Sandwitch Island. The Dakota discharged rifles in the air to drive away the demon or the evil spirit that is causing an eclipse. The Sencis of Peru also shot arrows at the sun, in order to drive away the savage beast, with which, they supposed the sun was struggling. In Mexico the dragon of eclipse, is called Tezcatlipoca.

(vi) On the West coast of Africa an eclipse of the moon is attributed to the shadow of the sun, which is constantly in pursuit. The natives throng the streets shouting, "Leave her, Go away."

(vii) The Jugo-Slaves believe that a wolf-man Vukodlak (variously spelt as Vikodlak, Vrkodlak, Volkun, etc.) follows the clouds and devours the sun or the moon, thus causing an eclipse. They beat drums, ring bells and fire guns to drive away the demon.

(viii) Prof. Holmberg[7] has given the Buriat story of eclipse in details as follows: "According to the Buriat tales (in Siberia) an eclipse of the sun or the moon takes place when a certain beast, which is ever persecuting the lights of the sky, swallows the sun or the moon."

Once when this monster, 'Alkha', again darkened the world, the gods became so angry, that they cut his body in two. The hind part fell down, but the living forepart still haunts the Sky."

The Buriats shout and throw stones to frighten away the monster. The same tale[8] appears in another Buriat District, as follows: "Formerly Arakho lived upon the earth and consumed the hairs of the people's bodies. Seeing this God became angry and inquired of the moon, Arakho's hiding place. On finding the beast he struck it in two, and the living fore-part is forever eating the moon in consequence." It is also told that god Otshirvani, wishing to sweeten the life for people and animals let the sun and moon prepare drink of life, but Arakho drank it up and soiled the cup. Inquiring of the beast's dwelling place from the moon, God hurried there and cut him in two. The fore-part, having thus become immortal persues the moon. This Arakho, causing eclipses, is known to Mongols also.

(ix) The Altai Tatars say that the eclipse of the moon is the work of a man-eater living in a star. The Russian Tatars and Chuvachs speak of a Vampire, which sometimes swallows the moon, and sometimes the sun.

One can easily mark that there is a uniform notion at the basis of all these eclipse-myths. Out of all these myths those in India and Siberia are fully developed. Prof. Holmberg holds that the myth has come to Siberia from India. He says,[9] "The tale originates in India, where the monster's name is Rāhu. Arakho and Alkha are corrupt variants of this name."

It can thus be seen that the eclipse-myths in their bare outlines are common to all races and nations. Hence this Rāhu-Ketu myth of the Indian mythology also must have arisen out of the popular idea of eclipse only. Its source is, thus, the floating mass of folk-literature, which is common-stock of all nations.

In most of the myths there is only one demon of eclipse, who persues the sun and the moon. In the Indian and the Teutonic myths there are two separate demons running after these luminaries. In Indian astronomy Rāhu and Ketu are the ascending and descending nodes. The idea of these two nodes might have suggested the additional demon Ketu. Further Rāhu and Ketu are two planets in Indian astronomy. This also is a part of popular folk mythology. As Donald Mackenzie has said stars and planets are often looked upon as the ghosts of the mighty dead. That is why we have similar myths about the constellations like the Great Bear. According to the Greek mythology Orion, after his death was placed among stars, where he appears as a giant, with a girdle, a sword, a lion's skin and a club.

Conclusion

As already noted this Rāhu-Ketu story, in its fully developed form appears for the first time in the *MB* and right from there it has always been forming a part of the *amṛta-manthana* legend. The reason for this is not far to seek. Right from the days of the *Ṛgveda* the word *samudra* has been used in both the senses, viz., (1) 'the ocean of the firmament' as well as (2) 'the terrestrial ocean.' The *Kṣīrasāgara* of this legend is nothing but the ocean of the firmament. That being so this eclipse myth of the luminaries in the heaven could be easily inserted here.

The basic notion of Rāhu and Ketu being evil spirits persists even today. Not only this but in addition, as described by Prof. Keith[10] and Prof. Carney, Rāhu and Ketu have now fallen on evil days. They point out that Ketu is now a demon of disease and Rāhu is the divinity of two minial tribes in the N.W. Provinces. He has been further degraded as the ghost of a leader of *Duṣāḍha* tribe or as a *Ḍom* from whom the sun and the moon had borrowed money.

References

1. *Classical Dictionary of Hindu Mythology, Religion etc.*, pp. 252-53. Dowson John, Kegan Paul, Trench, T.R. Buner & Co., London, 1903.
2. *Indian Myth and Legend,* p. 64, The Gresham Publishing Company, London.
3. *Orion,* B.G. Tilak, p. 159, Tilak Brothers, Poona, 1893.
4. *Ibid.,* p. 140.
5. *Encyclopaedia of Religion and Ethics,* Vol. X, p. 368.
6. *Teutonic Myth and Legend,* p. 8, Mackenzie Donald, Gresham Publishing Company, London.
7. *The Mythology of All Races,* Volume IV, p. 424, Marshall Jones Company, London, 1927.
8. *Ibid.,* p. 424.
9. *Ibid.,* p. 425.
10. *Ibid.,* Vol. VI, pp. 232-33, 1917.

13

A Critical Study of Dhanvantari

It is well-known that the two epcis, the *Mahābhārata* (*MB*) and the *Rāmāyaṇa* (*R.*), so also the various *Purāṇas* are replete with myths and legends, which are later drawn upon by classical poets and playwrights. The legend of *samudra-manthana* or *amṛta-manthana* is one of these popular legends. It occurs in the *MB* (*Critical edition, Ādiparvan,* chapters 17-19; Southern recension — *Ādiparvan,* chapters 12-14), in the *R.* (Gujarati Press, *Bālakāṇḍa,* 45, Bengal recension *Ādikāṇḍa,* 46, North-Western recension, *Bālakāṇḍa,* 41), and in a number of *Purāṇas* like *Viṣṇu,* IX; *Padma, Sṛṣṭikhaṇḍa,* IV, *Brahmakhaṇḍa,* IV; *Matsya,* 249-251; *Skanda,* IX; *Bhāgavata,* VIII; *Agni,* III, etc.

It has been frequently drawn upon by classical poets like Kālidāsa, Bāṇa, Bhavabhūti, etc. The whole legend is full of interesting details. It ends with the appearance of various gems, one after the other, on the surface of the Milky Ocean. The details regarding the number of gems, the order of their appearance, the ownership of the individuals gems, etc., differ with every version of the story. The popular list recorded in the *Subhāṣita: Lakṣmīḥ kaustubha,* etc., mentions 14 gems. This chapter intends to make a critical study of one of these gems, viz., Dhanvantari.

Dhanvantari in Different Versions

As pointed out above, the list is differently given in every version of the story; yet Dhanvantari finds his place in each version. The following is a table, indicating the number of gems and

Dhanvantari's place in some important versions:

Name of the text	*Number of gems mentioned*	*The order in which he occurs*
MB (Cr. Ed.)	7	6th
MB (N.R.)	9	6th
MB (S.R.)	12	11th
R. (Guj. Press)	7	2nd
R. (Bengal R.)	7	6th
R. (N.W.R.)	7	6th
Viṣṇu Purāṇa	15	12th
Padma, Sṛṣṭikhaṇḍa	10	7th
Padma, Brahmakhaṇḍa	12	5th
Matsya	14	9th
Skanda	15	15th
Bhāgavata	11	10th

In the popular *Subhāṣita-Lakṣmiḥ kaustubha,* etc. Dhanvantari is the 5th out of the 14 *ratnas.*

Let us take a survey of his description in these different accounts.

The *MB* and the *R.* (Guj. Pr.) describe him as follows:

tato dhanvantarirdevo vapuṣmānudatiṣṭhata;
śvetam kamaṇḍalum bibhradamṛtam yatra tiṣṭhati.

He is a deity, holding a white pitcher containing nectar. According to the *R.* he is pious-minded and carries a staff in his hand. It is in the Bengal and the N.W. recensions of the *R.* that he has been associated for the first time with the science of medicine. These recensions call him *Vaidyarāja,* the best of physicians. The *Purāṇas* have accepted his proficiency in medical art as an established fact and have repeated it time and again. They have also embellished his description by adding details of their own. The *Vāyu Purāṇa* describes him as *śvetāmbaradhara* (wearing a white garment). The *Padma Purāṇa* repeats the same. The *Matsya* calls him *Āyurveda-Prajāpatiḥ* (the progenitor of the medical science). Then it goes on to describe as to who among the gods appropriates which particular gem and says:

gajendram ca sahasrākṣo hayaratnam ca bhāskaraḥ
dhanvantarim ca jagrāha lokārogya pravatakam.

(Indra took possession of Airāvata; Bhāskara, the sun, took over the horse Uccaiḥśravas and Dhanvantari, who takes care of health of the people).

In the *Skanda Purāṇa*, Dhanvantari is described as follows:

mathyamānāttataḥ sindhorjajñe dhanvantariḥ punaḥ
visnoraṁśena gaurāṅgaḥ sudhākumbhaṁ kare dadhat.
ghṛtādīnām hi sarveṣām rasānāṁ sāramuttamam
amṛtam tad gṛhītvāsau śriyo'ntikamupāyayau.

He had a fair complexion, because he was a partial incarnation of Viṣṇu. He brought ambrosia, the essence of all savours, and with it he approached Lakṣmī.

In the *Bhāgavata Purāṇa* Dhanvantari's description runs as follows:

athodadhermathyamānāt kāśyapairamṛtārthibhiḥ,
udatiṣṭhanmahārāja puruṣaḥ paramādbhutaḥ.
dīrghapīvaradordaṇḍaḥ kambugrīvo'ruṇekṣaṇaḥ,
śyāmalastaruṇaḥ sragvī sarvābhāraṇabhūṣitaḥ.
pītavāsā mahoraskaḥ sumṛṣṭamaṇikuṇḍalaḥ,
snigdhakuñcitakeśāntaḥ subhagaḥ siṁhavikramaḥ.
amṛtapūrṇakalasam bibhradvalayabhūṣitaḥ.
sa vai bhagavataḥ sākṣād viṣṇoraṁśaṁśasambhavaḥ,
dhanvantaririti khyāta āyurvedadṛgijybhāk.

This *Purāṇa* calls him *paramādbhutaḥ puruṣaḥ* (a person highly miraculous). He is described as a youth, very strong in physique, his massive arms were long, his neck well-shaped, the eyes reddish, and he possessed lion-like valour. He sprang from Viṣṇu's portion. Like Viṣṇu he wears a yellow garment, bright jewelled ear-ornaments and garlands of flowers. Surprisingly Dhanvantari is here *śyāmala* and not *gaurāṅga* as in other versions. This feature is probably drawn from Kṛṣṇa, an incarnation of Viṣṇu. The *Bhāgavata* calls him *āyurvedadṛg* (a seer of the science of medicine) and mentions that he even claimed a share in the sacrificial offerings (*ijyabhāk*). Thus in the days of the *Bhāgvata Purāṇa* Dhanvantari was a fully developed personality.

The *Agni Purāṇa*, the *Brahmāṇḍa Purāṇa*, the *Vāyu Purāṇa* and the *Harivaṁśa* glorify Dhanvantari as an incarnation of Viṣṇu and further add that Dhanvantari was worshipped by king Dhanva and was born as his son.

After the epcis and the *Purāṇas* we find Dhanvantari mentioned only in connection with his proficiency in medical science. In the first chapter of *Śalyatantra* in the *Suśruta Saṁhitā*, Suśruta approaches *Kāśīrāja* Divodāsa and requests that Divodāsa should teach him the science of surgery. Upon this the teacher says:

> *aham hi dhanvantarirādidevo jarārujāmṛtyuharo'marāṇām,*
> *śalyāṅgamangairaparairupetaṁ prāpto'smi gām bhūya uhopadeṣṭum.*

In the same chapter, he is described as *dharmabhṛtāṁ variṣṭhaḥ* (the best of the upholders of law) and *amṛtodbhava* (arising out of the nectar, or the source of nectar).

After Dhanvantari's identifications with Viṣṇu of the ancient times and Divodāsa of the medieval period, his personality has not developed further. Many medical formulae are named after him and the authorship of some medical works is attributed to him.

There are some interesting problems connected with the various aspects of Dhanvantari, which deserve a critical study. It is presented in the following sections:

(A) *The Original Phenomenon*

Dhanvantari is not referred to in the *Vedic* literature. Medicine was not unknown to the Vedic India. There are references to medicine even in the *Ṛgveda*. The *Atharvaveda* is the most ancient source of Indian medicine. The Vedic twin-deities Aśvinau are frequently described as excellent physicians and surgeons. Various medical and surgical feats are recorded to their credit. Yet Dhanvantari is totally absent from the Vedic literature. This has led Prof. Zimmer to suggest that Dhanvantari might have been inherited from the aborigines of India. However, there is no decisive proof that the aborigines had a divine physician, possessing the same features as those of Dhanvantari. Until such proof is available the surmise cannot be accepted. Let us, therefore, study the origin and development of Dhanvantari within the range of Sanskrit literature itself.

As already noted, the earliest reference to Dhanvantari is found in the *MB* and the *R*, as a gem churned out of the Milky Ocean. In this context, Dhanvantari possesses the following features: (i) He comes out of the ocean. (ii) He has a very white complexion. (iii) He is clad in white. (iv) He brings a pitcher of nectar. (v) According to the two recensions of the *R*. he is the best of physicians, suggesting that he was the progenitor of medical science. Later on in the *Purāṇas* one more feature has been added, and (vi) Dhanvantari has been identified with Viṣṇu's partial incarnation.

Let us try to trace Dhanvantari's origin on the basis of these features. We can begin with the derivation of his name. Since there is no reference to Dhanvantari in the Vedic literature, Yāska has not attempted the derivation of this name. However, Yāska gives the etymology of the word *dhanvan,* which is — *dhanva antarikṣam; dhanvantyasmādāp iti* (*Nirukta*, V.5). '*Dhanvan* is the mid-region or firmament, from which the waters flow.' Later on commentators of the works on *Āyurveda* derive Dhanvantari's name as: *dhanuḥ śalyaśāstram, tasya antaṁ pāraṁ iyarti gacchati iti dhanvantariḥ* (*dhanu* + *anta* + *riḥ* — from the root *ṛ* to go; *dhanu* means the science of surgery and Dhanvantari is one who goes to the end of it, i.e., who has mastered it). This derivation has been obviously given with a bias for *Āyurveda*. St. Petersburg Dictionary derives the word as follows: *dhanvan* + *tariḥ* (from the root *tṛ* to cross): *dhanvanā tarati iti,* i.e., one who moves in the manner of a bow.

Taking a hint from Yāska's derivation of the word *dhanvan,* the present author would explain the word as follows: *dhanvānam antarikṣam tarati iti dhanvantariḥ*. He is one who crosses the firmament. This immediately suggests the sun, that traverses the wide mid-region daily. This also agrees with the derivation given in the St. Petersburg Dictionary. The firmament from the east to the west, which is traversed by the sun daily, appears to be a bow to the popular notion. Thus Dhanvantari would be the personification of the sun, that rises in the east in the morning, crosses through the bow-shaped firmament during the day and sets in the west in the evening.

According to prof. Adalbert Kuhn, Dhanvantari represents the lightning-aspect of the fire, 'the *antarikṣāgni*' in the threefold analysis of Yāska; but I think he can better be explained as *sūrya,* the sun, 'the *dyulokāgni*' according to Yāska. My reasons for saying so are as follows:

(i) This identification suits the etymology very reasonably. (ii) The sun posseses exceptionally bright white lustre. This agrees with Dhanvantari's fair complexion and white garment. (iii) The light of the sun is full of vigour. Even in the *Ṛgveda,* the sun is called the very life-vigour of the universe: *sūrya ātmā jagataḥ tasthuṣaśca* (I.115.1). The light of the sun is as benevolent as the elixir of life. This explains the description of Dhanvantari as one who brought a jug of nectar from heaven, and his connection with the science of medicine. (iv) The *MB,*[2] III.155 identifies Dhanvantari with the sun. (v) Later, in the *Purāṇas,* Dhanvantari is identified with Viṣṇu. In the *Suśruta Saṁhitā* he calls himself *Ādideva.* In the *Ṛgveda,* Viṣṇu is a solar deity. Dhanvantari as the sun offers immediate explanation of this identification. (vi) In the *Matsya Purāṇa* when the various gems are taken up by the appropriate deities, Dhanvantari is taken up by *Bhāskara,* the sun. (vii) As Prof. G.N. Mukhopadhyaya[3] points out, the sun (*Bhāskara*) is the fountain-head of all knowledge in medicine. (viii) In the *Brahmavaivarta Purāṇa* Dhanvantari is described as a pupil of Garuḍa, the son of Vinatā. Prof. Zimmer[4] explains Vinatā as the vault of the heaven and Garuḍa is associated with Viṣṇu as his vehicle. (ix) This also supports Dhanvantari's identification with the sun. Prof. Kuhn's suggestion that Dhanvantari represents the *antarikṣāgni* cannot be accepted, because throughout the Sanskrit literature Dhanvantari is intimately associated with *amṛta* and the lightning does not possess the benevolent nature of *amṛta.* (x) Dhanvantari, as the personification of the sun, can also be explained in the light of the legend of *samudra-manthana.*

Elsewhere I have tried to trace the original idea underlying this legend. It appears that the Milky Ocean in this legend originally stands for the imaginary ocean of the firmament, the vault of the heaven, and the later on it was transferred to the terrestrial ocean. The sun is as if dialy moving through that ocean, the invisible half of it being underground. This very well suggests to an imaginative mind Dhanvantari, bringing *Amṛtakumbha* from the *Kṣīrasāgara.*

(B) *Dhanvantari's Relation with Viṣṇu*

We have seen in the foregoing section that Dhanvantari was originally a personification of the sun. Viṣṇu being a solar deity, Dhanvantari could naturally be identified with him. Moreover, since Dhanvantari is credited with the bringing of the *amṛta,* he was naturally associated with preservation of life and sound health of the people. According to the Purāṇic distribution of cosmic functions, Viṣṇu in the Trinity is the god in charge of the preservation of the universe. This common characteristic between Dhanvantari and Viṣṇu strengthened the identification. According to the *Suśruta Saṁhitā,* Dhanvantari, who was an incarnation of Viṣṇu, was reborn as *Kāśīrāja* Divodāsa and became a great teacher of surgery. There Dhanvantari explains how this knowledge was of yore, imparted by Brahmā to Dakṣa, by Dakṣa to the *Aśvins,* by the *Aśvins* to Indra and by Indra to himself.

(C) *Dhanvantari's Connection with the Science of Medicine*

When the legend of *samudra-manthana* developed in a full-fledged form, Dhanvantari appeared as a miraculous person, carrying the pitcher of *amṛta,* the drink of immortality. Now immortality implies freedom from death and diseases. Hence Dhanvantari was looked upon as the divine physician come to the world of the mortals. In this legend, Dhanvantari comes out of the ocean. Waters have been looked up as the best of medicines. Hence his connection with the science of medicine appears quite reasonable.

Though Dhanvantari is not referred to in the *ṚV*, his prototype, the twin deities Aśvinau were well-known in the Vedic literature as expert physicians and surgeons. When in the epic period Dhanvantari was recognised as the heavenly physician and the first propounder of the medical science, the feats and epithets of the Vedic Aśvins were transferred to him. Later, the *Purāṇas* accepted Dhanvantari as the divine physician. In the *Suśruta Saṁhitā*, as we have already seen, Dhanvantari proclaims himself as the Primeval god, come to the earth in order to relieve people from different ailments. Since then his name was associated with the origin of medical science in India. Several medical formulae in *Āyurveda* are named after him. In the *Brahmavaivarta Purāṇa* he is stated as the author of *Cikitsātantravijñāna*. This *Purāṇa* describes Dhanvantari's strife with Manasā, the divine mother of serpents and brings out Dhanvantari's connection with the snake-charms also. Later the works like *Rogavijñāna* and *Vaidyacintāmaṇi* have been attributed to the authorship of Dhanvantari. There is a medical dictionary named after him, viz., *Dhanvantari-Nighaṇṭu*. The date of this work is about sixth century A.D. After this when the works in *Āyurveda* were composed by the *Vaidyas* known to history, this mythical physician receded to the background.

(D) *The Origin of Medical Science in Comparative Mythology*

This Dhanvantari, the first physician of ancient India, is a divine person and is described as possessing magical powers. Now these are the features, which are commonly found in many other mythologies of the world.

Dr. Ryan[5] says, "All medicine is derived from God, and without his will it cannot exist or be practised." Even the Bible has attributed the origin of medicine to a deity. In the Greek mythology *Aesculapius*, the son of Apollo was the first physician. In the Italian mythology there is no separate god of medicine. Aesculapius of the Greeks is supposed to have come to Rome in the disguise of a snake. In the Egyptian mythology, the art of a physician was revealed to the mankind by the god Thyoth or Thoth. In the Babylonian mythology, the earliest deity of medicine was the Moon-god. Later the god Marduk took that place. In the Iranian mythology also the origin of medicine is divine. From the *Avestā* we learn that their supernatural physician was Thrita, who was heroic, active, benevolent and possessed magical powers. Ahura Mazda gave him a metal-knife and several plants. In this mythology the amulets are named after the mystical Faridūn. Moreover Airman (probably a personification of prayer) also is intimately connected with the medical art. The Celtic deities also possess powers, generally attributed to medical-men. According to the Chinese mythology Sheh Ha Nang, a legendary emperor of the period 2838-2668 B.C., invented agriculture and medicine, under the inspiration of 'Pan Ku', the God of creation.

About the magical and miraculous powers possessed by the Aśvins of the Vedic period and by Dhanvantari of the epic period, it must be said, that this feature also is shared by other mythologies of the world. In all nations the medicine-man first begins as a conjurer and then tends to be a god or a divine being. In the North-American mythology the earliest medicine-man, called a Shaman, possessed magical powers and was a mediator between gods and spirits on the one hand, and human beings on the other. The Shaman, in fact, was a priest, a magician and a medicine-man, combined in one.

Conclusion

As already noted, Dhanvantari arose out of waters. This can be traced to a very early period in Indian mythology. Right from the days of the *Ṛgveda* waters have been looked upon as the best of medicines and the herbs are their off-springs. In the *Atharvaveda,* the plants are described as staying in primeval cosmic ocean. According to a Latin-American legend, Yauhana inflicted continued misery on mankind. Arwak, who was walking by the side of a lake, saw the goddess Orehu rise from the stream with a branch of a tree in her hand. At her bidding he planted the branch and all medicines grew from it.

In the Ice-landic mythology Guabontio, the woman of the sea, taught the use of amulets, pebbles, etc., to the medicine-hero Guagugiana.

Thus the origin of medical science or of the ancient physician from water is also a common feature of many mythologies. Taking into account the inevitable need of water for every living being this sounds quite reasonable.

References

1. *Hindu Medicine*, p. 36, H. Zimmer, The Johns Hopkins Press, Baltimore, 1948.
2. *Index of the names in the Mahābhārata*, Sorensen.
3. *History of Indian Medicine*, Vol. 1, pp. 83-98, University of Calcutta, 1923.
4. *Hindu Medicine*, p. 37.
5. *Medical Jurisprudence*.

14

MM. Dr. Kane's Contribution to Sanskrit Poetics

IT is really very interesting to note that this profound scholar, who is well-known for his gigantic work on the dry and obstruse subject of *Dharmaśāstra*, not only in India but even abroad, began his literary career with the delicate topic of *Sāhityaśāstra*. With the bubbling enthusiasm of a fresh graduate, Dr. Kane wrote an essay on 'The History of *Alaṅkāra*-Literature' in 1906, and was awarded the covetable V.N. Mandlik Gold Medal for the same. In 1910 he published an edition of[1] *Viśvanātha's Sāhitya-darpaṇa (Paricchedas* I, II and X) with exhaustive notes and introduction, giving the information about Viśvanātha's life and date. Even this small work on Viśvanātha highly impressed the Western scholars like Sylvain Levi and Dr. Kane was requested to write a 'History of Literary theories in India'. This inspired the profound scholar to take greater pains over the subject and he published several articles on it in the various issues of the *Indian Antiquary*. As all copies of the *Sāhitya-darpaṇa* were sold out in the next 12 years, he brought out the second edition of that book in 1923. To this was pre-fixed an exhaustive introduction of 177 pages, in which Dr. Kane dealt with 'The History of *Alaṅkāra*-Literature'. Surprisingly *The History of Sanskrit Poetics*, Part I by Dr. S.K. De was published in the same year from Calcutta. Both these eminent scholars had worked absolutely independently. There can rarely be a better instance of the maxim 'Great minds think alike'. Both admired each others efforts. Here we realise the truth of the Subhāṣita — *vidvānneva vijānāti vidvajjana-*

pariśramam. In 1925 Dr. De brought out the second part of his history. The credit of doing pioneering work in the field of Sanskrit Poetics thus goes to these two eminent Sanskritists.

Within the next 28 years Dr. Kane's edition of *Sāhitya-darpaṇa* had gone out of stock again. In 1951 he published the third edition of the book. This time *The history of Sanskrit Poetics* in the introduction was fully revised by the *Mahāmahopādhyāya*. It was also published separately, being the second edition of the history. This time it comprised of 423 pages. It will not be out of place to quote here, what Dr. Kane says in its Preface — "Our books led many scholars to study the numerous works on *Alaṅkāra*, to point out defects and mistakes, to produce papers dealing with several aspects of *Alaṅkāraśāstra* and to publish several important texts." He mentions how several texts like *Abhinavabhāratī*, *Nāṭyadarpaṇa*, *Sāhityamīmāṁsā*, etc., were published during the intervening period of 28 years. The source of inspiration for all this lay in the books of Dr. Kane and Dr. De. Towards the conclusion of the Preface the *Mahāmahopādhyāya* remarks — "Now that I am over 71 years of age and have yet to complete my *History of Dharmaśāstra*, I am afraid that I shall hardly have the time or energy to revert to this subject again and therefore, I bid farewell to these studies of my youth." And yet the Sanskrit readers would not allow the aged *Mahāmahopādhyāya* to bid farewell to his first love even now. Again in the next 9 years all copies of this history were already sold out and in 1961 Motilal Banarsidass of Delhi brought out the third edition of Dr. Kane's *History of Sanskrit Poetics*. This revised edition comprised of 446 pages. In the Preface to this edition the *Mahāmahopādhyāya* says, "During the last 9 years a good deal has been written on the subject of this work. I tried to read as much as I could and have made substantial additions and changes in this edition. But I am unable to say that I read everything that has been written during the last nine years on Sanskrit Poetics. I hope, however, that I have not missed much of valuable matter." No wonder that the profound scholar, aged over 80, feels delighted that his book is even now held in high esteem. In the same Preface he continues, "It gives me great satisfaction that this history, which I first wrote over fifty years ago still continues to be popular with students of Sanskrit

Poetics." The great scholar fortunately lived to see that even this edition of his history went out of stock within the next 10 years only. Motilal Banarsidass had to publish the fourth edition — a reprint of the third edition in 1971. There are, indeed, very few books, which enjoy such enviable popularity. His *History of Sanskrit Poetics* has been translated into Marathi by Shri K.L. Ogale, into Hindi by Professor Indrachandra Shastri, and into Kannada by Shri S. Kaujalgi.

In addition to this valuable book MM. Dr. Kane has also contributed the following learned articles to the subject of Sanskrit Poetics:

(1) Bhāmaha and Daṇḍin — *JRAS*, Vol. XXIII, 1908.

(2) The Joint Authorship of the *Kāvyaprakāśa, Indian Antiquary,* Vol. 40, 1911.

(3) Outlines of the History of *Alaṅkāraśāstra, Indian Antiquary,* Volume 40, 41, 46 (1908-12).

(4) Fragments of Kohala — *Proceedings of the Sixth Session of the AIOC,* Patna, 1930.

(5) Gleanings from the *Abhinavabhāratī, Journal of the BORI, Professor K.B. Pāthak Commemoration Volume,* Poona, 1931.

In Marathi:

(1) *Bharatāce Nāṭyaśāstra,* Sarasvatī Mandira, 1907.

(2) *Sāhitya Śāstra.* Vividhajñānavistāra, Silver Jubilee Volume.

This list of his article on *Alaṅkāraśāstra* would have been very lengthy, had not the great *Mahāmahopādhyāya* deserted this study of his youth, in order to render more invaluable service to the neglected and difficult subjects of *Dharmaśāstra* and *Mīmāṁsā.*

Though it is only one memorable book that the great Doctor has contributed to Sanskrit Poetics, the service that he has rendered is really beyond measure. Dr. Kane wrote at a time, when the chronology of the different works on the subject was all in a jumble. Very little was known with certainty about most of the works and authors in *Alaṅkāraśāstra.* Very few works had been in print. Much of the material upon which the great scholar worked was available in manuscript form only. The research-work done under such circumstances is far more difficult, labourious and therefore far more precious than the work that is being done by modern scholars.

Even then with his sharp intellect, deep insight, industrious habits and perseverence, Dr. Kane surmounted all difficulties and could establish important conclusions by way of land-marks in the *History of Sanskrit Poetics*. The following short summary of the conclusions arrived at by Dr. Kane in this regard will give us a glimpse into his important contribution to this field of Indological studies.

Part I[1] (pp. 1-325). Important works on the *Alaṅkāraśāstra* and analysis of the contents, Chronology of the authors.

Part II (pp. 326-95) Topics in *Alaṅkāraśāstra:* Theories of Poetics and their history.

Index of Authors and Works (pp. 397-446).

Part I

Dr. Kane has collected all available references to Nandikeśvara, an ancient authority on *Rasa,* who has been referred to by Rājaśekhara, Śāradātanaya, Abhinavagupta, etc. For want of difinite date, he could not fix the date of this ancient teacher. Because of its claim as a *Purāṇa, Agni Purāṇa* was wrongly considered to be the original source of all later teachings on *Alaṅkāraśāstra.* Dr. Kane proves that it belongs to a much later date and that the section on poetics in that work was probably composed after 1050 A.D. He first brings it to our notice that it is an encyclopaedic work, dealing with all sorts of subjects in which medieval India was interested. A comparison of the different versions leads him to say[2], "It appears that the old *Agni Pūraṇa* was recast and then it assumed its present form." With a critical study he points out that the *Agni Purāṇa* quotes from Bharata's *Nāṭyaśāstra,* Daṇḍin's *Kāvyādarśa,* Bhāmaha's *Kāvyālaṅkāra,* etc. Contrary to Batuknath Bhattacharya's view, Dr. Kane feels that the *Agni Purāṇa* seems to be acquainted with the theory of *Dhvani.* He does not agree with Professor S.K. De that Ānandavardhana quotes 2 verses from this *Purāṇa.*

Finally he concludes,[3] "The *Agni Purāṇa* is later than the seventh century at least and the section on Poetics was certainly compiled about or a little after 900 A.D. and probably after 1050 A.D."

Dr. Kane rightly refers to the *Nāṭyaśāstra* of Bharata as "the oldest extent work on the theory of Sanskrit poetics." Before the third edition of his *History,* the editions of the *Nāṭyaśāstra* available to him were as follows:

(1) The *Nāṭyaśāstra-Kāvyamālā series:*

(2) The *Nāṭyaśāstra-Kāśī Sanskrit series* or *Chowkhamba Sanskrit Series*

(3) The *Nāṭyaśāstra* with the *Abhinavabhāratī* Chapters 1-27 — *Gaekwad Oriental Series.*

(4) Translation into English of Chapters 1-27 and a lengthy introduction by Professor Manmohan Ghosh.

After a critical survey of this material the great scholar comments,[4] "The text of the *Nāṭyaśāstra* is unsatisfactory and has been tampered with in almost every chapter." He rightly points out that it is difficult to constitute the text of the *Abhinavabhāratī* because of unsatisfactory material.

About the much-discussed problem of the original kernel and the recensions of the *Nāṭyaśāstra* the *Mahāmahopādhyāya* rightly observes, "It appears that the first chapter of the *Nāṭyaśāstra,* — and probably the next four were added some centuries before the 5th century A.D. . . . The most of the Chapters now found were in existence from at least the 3rd or the 4th century A.D." Coming to the problem of the date of this important text he discusses it in all details and concludes,[5] "At least some time before the 3rd or the 4th Century A.D. there was a recast made by one man in which were included prose passages in *Sūtra-bhāṣya* style, ancient *Āryā* verses and *ślokas,* together with the composed *Kāṇḍas* by the recaster. Then in different places and at different times some verses came to be added here and there by people learned in the *śāstra.*" He, however, feels that the question cannot be settled till dramatic works of earlier commentators like Kohala and Nandikeśvara are discovered. "One can only say that before 300 A.D. there existed a work known as the *Nāṭyaśāstra* of Bharata. It contained the *Rasa* theory and dealt with dramaturgy."

Dr. S.K. De suggests[6] fourth or fifth century A.D. as the lower limit for the original *Nāṭyaśāstra* and assigns the present form of the text to a date before the eighth century A.D.

About the commentaries on the *Nāṭyaśāstra,* Dr. Kane feels that Udbhaṭa (about 800 A.D.) Lollaṭa (800-840 A.D.), and Śaṅkuka (about the end of the 9th century) must have commented upon the whole of the *Nāṭyaśāstra.* He feels that Mātṛgupta, who has been mentioned by Abhinavagupta, Śāradātanaya and Sāgaranandin, did not compose a commentary on the *Nāṭyaśāstra* but probably wrote an independent treatise on the *Nāṭyaśāstra* Dr. S.K. De is not inclined to accept that this *Nāṭyaśāstra* is the same as that of the poet Mātṛgupta mentioned in the *Rājataraṅgiṇī* but Dr. Kane accepts the identity. About Bhaṭṭanāyaka's *Hṛdayadarpaṇa* both Dr. Kane and Dr. De feel that it was not a commentary on the *Nāṭyaśāstra,* but a work in verse and prose, composed for establishing a theory of poetics and controverting the position of the *Dhvanyāloka.*

Then coming to the ancient commentators whose works have not yet been discovered even in some portions, Dr. Kane has collected a lot of information about Kohala. He had already dealt with this ancient teacher in his paper 'The Fragments of Kohala', published in the *Proceedings of the AIOC,* Patna 1930. Dr. Kane feels that Kohala must have written on all topics of the *Nāṭyaśāstra,* especially on music, acting and dance. He further remarks that Kohala might have written on Prakrit dramatic pieces also. About the *Vārtika* of Harṣa or Śrīharṣa, which has not yet been discovered and which seems to be a commentary on the *Nāṭyaśāstra,* Dr. Kane surmises.[7] "It follows that the *Harṣavārtika* probably dealt with all the chapters of the *Nāṭyaśāstra,* that it was composed mostly in Āryā verses with prose-passages and illustrations from dramatic literature."

About the *Bharatabhāṣya* or *Bharatavārtika* of Nānyadeva, available only in manuscript form, Dr. Kane says that it is not a commentary on the *Nāṭyaśāstra,* though, that treatise is profusely quoted in it. The reference to Niḥśankadeva in 1.4 presents a difficulty in fixing the date of this work.

In the first Volume of the *Nāṭyaśāstra,* published by the *G.O.S.* a list of works and authors connected with the *Nāṭyaśāstra* was included. MM. Kane noticed that the list required numerous corrections and in his article 'Gleanings from *Abhinavabhāratī*', he gave all these corrections and also added important notes of his own.

Because of the reference *Baudhasaṅgatimivālaṅkārabhuṣitam* in Subandhu's *Vāsavadattā* many scholars like Aufrecht, Hall, Peterson, Telang, etc., thought that the Buddhist logician Dharmakīrti had written a work on Poetics. Professor S.P. Bhattacharya repeats[8] the opinion; but Dr. Kane emphatically disagrees.

The *Mahāmahopādhyāya* places *Viṣṇudharmottarapurāṇa* after the *Nāṭyaśāstra* and before the *Bhaṭṭikāvya*. *Bhaṭṭikāvya,* though illustrating rules of grammar, has discussed a number of topics from Poetics in the section known as *Prasannakāṇḍa* (Chapters X-XIII). Dr. Kane feels that Bhaṭṭi can be assigned to about 600-640 A.D. at the latest. He does not accept the identification of this Bhaṭṭi with Vatsabhaṭṭi of Mandasor Inscription, as was suggested by Shri Mazumdar in *JRAS*, 1904.

After this the *Mahāmahopādhyāya* comes to Bhāmaha. Though in 1960 he still held the view that Daṇḍin was earlier to Bhāmaha, he deals with Bhāmaha first 'out of reverence to the opinion of a majority of scholars'. He does not fight shy of making the bold statement,[9] 'I still hold that this view of the majority is wrong'. To begin with, Dr. Kane points out that 'A scholarly edition of Bhāmaha's work is a great desideratum'. Then he gives a summary of the *Kāvyālaṅkāra* and turns to the problem whether Bhāmaha was a Buddhist. He refutes the arguments of Professor M.T. Narasimhiengar and Professor A.B. Dhruva and concludes, that Bhāmaha was probably a Hindu steeped in the ancient culture, but with an admiration for Buddha's noble life.

After that Dr. Kane takes a critical survey of Daṇḍin's *Kavyādarśa* and remarks that it expounds the *Rasa* school, and to some extent the *Alaṅkāra* school also. In Dr. Kane's opinion Daṇḍin has higher poetic excellence, while Bhāmaha is superior in point of logical acumen.

The *Mahāmahopādhyāya* incidentally refers to the problem whether Daṇḍin of *Kāvyādarśa* is identical with Daṇḍin of the *Daśakumāracarita*. Admitting the identity, he explains[10] the discrepancy in the literary tastes of the two books as follows: "The *Daśakumāracarita* may have be composed while Daṇḍin was comparatively young and inexperienced, while the *Kāvyādarśa* is a product of mature years." Dr. Kane is also inclined to accept the *Avantisundarīkathā* as Daṇḍin's work. (A few remarks about Dr. Kane's view as regards 'The Relative Position of Bhāmaha and Daṇḍin' will be added later).

Coming to Udbhaṭa the great scholar has made a detailed study of his *Alaṅkāra-saṅgraha,* all available commentaries on it, and all traceable references to Udbhaṭa, and his work. He refutes Col. Jacob's view that Udbhaṭa is a propounder of the *Rasa* school and establishes that Udbhaṭa is the foremost representative of the *Alaṅkāra* school. The date of Udbhaṭa (750-850 A.D.) presents no difficulty. Dr. Kane feels that the commentary, published in *G.O.S.* in 1931 is Tilaka's *Udbhaṭa-viveka.* Dr. De thinks that it belongs to a very late period.

Then the *Mahāmahopādhyāya* points out that the *Kāvyālaṅkāra-sūtravṛtti* of Vāmana, the great propounder of the *Rīti* school is of great importance in setting the chronology of many Sanskrit works, from which it quotes very often. Vāmana is always remembered in connection with the theory of *Rīti,* the distinction between *guṇas* and *alaṅkāras* and the new theory of *Pāka*. Dr. Kane has added a comparative list of the *alaṅkāras* dealt with by Bhaṭṭi Daṇḍin, Bhāmaha, Udbhaṭa and Vāmana. He then points out the special features of Rudraṭa's contribution to *Alaṅkāraśāstra* as follows: (1) Some basis for the classification of figures of speech (2) *Preyas* as the 10th *Rasa* (3) *Rīti* looked upon as insignificant (4) No treatment of *guṇas.* Dr. Kane fixes his date as 825-50 A.D. Then he turns to the problem whether Rudrabhaṭṭa, the author of the *Sṛṅgāratilaka* is the same as Rudraṭa. Weber, Bühler, Aufrecht and Pischel believed in the identity, while Pandit Durgaprasad, Dr. Jacobi and Dr. Harichand disagreed. After a critical study of the problem the *Mahāmahopādhyāya* concludes,[11] "Taking all the above circumstances together I think that Rudra is later than Rudraṭa, elaborates the dicta of Rudraṭa with illustrations, bases his *Śṛṅgāratilaka* on the *Kāvyālaṅkāra* and flourished between 950-1000 A.D."

Righly does Dr. Kane admire the importance of *Dhvanyāloka* of Ānandavardhana as — "The *Dhvanyaloka* is an epoch-making work in the history of *Alaṅkāra* literature. It occupies the same position in the *Alaṅkāraśāstra* as Paṇini's *Sūtras* on grammar or the *Vedāntasūtras* on *Vedānta.*" It is well-known to the students of *Alaṅkāra* literature for the controversy it evokes about the Authorship-problem. Dr. Kane could not avoid discussing it in details. He has devoted 37 pages (pp. 163-99) to it. A note on 'The Problem of the Authorship of the *Kārikās* and the *Vṛtti*' will be added later. Dr. Kane takes a survey of all the important topics dealt with in this treatise, e.g., the treatment of *Dhvani* from all points of view, its nature, its divisions, its relation to the *Rasavadalaṅkāra*, the *pratibhā* of poet and so on. With precision he notes the date of Ānandavardhana's literary activity as 860-90 A.D.

About Bhaṭṭenduraja, the teacher of Abhinavagupta, there is a problem whether he is identical with Pratihārendurāja, the commentator of *Udbhaṭa*. Professor K.C. Pandey advocates the identity, but Dr. Kane rejects it.

About Rājaśekhara's *Kāvyamīmāṁsā*, which is a unique work and a practical handbook for poets Dr. Kane remarks — "It is a mine of information on numerous matters." Unlike many other Sanskrit authors Rājaśekhara gives a lot of information about himself in other works of his. Hence there is no difficulty about his date (end of the 9th and the beginning of the 10th century A.D.). Then the great scholar disposes off the problem whether Rājaśekhara was a brāhmaṇa or a kṣatriya and opines that he was a brāhmaṇa.

After mentioning *Abhidhāvṛttimātṛkā* of Mukulabhaṭṭa and *Kāvyakautuka* of Bhaṭṭatota, he comes to Kuntaka's important work *Vakroktijīvita*. After giving useful summary of the 4 *Unmeśas* he points out how Kuntaka includes *vyaṅgyārtha* under his *Vakrokti* and attaches great importance to *Kavivyāpāra*. About this Dr. De has remarked,[12] "*Kuntaka* 'discovered' poetic imagination." Dr. Kane stresses the importance of the *Vakroktijīvita* and the original thinking on the part of *Kuntaka*. He feels that the work should be rescued from the oblivion into which it has fallen. Consequently Dr. S.K. De has brought out an excellent edition of the work.

In case of Abhinavagupta, the intellectual giant of his period, a lot of work has been done by different scholars on his life and works. Professor K.C. Pandey's *Abhinavagupta* is quite well-known and exhaustive. Among his varied and numerous works his commentary Locana on the *Dhvanyāloka* and his commentary *Abhinavabhāratī* on the *Nāṭyaśāstra* are the most illustrious. The date of his literary activity (1030-70 A.D.) presents no problem.

In connection with the *Daśarūpa* of Dhanañjaya the great Professor agrees with Dr. De that Dhanika, the commentator, is the younger brother of Dhanañjaya. About the *Vyaktiviveka* of Mahimabhaṭṭa (1020-1100 A.D.) also there is no critical problem. His work is admired by the great scholar as[13] "His work is one of the master-pieces of the *Alaṅkāra* literature and deserves to be saved from the unmerited oblivion in which it has fallen." Consequently the work has been studied by scholars like Dr. De. Smt. Asha Toraskar got her Ph.D. degree for her thesis on *Vyaktiviveka — a Critical Study*.

About the *Sarasvatīkaṇṭhābharaṇa* of Bhoja, Dr. Kane, who is later followed by Dr. V. Raghavan, does not agree with Dr. S.K. De that Bhoja in the *Sarasvatīkaṇṭhābharaṇa*, II.2.39 and 75 is borrowing from the *Agni Purāṇa*. He remarks[14] "It is, therefore, proper to hold that the *Agni Purāṇa*, which is not an original work on any subject, but a mere encyclopaedic compilation most probably derived its inspiration from Bhoja."

Coming to his *Śṛṅgāraprakāśa* Dr. Kane points out that it is a very voluminous work, longer than any work on Sanskrit poetics. Till 1960, when the *Mahāmahopādhyāya* brought out the third edition of his history, only Volume I (*Prakāśas* 1-8) had been edited by Shri G.R. Joyser for the International Academy of Sanskrit Research, Mysore 1955, but consequently Vol. II (*Prakāśas* 9-14) was published in 1963 and Vol. III (*Prakāśas* 15-24) was published in 1969. Thus now 2/3 of the Voluminous work has been in print. Till 1923 Dr. V. Raghavan had brought out only the first Volume of his critical study of the *Śṛṅgāraprakāśa*. Now he has published his 'Critical Study' of the whole of the text in 1963.

Dr. Kane first gives a title-summary of all the 36 chapters and points out how it deals with both poetics and dramaturgy and propounds that *Śṛṅgāra*, identified with *abhimāna* and *ahaṅkāra* is the only *rasa*. Bhoja is credited with having composed 84 works on almost all sciences of medieval India. Dr. Kane does not agree with Dr. V. Raghavan, who feels that Bhoja might have composed a good many works out of this list.

Then having introduced the readers to the *Aucityavicāracā* and *Kavikaṇṭhābharaṇa* of the voluminous writer Kṣemendra, Dr. Kane comes to Mammaṭa's *Kāvyaprakāśa.* There was no critical problem to be discussed about this text. Long back in 1911 in Vol. No. 40 of the *Indian Antiquary* he had published a critical note on "Joint Authorship of Mammaṭa's *Kāvyaprakāśa.*" He accepted that Mammaṭa's incomplete *Kāvyaprakāśa* was completed by the Kashmirian rhetorician Alaka. Depending on Arjunavarmadeva's statement Dr. Kane felt that *Alaka* had a hand in the 7th *Ullāsa* also.

Coming to Ruyyaka's *Alaṅkārasarvasva* he discards the tradition prevalent in Kashmir that the *vṛtti* was composed by Maṅkhaka.

Taking up the debatable problem about the authorship of the *Śahitya-mīmāṁsā* published in the *Trivandrum Sk. Series* Dr. Kane remarks[15] — "The *Sāhityamīmāṁsā* does not speak of *vyañjanā* function of the words at all. The author of the *Alaṅkārasarvasva* was a staunch advocate of the *Dhvani* theory. The only way in which the contradiction between the same author's viewpoints in the two works can be explained is by supposing that *Sāhityamīmāṁsā* was composed by him when the author was comparatively young and under the influence of the *Vakroktijīvitakāra,* while the *Alaṅkārasarvasva* was composed when he was of mature intellect and came completely under the influence of the *Dhvanyāloka* of Ānandavardhana." Dr. Raghavan, however, doubts about it being Ruyyaka's work.

Then, having just introduced the readers to the *Kāvyālaṅkāra* of Vāgbhaṭa 1, the *Kāvyānuśāsana* of Hemacandra, the *Candrāloka* of Jayadeva, the *Ekāvalī* of Vidyādhara, the *Pratāparudrayaśobhuṣaṇa* of Vidyānātha, the *Kāvyānuśāsana* of Vāgbhaṭa II, the *Mahāmahopādhyāya* turns to the *Sāhityadarpaṇa* of Viśvanātha, the text that he edited. He calls Viśvanātha whose date is fixed as 1300 to 1380 A.D., 'a star of second magnitude only'. While introducing the *Rasamañjarī* and *Rasataraṅgiṇī* of Bhānudatta, Dr. Kane discusses the problem whether the lyrical poem *Gītagaurīśa* is his work and says that it is not so. Then he discusses the question whether Bhānudatta is the same as Bhānukara, patronised by Vīrabhānu (beginning of the 16th cent. A.D.). Dr. H.D. Sharma accepts the identity while Dr. Kane and

Dr. De hold the opposite view. Then after mentioning Rupagosvamin and Kesavamisra, Dr. Kane passes to the prolific writer Appayya Dīkṣita. He says that Appaya was born a little before 1554 A.D. and died as an old man. As pointed out by Dr. Raghavan there were three persons named Appayya in the same family in three generations. Dr. Kane rightly feels that the confusion in deciding the accurate date is due to this fact. Coming to Jagannātha's *Rasagaṅgādhara*, Dr. Kane remarks "The *Rasagaṅgādhara* stands next only to the *Dhvanyāloka* and the *Kāvyaprakāśa* in the field of Poetics." There is no difficulty in fixing the period of Jagannātha's literary activity as between 1620 to 1665 A.D. In connection with the anecdote about Jagannātha's liason with a Yavana damsel named Lavaṅgī, Dr. Kane feels[16] that it is a myth spread by those who were offended by the biting tongue of Jagannātha.

Part II

Dr. S.K. De had blamed[17] MM. Dr. Kane for laying undue emphasis on the use of Poetic figures in Vedic literature. MM. Kane says, "He is wrong." On the basis of the dialogue-hymns in the *ṚV*, the use of figures of speech by the Vedic poets, the development of music, dance and dialogue in the *Brāhmaṇas* and the *Upaniṣads,* Dr. Kane feels that even the earlier period of Vedic literature knew dramatic spectacles of religious character. Then on a close study of the two epics and the references to the actors and the *Upamās* in the ancient works on grammar Dr. Kane points out that from 500 B.C. to 100 B.C. great deal of poetical material of a secular character had accummulated. He says[18] "This must have naturally led to speculations about the functions and objects of poetry, . . . to attempts, more or less crude to establish a theory of poetics and literary criticism." In the second revised edition of his History, Dr. De notes MM. Kane's opinion in the footnote 1, page 3 and once again repeats his view. He says,[19] "There is hardly any material in the ancient literature itself to enable us to trace the origin of poetics to a very remote antiquity." He, further explains,[20] "Between this unconscious employment of figures of speech and the conscious formation of a definite system there must necessarily be a long step." However Dr. Kane seems to be dogmatic about the origin of poetics in the Vedic period.

Then the great Professor enters into the discussion about the name of the *Śāstra*. Having explained the names *Alaṅkāraśāstra* and *Sāhityaśāstra* he discusses Dr. Raghavan's suggestion[21] that the oldest name of this poetic discipline was *Kriyākalpa*. One of Dr. Raghavan's arguments is the use of the term in the *Lalitavistāra*. Dr. Kane has doubts as regards the reading *Kriyākalpa*. Moreover he says that in the passage under consideration it can only mean *Śradhakalpa*. Thus he does not accept, Dr. Raghavan's opinion in this matter.

His sections on 'The purposes of Poetry', 'The equipment of the poet'. 'The definition of Poetry' are purely of a textual nature. Then he proceeds to acquaint the readers with the different schools of poetics.

1. *The Rasa school* — Dr. Kane rightly points out that though the theory of *Rasa* was not systematically dealt with till the days of Ānandavardhana, it does not mean that the earlier critics like Bhāmaha and Daṇḍin were ignorant about the importance of *Rasa*. Dr. Kane then deals with the psychological aspect of *Rasa* and explains the technical terms like *vibhāva, anubhāva,* etc. He then adds[22] a list of the Research-papers dealings with *Rasa* published till 1959.

2. *The Alaṅkāra school* — He explains how the ancient rhetoricians like Bhāmaha, Udbhaṭa, Rudraṭa attached importance to the *alaṅkāras*.

3. *The Rīti school* — About this school MM. Kane rightly remarks[23] — The *Rīti* marks a very real advance over the *Alaṅkāra* school. Though it did not reach the essence of poetry it approached very near it. A list of the Research-papers on the aspects of *Rīti* has been added on pp. 385-86.

4. *The Vakrokti school* — Dr. Kane clearly explains what *Kuntaka* means by *Vakrokti* and how it differs from the *Arthālaṅkāra Vakrokti,* discussed by earlier rhetoricians.

5. *The Dhvani school* — MM. Kane rightly comments that the *Dhvani* theory is only an extension of the *Rasa* theory. He explains how a single verse may not contain a particular *Rasa* but can suggest some aspect of *Rasa*. Since *Rasa* is always suggested, *Dhvanyāloka* logically came to the conclusion that the best poetry

is that which contains a charming suggested sense. Dr. Kane speaks of the great popularity which this school enjoyed; but he also points out that before the theory secured general acceptance it had to pass through an ordeal of fierce criticism at the hands of Kuntaka, Pratihārendurāja, Bhaṭṭanāyaka and Mahimabhaṭṭa.

Towards the end Dr. Kane adds the textual sections on 'The Divisions of Poetry' and 'The poetic Defects'. He explains how poetics has influenced other branches of Sanskrit learning.

In the end he has added a very useful 'Index of Authors and works on Sanskrit Poetics', which runs over 50 pages. It is extremely helpful for finding ready reference to the various topics in Sanskrit Poetics.

Dr. S.K. De has referred to Dr. Kane 30 times in his *History of Sanskrit Poetics.* Generally he refers to the great *Mahāmahopādhyāya* in order to support his own conclusions, while only in 6 places he differs from Dr. Kane.

A brief survey of the important debatable topics in Sanskrit 'Poetics' discussed by Dr. Kane.

I

The Relative Position of Bhāmaha and Daṇḍin. The Sanskrit scholars are sharply divided in two groups.

(a) Those who advocated Bhāmaha's priority. Prof. K.P. Trivedi, Dr. Jacobi, Prof. Rangacharya, Pandit G. Shastri.

(b) Those who place Daṇḍin earlier — Dr. Kane, Prof. M.T. Narasimhiengar and Prof. A.B. Keith.

Prof. K.B. Pathak earlier (*Introduction to Kavirājamārga*) belonged to group (a) but later (*Indian Antiquary* 1912) he changed over to Group (b).

The important arguments of Group (a) are as follows:

(1) Bhāmaha is always honoured as *pūrva-cirantana,* etc., by earlier rhetoricians like Ruyyaka and Vidyānātha.

(2) Bhāmaha's divisions of *Alaṅkāra* are less minute. So also his treatment of *Alaṅkāras* and distinction of *Kathā-Ākhyāyikā* are less detailed.

(3) In some places Daṇḍin's commentator Taruṇa Vāscaspati

clearly remarks that Daṇḍin is criticising Bhāmaha.

Dr. Kane refutes these points as follows:

(1) This does not mean that Daṇḍin also is not *pūrva,* or *cirantana,* Namisādhu refers to Daṇḍin as earlier and he is a commentator much earlier than Ruyyaka and others.

(2) Daṇḍin's treatment of *Alaṅkāras* is unscientific, while Bhāmaha gives the divisions of *Upamā* on grammatical basis, for the first time.

(3) Taruṇa Vācaspati is a comparatively later commentator.

Dr. Kane then puts the following additional arguments:

(1) Daṇḍin's treatment of *Upamā* is unscientific. His divisions *Nindopamā, Praśaṁsopamā* and *Ācikhyāsopama* are criticised by Bhāmaha.

(2) Bhāmaha later reduced the 10 *guṇas* of Daṇḍin to 3. Later on Ānandavardhana and Mammaṭa followed 3 *guṇas* only.

(3) There are other portions like *Vaidarbhī-Gauḍī* distinction, *Svabhāvokti* and *Punarukta* where Bhāmaha seems to criticise Daṇḍin.

Nevertheless, about Daṇḍin's priority over Bhāmaha Dr. Kane is not dogmatic. He concludes,[24] "It seems probably that Bhāmaha and Daṇḍin follow independent traditions, the former having more affinity with the *Alaṅkāra* schools and the latter with *Bharata's* school. Whoever may be earlier, both are very near to each other and are to be placed between 650-750 A.D." However if the priority is to be declared in favour of one, Dr. Kane continues, "then I would declare myself in favour of Daṇḍin's priority over Bhāmaha."

II
The Mutual Relation of Bhāmaha — Nyāsa-Māgha

The following Sanskritists have entered into the discussion of this problem:

(1) Professor K.P. Trivedi, (2) Dr. P.V. Kane, (3) Professor K.B. Pathak, (4) Shri Narasimhachariar, and (5) Mr. Rice.

Bhāmaha has referred to Nyāsakāramata in *Kāvyālaṅkāra*, VI.36. There is a difference of opinion among these scholars whether Bhāmaha is referring to the Nyāsa of *Jinendrabuddhi* or to some other Nyāsa. Professor Trivedi, Shri Narasimhachariar and Mr. Rice feel that it is some other Nyāsa, while Dr. Kane and Professor Pathak claim that it is the Nyāsa of *Jinendrabuddhi* only. Depending upon It-sing's statement Professor Pathak places Nyāsa in 700 A.D., Bhāmaha later than it and Māgha still later in the close of the eighth century A.D.

With a critical survey of all available references, Dr. Kane gives the dates of the different important texts, involved in this problem as follows:

(1) Kāśikā of Vāmana and Jayāditya (before 661 A.D.), (2) Daṇḍin (660-80 A.D.), (3) Nyāsa of *Jinendrabuddhi* (about 700 A.D.), (4) Bhāmaha (about 725-50 A.D.), (5) Māgha (about 750 A.D.).

The Problem of the Authorship of *Dhvanyāloka*

Are the authors of the *Karīkās* and of the *Vṛtti* identical or different?

This is one of the most debatable problems in the field of Sanskrit Poetics. Dr. Kane remarks[25] — "From the days of Bühler, i.e., about 72 (now about 95) years ago up to the present-day (i.e., 1974 A.D.) the question, whether the author of the *Kārikās* and that of the *Vṛtti* in the *Dhvanyāloka* is one and the same person, has been discussed at great length and it cannot be said that it has been settled beyond cavil." Practically every scholar in the field of Sanskrit Poetics has written pages after pages on this problem. MM Dr. Kane has devoted more than 35 pages (pp. 163-99) to this problem even in his 1961 edition.

The Scholars fall into two groups on this issue:

(A) Those who believe in the identity of the authorship:

(1) MM. Professor Kuppaswami, (2) Dr. A. Sankaran, (3) Dr. Satkari Mookerjee, (4) Professor K.C. Pandey, (5) Dr. K. Krishnamoorthy, (6) Professor B.R. Mankad, (7) Professor T.R. Chintamani.

(B) Those who hold that the authors are different:

(1) MM. Dr. P.V. Kane, (2) Dr. S.K. De, (3) Professor S.P. Bhattacharya, (4) Mr. K. Goda Verma.

Though Dr. Kane belongs to Group (B) he introduces[26] this discussion with words — "It was I who first collected almost all important external evidence, which was almost unanimous in holding the identity of the two. I should be glad, if ultimately it be proved that the same person is the author of both the *Kārikās* and the *Vṛtti*." After going through all the arguments of the Protagonists, who had expressed their view up to 1960 he still holds fast to his opinion and remarks, "I still hold that the hypothesis of non-identity cannot in the language of the law be said to be disproved. It is very near its being proved."

In this *HSP* (1961) he aruges the case as follows:

He points out 8 passages from Abhinavagupta's Locana, which according to him, can be explained satisfactorily on the basis of different authorship only, e.g., in one place the Locana says *na caitamayoktam. api tu kārikākārābhiprayenetyāha.* This is explained by Dr. Mookerjee by pointing out that this distinction is a matter of form, lapse from which was very seriously regarded as an unpardonable offence. Upon this Dr. Kane remarks that there is no such rule. He points out that as old as 800 A.D. Vāmana expressly tells us that he composed both the *sūtra* and the *vṛtti* in his *Kāvyālaṅkārasūtravṛtti*. Dr. Kane feels that there can hardly be an instance when the *Vṛttikāra,* who is identical with the *Kārikākāra* would refer to himself as *Asmanmūlagranthakṛt*. Further he points out that the Locana always uses the word *Granthakṛt* as referring to the *Vṛttikāra,* i.e., Ānandavardhana and the word *Mūlagranthakṛt* to refer to the *Kārikākāra.*

While Dr. Mookerjee claims that it is an offence against the rules of exegesis to introduce *Utsūtra* explanations, Dr. Kane points out that in practice the rule is not followed except in the commentaries on grammatical treaties. MM. Kane further feels that if the author is the same there cannot be mutual contradiction in the views of the *Kārikākāra* and the *Vṛttikāra,* which is later to be reconciled by the commentator Abhinavagupta.

In his *Abhinavagupta* Professor K.C. Pandey cites the instances of Utpaladeva, the commentator of Abhinavagupta's *Iśvarapratyabhijñāsūtra*. In his *Vimarśinī* Utpaladeva does not expressly say that both the *sūtras* and the *vṛtti* came from Abhinavagupta.

Similarly these Protagonists claim that Abhinavagupta might not have made a clear statement to that effect. Dr. Kane refutes this by pointing out that in the introduction to his *Vimarśinī*, Utpaladeva has said so clearly and hence he does not find it necessary to repeat it in the body of the commentary. Dr. Kane then points out to Dr. K. Krishnamoorthy that he has never said that a circle of *Sahṛdayas* composed the original *Kārikās*. Further as pointed out by the opposite group, in his *Abhinavabhāratī* Abhinavagupta seems to regard Ānandavardhana as the author of both the *Kārikās* and the *Vṛtti*. Dr. Kane explains that this is so because he is under the influence of Bhaṭṭatota, his teacher in *Nāṭyaśāstra*. Dr. Kane points out that the Commentary *Candrikā*, which is older than Locana, seems to favour non-identity. He feels that if the author was the same he would not have relegated the *Parikaraślokas* and *Saṅgrahaślokas* to a subordinate position in the *Vṛtti*. The *Mahāmahopādhyāya* also points out that there is discrepancy in splitting the *Kārikās* and the interspersing prose portions of the *Vṛtti*.

About the name of the work Dr. Kane says that the work was called *Dhvani*, *Dhvanyāloka*, *Kāvyāloka* and *Sahṛdayāloka*. Professor Sovani had suggested that *Sahṛdaya* was the name of the author of the *Kārikās*. The *Mahāmahopādhyāya* adds fresh evidence to support it and says,[27] "The passages make it probable that *Sahṛdaya* was the name of the author, who propounded the theory of *Dhvani* or (more probably) was the title given to him by the admirers." Dr. Kane then winds[28] up this hair-splitting discussion about the authorship — problem with the words — "On going over all the arguments for and against the identity or non-identity of authorship I cannot help suspecting that soon after Ānandavardhana, those who believed in identity tried to tamper with the text of the *Dhvanyāloka* in various ways such as introducing the spurious verse *iti kāvyārtha* — After III.9, reading *Ityākliṣṭa* for *Nityākliṣṭa*, the splitting up of the *Kārikās* and so on".

After this Dr. K. Krishnamoorthy published his book *Dhvanyāloka and its Critics* in 1968. In the Preface to this book he says that he has thoroughly revised his original thesis, which he had submitted to the University of Bombay for the degree of 'Doctor of Letters'. He continues that he has added fresh material in the chapter on "Authorship of the *Kārikās* and the *Vṛtti*", in order to meet the points newly raised by Dr Kane. He has suffixed to Chapter III an "Addendum" covering 18 pages (pp. 73-90) for this purpose. He brings forth some important and fresh arguments:

(1) He explains why Abhinavagupta makes an apparent distinction between the *Kārikākāra* and the *Vṛttikāra* in his Locana and not in *Abhinavabhāratī*. "The simple answer is that Abhinava makes this distinction only in the Locana, where it serves an exegetical purpose and not elsewhere as in the *Abhinavabhāratī*, where the said purpose is absent."

(2) He explains in details why the Locana blames the Candrikākāra for having failed in his duty as a commentator, while explaining the passage *evam vyaṅgyamukhena dhvaneḥ, pradarśite saprabhede svarūpe punarvyañjakamukhena tat prakāśyate*. The Candrikākāra had made a cross-reference to the *vṛtti* in explaining the *Vṛttikāra's* introduction to a new *Kārikā* at the beginning of a new *Udyota*.

(3) In order to prove that there was a tradition in Kashmir to assume the functional distinction between the *Kārikākāra* and the *Vṛttikāra*, though identical, Dr. Krishnamoorthy cites the instance of Vidyādharacakravartin, an old commentator of Mammaṭa's *Kāvyaprakāśa*, who makes a functional distinction between the *Kārikākāra* and the *Vṛttikāra* of the *Kāvyaprakāśa* in almost every opening sentence of his commentary on the different *Ullāsa*.

(4) About the criticism of *Dhvani* by Manoratha, contemporary of Ānandavardhana according to Abhinavagupta, Dr. Krishnamoorthy explains that Manoratha was not criticising *Dhvanyāloka*, but only the germs of the *Dhvani* theory known before Ānandavardhana.

(5) About the discrepancy in the splitting of the *Kārikās* and the *Vṛtti* portions, the Doctor points out that such discrepancies are mostly found in *Udyota* IV, *Dhvani* theory being already established by the end of *Udyota* III. In this connection he remarks,[29] "I am constrained to think that the first draft of the *Dhvanyāloka* consisted of only the first three *Udyotas* and the fourth was an after-thought and a later addition by the author himself."

When Dr. Krishnamoorthy's book was published, MM.

Dr. Kane was nearly 90 years of age. I do not know whether he was aware of these fresh arguments. Even if he had read these arguments, I think, his delicate health might not have allowed him to answer them.

Dr. Kane used to refer to all important books and articles in the field of Sanskrit Poetics in all the editions of his History. He has taken a note of such books and articles published up to 1959. After that more than 20 important works on this subject have been published. For want of space it is not possible to add a list here. Most of these books refer to Dr. Kane's views in different contexts.

This contribution by Dr. Kane to Sanskrit Poetics sounds all the more impressive when we take into account the fact that he had to bid farewell to this 'first love' of his youthful age very early and then throughout his life he remained faithful to his 'second love', the *Dharmaśāstra,* in which he has done magnificent work. Nevertheless, the present author is sure, all present and future writers on Sanskrit Poetics will ever remain grateful to MM. Dr. P.V. Kane and Dr. S.K. De, the great pioneers in this field and would say:

ūrdhvordhvamāruhya yadarthatatvaṁ,
dhīḥ paśyati śrāntimavedayantī,
phalam tadādyaiḥ parikalpitānām
vivekasopānaparamparāṇām.

(*Abhinavabhāratī,* Stz. 2, Chapter VI.).

"The truth which is perceived by our tireless intellect, climbing higher and higher, is the result of the ladders of thought designed by earlier thinkers."

(Tr. by K. Krishnamoorthy)

References

1. *Kane's HSP,* 3rd Edition, 1961.
2. *HSP,* p. 5.
3. *HSP,* p. 9.
4. *HSP,* p. 12.
5. *HSP,* p. 23.

6. *History of Sanskrit Poetics*, De, p. 31.
7. *HSP*, p. 60.
8. 'Neo-Buddhist nucleus in *Alaṅkāraśāstra*', *JASB*, Vol. 1950.
9. *HSP*, p. 78.
10. *HSP*, p. 95.
11. *HSP*, p. 160.
12. *Sanskrit Poetics as a study of Aesthetic*, Dr. S.K. De.
13. *HSP*, p. 254.
14. *HSP*, p. 9.
15. *HSP*, p. 283.
16. HSP, p. 321.
17. De's *HSP*, 1st Edition, Vol. I, p. 341.
18. *HSP*, p. 335.
19. De's *HSP*, 2nd Edition, p. 2.
20. *Ibid.*, p. 3.
21. *Some Concepts in Alaṅkāraśāstra*, pp. 264-67.
22. *HSP*, p. 366.
23. *HSP*, p. 381.
24. *HSP*, p. 115.
25. *HSP*, 1951 Edition, p. 154.
26. *HSP*, p. 163.
27. *HSP*, p. 192.
28. *HSP*, p. 199.
29. *Dhvanyāloka and its Critics*, p. 79.

15

The Legend of Udayana

THE immense popularity that the legend of Udayana has enjoyed in Indian literature is evident from the fact that it has been drawn upon by many Sanskrit, Pāli and Prakrit authors and has been referred to at many places in Indian literature. Two of Bhāsa's plays (about 4th B.C.), viz., *Svapnavāsavadatta* and *Pratijña-yaugandharāyaṇa* have the Udayana legend as the central theme. Udayana is the hero of two of Śrīharṣa's plays (606-47 A.D.), viz., *Ratnāvalī* and *Priyadarśikā*. There is an incomplete and anonymous play *Vīṇāvāsavadattā* which also deals with an important event in Udayana's life.

Tāpasavatsarāja, a play by Anaṅgaharṣa or Māyurāja and *Vatsarājacarita*, a poem by Śūdraka also deal with the same hero. The legend is given in full in the *Kathāsaritsāgara* of Somadeva (between 1062 and 1082 A.D.) and *Bṛhtkathāmañjarī* of Kṣemendra (about 1035 A.D.) The available fragments of *Bṛhatkthāśloka-saṅgraha* of Budhasvāmin (about 6th cent. A.D.) give details of some parts of the legend.

In the Buddhist literature the legend is given in Pāli *Dhammapada — Aṭṭhakathā* of Buddhaghoṣa, *Papañcasūdanī*, a commentary on *Majjhima Nikāya* by Buddhaghoṣa, *Sāmavatī-Jātaka* and in the Chinese *Mūlasarvāstitvavāda-Vinaya* and Tibetan *Kanjur*. In addition to these texts Buddhist canonical literature sporadically refers to some aspects of the legend.

In the Jain literature *Kumārapālapratibodha* of Somaprabha (1195 A.D.) gives the story of Udayana's birth in *Mṛgāvatī Kathā* and of his marriage with Vāsavadattā in *Pradyotakathā*.

In the classical literature, references to Udayana are available as back as the *Arthaśāstra* of Kauṭilya (4th cent. B.C.) which mentions Udayana's name to illustrate how a king can regain his lost power. In his *Meghadūta*, Kālidāsa refers to the elderly persons in the city of Avantī as being conversant with *Udayana-kathā* and enumerates some of the incidents in the story as follows:

pradyotasya priyaduhitaraṁ vatsarājo'tra jahre
haimam tāladrumavanamabhudatra tasyaiva rajñaḥ
atrodbhrāntaḥ kila nalagiriḥ stambhamutpāṭya darpādi
tyāgantūn ramayati jano yatra bandhunabhijñaḥ.

Mṛcchakaṭika of Śūdraka (between 4th and 8th cent A.D.) refers to the rescue of Udayana by *Yaugandharāyaṇa* through the words of *Śarvilaka*. Bhavabhūti in his *Mālatīmādhava* alludes to one event in Vāsavadattā's life through the words of *Kāmandakī: vāsavadattā, ca pitrā sañjayāya rājñe dattāmātmānam udayanāya prāyacchat.*

Looking to these and such other numerous references to the story of Udayana-Vāsavadattā one realises the truth of the following remark by Dr. V.S. Sukhthankar:[1] "The touching and romantic episode in their eventful life-history have formed the warp and woof of many an alluring tapestry of love-romance deftly woven."

A comparative survey of this romance is bound to be interesting. For convenience of study we can divide the legend in 6 parts as follows:

(A) The early history of Udayana or the story of Mṛgāvatī.
(B) Udayana-Vāsavadattā episode.
(C) Udayana-Padmāvatī episode.
(D) Udayana and other heroines.
(E) The birth of Naravāhanadatta.
(F) Udayana's end.

(A) The Early History of Udayana or The Story of Mṛgāvatī

Narrative of the *KSS*. — The second Lambaka, i.e., Kathāmukha gives the story of Udayana's birth as follows: Śatānīka the king of Kauśāmbī was a son of Janamejaya. When he was invited to the heaven by Indra in order to fight on behalf of the gods, he placed the yoke of administration on Yugandhara, the minister, and Supratīka, the commander-in-chief. Śatānīka was killed in the battle, queen Viṣṇumatī died after him, and then their son Sahasrānīka becomes the king of Kauśāmbī. Later on he also goes to the heaven on being invited by Indra. There he learns that in his former birth he was a Vasu named Vidhūma and the nymph Alambuṣā was his wife. Alambuṣā is now born as Mṛgāvatī, the princess of Ayodhyā. While returning he is engrossed in thoughts of Mṛgāvatī and as such does not even hear the words of Tilottamā, who is calling him. Enraged she curses him, *yayā hṛtamanā rājan na śṛṇosi vaco mama / tasyāścaturdaśasamā viyogaste bhaviṣyati.*

After his return to Kauśāmbī a messenger is sent to Ujjayinī and the marriage takes place. Now Yugandhara, Supratīka and Narmasuhṛda get sons named Yaugandharāyaṇa, Rumanvān and Vasantaka respectively. After some days Mṛgāvatī has a strange pregnancy-longing for a bath in a lake of blood. The king orders a pool to be filled with juice of lac. When she is taking her bath an eagle takes her off mistaking her for a piece of flesh. Sahasrānīka is consoled by Indra's charioteer Mātali, who had overheard *Tilottamā's* curse. Now Mṛgāvatī is dropped down on Udaya *Parvata* by the bird. She cries helplessly. She is saved from a boa by a divine figure. She falls before a wild elephant but is not crushed by it. Hearing her cry a young ascetic comes there and takes her to the hermitage of Jamadagni.

That sage, who has *divyadṛṣṭi* assures her that she will give birth to a son there and will be united with her husband. At the proper time she delivers a son.

At his birth are heard the following words from the heaven:

> *śrimānudayano nāmnā rājā jāto mahāyaśāḥ,*
> *bhaviṣyati ca putro'sya sarvavidyādharādhīpaḥ.*

Jamadagni performs all the sacraments for him and teaches him all lores. The mother puts on his arm an armlet with Sahasrānīka's name on it. Once Udayana, while hunting saw a snake being dragged by a *Śabara.* Udayana took pity on the snake and released it by giving the *Śabara* his armlet in exchange. The snake in gratitude said, "I am Vasunemi, elder brother of Vāsukī. I am pleased with you. Take this lute, these betel-leaves and the magic art of unfading garland and mark." Now the *Śabara* is caught by the guards while he was selling that armlet marked with the king's name. He gives out the facts of how he got it and at the same time a divine voice informs the king of the whereabout of his wife and son. The king then goes there and brings Mṛgāvatī and Udayana to Kauśāmbī with great pomp. Sahasrānīka installs Udayana on the throne. Again *divyā vāk* foretells how he will rule the entire earth with Yaugandharāyaṇa, Rumanvān and Vasantaka as his ministers. Then Sahasrānīka retires to the forest along with his queen and ministers.

The *BKM* gives a similar account in the first *guccha* of *Kathāmukhalambaka*. It differs from the *KSS* in a few minor details. At the time of Udayana's birth the voice from the heaven refers to him as *Bhaviṣyaccakravartin*. The *nāga* rescued by Udayana is described as *Kinnarādhīpa* and *Dhṛtarāṣṭrasuta*.

The *Vīṇā* is named as Ghoṣavatī and in addition to the lute, the betel-leaf and the unfading garland, Udayana gets Lalitā, the sister of that *nāga*.

The *BKSS* gives this story in the fifth *Sarga*, while describing the *dohadasampādana* of Vāsavadattā. Vāsavadattā says that she has a strange longing which she cannot give out. In order to induce her to do so Mṛgāvatī relates her own story. The narration differs from that of the *KSS* in the following points:

1. Mṛgāvatī had a desire to see herself clad in red and the whole city also dressed in red.
2. She is taken by the hermits to Vasiṣṭhāśrama.
3. There is no reference to the armlet.
4. Vasiṣṭha had warned the boy not to go to the woods.

One day while playing in a tank the boy sees some snakes who take him to the city of Bhogavatī in the under-world. When the boy informs Vasiṣṭha of his visit to Pātāla he advises him to go there once again. During this second visit he receives by way of present the lute Ghoṣavatī with which he can bewitch men and animals. When Udayana's education is over Vasiṣṭha sends the mother and the son to Kauśāmbī. The guards see Udayana and then the king receives them both.

Buddhist Literature

According to the *Aṭṭhakathā* of *Dhammapada,* Parantapa, the king of Kauśāmbī, is sitting on the terrace with his pregnant queen wrapped in a red shawl. Just in sport she removes the king's signet ring and puts it on her finger. Just at that time the vulture Hatthiliṅga comes there flapping the wings. The king being frightened runs inside the palace, but the queen cannot do so. The bird carries her off and leaves her between two branches of a fig-tree on the mountain Himavat. She passes that cloudy and stormy night miserably and gives birth to a son in the early morning. Hence she named him Udena. Nearby lived king Allakappa who had by now become a hermit. She thinks that under the circumstances the best way was to seduce him. They then live together happily. One day the hermit, observing the stars, exclaims, "King Parantapa is dead." She bursts into tears and reveals her identity. She is aggrieved that her son cannot inherit the kingdom. He promises that he would find a way out. He then gives Udena a lute and teaches him a secret formula to tame elephants. By the efficacy of the lute and the formula the head-elephant presents itself before Udena on the third day. The mother gives necessary instructions to the son, informs him of the names of the ministers, etc., and hands over the red mantle and the signet ring to him. With that Udena mounts the elephant and whispers something in its ear. The elephant is followed by a herd of elephants and thus Udena triumphantly enters Kauśāmbī and claims the kingdom. With the help of the instructions and the things given by his mother he convinces the people that he is the rightful heir to the throne and is crowned as king of Kauśambī.

Papañcasūdanī of Buddhaghoṣa gives this part of Udena's history in a condensed form. It is not recorded in the Chinese *Mūlasarvāstitvavāda-vinaya* and in the Tibetan *Kanjur.*

Jain Literature

Kumārapalapratibodha of Somaprabha gives the story of Mṛgāvatī to illustrate the importance of chastity.

In the city of Sāketa festivities were held annually in honour of Yakṣa Surapriya. Painting of his resemblance was an essential part of the worship. Unfortunately every year the painter of his portrait was soon deprived of his life. The painters in Sāketa tried to run away. It was then decided that the work would go to all families of painters turn by turn. When it was the turn of an old woman's son he was saved voluntarily by a painter from Kauśāmbī. He took a holy bath, worshipped the Yakṣa with great pomp, painted the portrait, and then begged of the Yakṣa to forgive him for the shortcomings, if any. The Yakṣa is propitiated and gives him two boons. He says, "Do not kill anybody hence forward and give me the skill of drawing the likeness of any *dvipāda* or *catuṣpāda* by simply looking at any one part of the body." The stranger then returns to Kauśāmbī. There king Śatānīka is told by his subjects that his glorious kingdom has one drawback, viz., that it cannot boast of a picture-gallery. The king orders for the same, and the same young painter sits to work. He happens to see a toe of Mṛgāvatī and draws her full-size portrait right up to the *masībindu* on her breast. The king gets suspicious and gets the young painter arrested and though the painter proves his innocence his right hand is cut off. He then decides to take revenge. Again he propitiates the Yakṣa and with his grace is able to paint with his left hand with equal skill. He paints Mṛgāvatī's likeness and sends it to the licentious Pradyota. As expected, Pradyota, being enamoured of her charms, asks king Śatānīka for her. Naturally a battle follows in which Śatānīka is killed. Mṛgāvatī is very much worried over her *śīlarakṣaṇa*. When Pradyota asks for her hand she sends messages twice. By one she asks him to build a rampart around Kauśāmbī, with bricks from Ujjayinī. By another she makes him fill the city of Kauśāmbī with food and wealth. Then she closes the doors of Kauśāmbī, so that Pradyota has to wait outside in a dejected mood. She began to think: "If Jina were to come here I shall take to renunciation." As desired by her Jina actually comes there. The gates are then opened and all including

Pradyota and Mṛgāvatī, listen to the sermon. The tale of a gold-smith, makes them all full of dejection. Mṛgāvatī salutes Jina, hands over Udayana to Pradyota and with Pradyota's permission she renounces the world. She is followed by queen Aṅgāravatī and seven other wives of Pradyota. The story ends with the conclusion:

> *śīlavaśena lahium kevalanāṇam migāvatī siddhā*
> *śīlarahio ya patto ayaśam kugaim ya pajjoo.*

A similar story occurs in *Mṛgāvaticaritra* of Maladhārī Devaprabha also.

From all these accounts we can come to the following conclusion about Udayana's history:

Some kind of mystery surrounds his birth and childhood. He was born when his mother was separated from her husband. The place where he was born is Jamadagnyāśrama according to *KSS* and *BKM*, Vasiṣṭhāśrama according to *BKSS* and the hermitage of Allakappa on the mountain Himavat according to *Aṭṭhakathā*. Thus the place of his birth is some distant hermitage. The name of his father is Sahasrānīka according to *KSS* and *BKM* but Śatānīka according to *BKSS* and *KPP* and Parantapa according to the *Aṭṭhakathā*. Śatānīka is the father of Udayana and the grandfather of Vahīnara according to the *Purāṇas* also. In *PY*, Pradyota inquires whether his prisoner is *Śatānīkasya putraḥ* and *Sahasrānīkasya naptā*. Tibetan *Kanjur* also refers to Udayana as son of Śatānika. In *KSS* and *BKM*, Śatānīka is Udayana's grandfather. It seems from all these references that Śatānīka is the name of Udayana's father. *KSS* might have given Sahasrānīka as his son to point out that he was more powerful than his father, and then made him the father of the illustrious Udayana. It cannot be definitely said as to why *Aṭṭhakathā* gives the name as Parantapa. Etymologically, the name suggests how he was a terror to his enemies and thus does not differ much from the name Śatānīka.

Except for *KSS* and *BKM*, we do not find a reference to the armlet worn by Udayana. It seems to have been inserted by the compiler of the Kaśmīrī version of the *BK* which is more ornate than that of the Nepālī version. Udayana was educated by a hermit like Sarvadamana-Bharata and Lava-Kuśa.

All versions of the story, except the Jain version refer to Udayana getting his Ghoṣavatī *vīṇā* in a miraculous way. It is a gift from the *Nāgaloka* according to all the three versions of the *BK;* but according to the *Aṭṭhakathā* it is a gift from the hermit Allakappa. Kaśmīrī version of the *BK* has elaborated the point by referring to the *vīṇā* as a token of gratitude on the part of the *Nāga,* and by introducing the *Śabara,* who, like the fisherman in the Śākuntala, becomes instrumental in bringing about the reunion. The ring which serves a similar purpose is present in *KSS, BKM* and *AK;* but the purpose served by it in *AK* is less dramatic than that in the Kaśmīrī version. The reunion is brought about by Vasiṣṭha himself without any fuss about it in the *BKSS.* In *KSS* and *BKM* it is brought about in a dramatic manner, while in the *AK* it begins with Allakappa's remark 'Parantapa is dead' and ends with the help of supernatural element, viz., the charm for elephant-taming.

According to the *AK* and the *Papañcasūdanī* there is no reunion of Mṛgāvatī and her husband, as Udayana claims his father's kingdom after his death. Here the narration of the *BK* seems more poetic.

As for the manner in which Mṛgāvatī lived when separated from her husband all versions except the Buddhist have depicted Mṛgāvatī as a chaste lady. But the *AK* and *Papañcasūdanī* depict Mṛgāvatī in bad colours, where she seduces the hermit Allakappa. This is the most natural and convenient thing that could have been done by a woman in her circumstances.

Prof. Lacote[2] believes that *Guṇāḍhya* must be drawing upon the same version as used by the Buddhist authors. If that is so why do we find this divergence in the story of Mṛgāvatī? Prof. Lacote says, "The story of Mṛgāvatī has been modified intentionally;" and the reason for this modification, according to him is, "The future *Cakravartin* (Naravāhanadatta) could not possibly be born from a family in which the least stain could be found."

It is, however, worthnoting that this dark side of Mṛgāvatī's life is found in the *AK* and *Papañcasūdanī* only. Jains are often supposed to use such myths and legends in a distorted form. Not only that the Jain versions of the story have not referred to this seduction of the hermit by Mṛgāvatī, but they have given Mṛgāvatī a high rank among persons whose example should be followed. Somaprabha gives her story to illustrate the importance of *śīla*. Hence the version of the story used by the *AK* of Dhammapada seems to be current in a very restricted locality, while the *Udayanacarita,* which Prof. Lacote describes as existing at Kauśāmbī and consisting of 'a cycle of stories either in writing or handed down by oral tradition, more comprehensive than what has passed into the Buddhist text,' seems to have a wider sway.

(B) Udayana-Vāsavadattā Episode

In the *KSS* the episode covers *taraṅgas* 3-6 of the *Kathāmukhalambaka*. In brief it is as follows:

Udayana, as king of Kauśāmbī leads a life of pleasure. He thinks,

> *kularūpānurūpā me bhāryā kvāpi na vidyate*
> *ekā vāsavadattākhyā kanyakā śrūyate, paraṁ*
> *kathaṁ prāpyeta sā ceti cintām ekām uvāha saḥ.*

Caṇḍa-Mahāsena of Ujjayinī is worried as to how he can get Udayana to be his son-in-law. He then decides to capture him taking advantage of his fondness for elephant-chase.

He propitiates Caṇḍi and she blesses him. He sends a messenger to Udayana saying, "Come here and instruct my daughter in music." Yaugandharāyaṇa comments on this —

> *bhuvi vyasanitākhyātiḥ prarūdhā te lateva yā*
> *idaṁ tasya mahārāja kaṣāyakaṭukaṁ phalam.*

But he advises Udayana not to have enmity with Mahāsena and gives an account of Mahāsena's family. When Mahāsena was celebrating *Indrotsava* for his sons Gopālaka and Pālaka, Indra promised him in dream that he would get a daughter. Hence he named her Vāsavadattā. At her birth a divine voice declared, "Her son, an incarnation of Kāmadeva, will be a sovereign of *Vidyādharas*."

Udayana then sends a counter-message, "If you want me to teach, send your daughter here." On hearing this reply Mahāṣena begins with his plan. A *Yantrahasti* is placed in the forest. Udayana cannot realise that it was a mechanical elephant because his mind was absorbed in music and also because of the evening dusk. Udayana is taken a captive and led to Ujjayinī. Yaugandharāyaṇa entrusts Rumanvān with the affairs of Kauśāmbī and goes to Ujjayinī, along with Vasantaka, in order to rescue his master. In the cemetery he makes friends with a *brahmarākṣasa* named Yogeśvara. With his help Yaugandharāyaṇa assumes the form of a madman, bald-headed and comic. Vasantaka also appears ugly. In the meanwhile the prisoner Udayana is asked to teach Vāsavadattā, the art of music; and during the lessons they learn something other than music. Yaugandharāyaṇa now manages to see Udayana and gives his some magic-lores to break off the chains and win over the heart of Vāsavadattā. Then Āṣāḍhaka, the elephant-driver in charge of Bhadrāvatī, is won over. Mahāmātra, the elephant-superintendent, is given liquor. One day Udayana kills the two guards and elopes on Bhadrāvatī with Vāsavadattā, accompanied by her friend Kāñcanamālā. Yaugandharāyaṇa and Vasantaka wait for them at the house of Pulindaka, the forest-king. When their absence is noticed in Ujjayinī Pālaka pursues them on Naḍagiri but the elephant refuses to fight against his mate. After some time Bhadrāvatī dies as she drinks the water of a stream. It is told by her that she was a Vidyādharī, temporarily born as a Kareṇu. She further informs that Vāsavadattā is a deity.

After some time Udayana comes to Pulindaka's house. Rumanvān joins him with a big army. They reach Kauśāmbī safely. Mahāsena sends his congratulations, Gopālaka comes to Kauśāmbī and the marriage is duly celebrated.

The *BKM* gives a similar account, with a few details, dropped. The available fragments of *BKSS* do not contain this episode, though Bhadra refers to it.

The episode forms the central theme of the play *Py*. Pradyota Mahāsena, the king of Ujjayinī is desirous of giving his daughter to Udayana, though he is receiving offers from different suitors everyday. Sālaṅkāyana, his minister captivates Udayana by means of a mechanical elephant. When the news reaches Kauśāmbī Yaugandharāyaṇa takes a vow to see that Udayana elopes with Vāsavadattā. A mad brāhmaṇa attending the *Śāntibhojana* gives him a clue for going to Ujjayini in *Unmattakaveṣa.* Now they enter Ujjayinī, Yaugandharāyaṇa as Unmattabrāhmaṇa, Vasantka as Ḍiṇḍika and Rumanvān as a Śramaṇaka. They manage to enter Pradyota's palace and stay there. Vasantaka entertains Vāsavadattā by narrating excellent tales and conveys to Udayana the hints given by Yaugandharāyaṇa, whenever possible. Many other spies of Yaugandharāyaṇa also are working in Ujjayinī under different garbs. One day Udayana elopes with Vāsavadattā when Vāsavadattā goes out on Bhadrāvatī under the pretext of going for *udakakrīḍā.* When the fugitives are being pursued Nalagiri refuses to fight against Bhadrāvatī. Finally Mahāsena declares that he looks upon the marriage as lawful and then the wedding festivities are celebrated in Ujjayinī with the portraits of Udayana and Vāsavadattā. Thus the *Pratijñā* of Yaugandha- rāyaṇa is fulfilled.

The *SV* describes a later romance of Udayana; even then it refers to the Udayana-Vāsavadattā episode off and on. In Act IV Padmāvatī inquires whether Udayana was loved by Vāsavadattā also with equal intensity. Vāsavadattā, now Avantikā, unconsciously replies, *ato'pyadhikam.* When Padmāvatī asks as to how Avantikā could know it, she replies *yadyalpaḥ snehaḥ, sā svajanaṁ na parityajati.*

In verse No. 1 of this Act the king remembers the incident in Ujjayinī when he fell in love with Vāsavadattā. In Act VI, verse No. 8, Udayana expresses his gratitude to Mahāsena and refers to the events in Ujjayinī as follows:

ahaṁ avajitaḥ pūrvaṁ tāvat sutaiḥ saha lālitaḥ
dṛḍhamapahṛtā kanyā bhūyo mayā na ca rakṣitā.

In verse No. 11 he refers to Vāsavadattā as

mahāsenasya duhitā śiṣyā devī ca me priyā.

In the message to Udayana, Vāsavadattā's mother says,

> *atha cāvabhyāṁ tava ca vāsavadattāyāś ca pratikṛtiṁ citraphalakāyāmalikhya vivāho nirvṛttaḥ.*

The *viṣkambhaka* of this Act refers to the loss and regaining of Ghoṣavatī *viṇā*.

The *VV* (incomplete up to the beginning of the Act IV and anonymous) gives the story of *PY* with a few but important deviations. The story runs as follows: In order to solve the problem of Vāsavadattā's marriage, Pradyota Mahāsena is propitiating god Śiva with austerities. After some days he stops the austerities as god Śiva has bestowed favours on him in a dream. Śiva appeared before him in his dream and asked him to hand over Vāsavadattā to an ideal youth as described by the god in a verse. Bharatarohaka, the prime-minister, explains to him that every king whom he knew had one or the other defect, e.g., Sañjaya, the son of Aśmaka was suffering from a disease causing blood-vomitting and was much addicted to liquor. Darśaka of Magadha was cruel. Then suddenly he remembers that Maheśvara must have referred to Udayana Vatseśvara in that verse. Now the difficulty is how to bring about the marriage. Again Bharatarohaka suggests that if he is taken a captive he would be put to a hard test of adversity to find out if he satisfied the standards laid down by Śiva. Upon this Pradyota puts forth the difficulty that he would be liable to ignominy that he did not keep the engagement fixed with Sañjaya. The difficulty is solved by Bharatarohaka by foretelling that it would not be so, since Udayana will elope with Vāsavadattā in the manner of *Subhadrāharaṇa*. How to bring Udayana to Ujjayinī? Bharatarohaka is ready with a plan to entrap him with the help of an artificial elephant. He then informs about a curse pronounced on Udayana by the sage Aṅgāraka. Udayana, when a boy, was playing the part of an elephant. His playmates were following him. In the manner of an elephant he tossed about dust, which troubled the sage Aṅgāraka, passing by. Irritated, the sage cursed, 'You will be subject to imprisonment and humiliation at the hands of your enemy because of an elephant." The minister Sālaṅkāyana begins with the plan and goes to Nāgavana. Udayana goes forth accompanied by Aupagāyaka, carrying *vīṇā*. Udayana plays on the lute, and is all of a sudden surrounded by an army led by Sālaṅkāyana. Sālaṅkāyana explains to him that Mahāsena desires to take him safe to Ujjayinī. Udayana persuades Sālaṅkāyana to be his minister, but cannot succeed. A battle ensues and Udayana is taken captive. When Yaugandharāyaṇa knows of the incident, he asks Haṁsaka to speed up to Ujjayinī. He himself spreads a rumour that Udayana is dead and writes a letter in a code-language that could be understood only by Udayana and Rumanvān. He further says, "I know *cakṣurmohinī vidyā*. I shall enter pyre and secretly go to Ujjayinī to rescue my master. I shall freely wander in that city in the disguise of a mad-man and shall enter Kauśāmbī along with my master."

The play is left unfinished with the remark of Haṁsaka in the disguise of Ḍiṇḍika, "I have wandered throughout the city of Ujjayinī, let me rest a while in this temple."

Buddhist Literature

In the *AK* after describing the marriage of Udayana with Sāmavatī, the story turns to Vāsavadattā-episode. Udena had another wife, called Vāsuladattā, daughter of Caṇḍapajjota, king of Ujjayinī. Pajjota heard that Udena's splendour surpassed his own mainly because he could charm the elephants with his magic-lute. Hence out of sheer jealousy he contrives to captivate him with the help of a mechanical elephant. In the course of the chase Udena is separated from his retinue and is taken to Ujjayinī as a prisoner. Pajjota demands that his prisoner should reveal to him the secret elephant-charms. Udena would teach only to one who paid him homage as a teacher. This, Pajjota would never do. He then thought of giving his daughter as a pupil to Udena. He said to Udena, "I have in my house a girl who is hunch-backed. She will stand behind a curtain, yourself in front of it, and then you teach her the formula." He tells Vāsuladattā that she is going to be taught by a leper. The lessons begin. For many days Udena tries to teach, but the pupil cannot learn. Out of impatience he calls her, 'hunch-backed girl', 'leper' she retorts. Thereupon Udena lifts up the curtain and thus the mystery is solved. Now, instead of the elephant-charms they speak of the elopement-plan. Vāsuladattā manages to get a conveyance, viz., Bhaddāvatī and permission to use a gate of the city. She says that in order to learn the practical part of the charms, they require a certain herb, which can be obtained at night only at a particular hour indicated by the stars. Now people get used to seeing them passing together through that gate. One day when Pajjota was out on a pleasure-trip, Udena loads Bhaddāvatī with gold and silver coins, mounts her along with Vāsuladattā and they run away. When they are being pursued by the guards of Ujjayinī, Udena scatters the gold coins, which detain the guards. They then safely reach Kauśāmbī, where the marriage is duly celebrated.

The Tibetan *Kanjur* gives a similar version of the story but with a different beginning. When Udena knew that Caṇḍapradyota of Ujjayinī has given leave to the ladies in his harem to move out at night, he goes there in spite of Yaugandhara's warning. Tārā, a *Pāṇḍavī*, attracts him. At the sound of drums she goes away, after stealing Udayana's ring. Because of it Pradyota comes to know of Udayana's audacity. Once again Udayana and Yaugandhara go to Ujjayinī and stay there. Bharata, the minister of Pradyota causes the house to be surrounded by soldiers. Yaugandhara and Udayana disguised as a maid-servent, make good their escape. For this Bharata is threatened to death if Udayana is not captured. He then begins his plans. He causes a notice to be issued that the elephant Naḍagiri has run away. A big mechanical elephant is placed in woods nearby Kauśāmbī. As expected Udayana approaches it and is brought as a prisoner to Ujjayinī. When Pradyota orders that he be killed Bharata says, "Let him teach the art of elephant-taming first and then we will kill him." Of course Pradyota cannot be humble before him. If he teaches it to Bharata, he cannot kill his own preceptor. Bharata suggests that he should teach Vāsavadattā. The teacher and the pupil are separated by a curtain. Vāsavadattā has been told that the sight of the prisoner-teacher would be mortal to her. Now anxious Yaugandhara sends his sister Kāñcanamālā to get some news of Udayana. She manages to enter the palace in the disguise of a female beggar and reveals the mystery to the teacher and the student. Now Yaugandhara comes to Ujjayinī as a mad-man named Vasantaka. Vāsavadattā informs her father that now she needs a little practice in the charms. Both get used to going out on Bhadrāvatī. Yaugandhara once collects elephant-excrements and puts these at two places on the road to Kauśāmbī.

Udayana, Vāsavadattā, Yaugandhara and Kāñcanamālā run away mounted on Bhadrāvatī. Bharata pursues them on Naḍagiri. The elephant loses time in smelling the excrements. The fugitives reach Kauśāmbī, where the marriage takes place. Udayana gives out his intention of avenging the insult and says that he would not rest till Pradyota is taken a captive and made to learn weaving. A similar story in brief is given in *Divyāvadāna,* XXXVI. The *MSVV* of the Chinese does not relate Udayana-Vāsavadattā episode.

Jātaka, III.384 (Fausboll) has an allusion to the abduction of Vāsavadattā, which, though brief, presupposes that the readers are familiar with the details of the legend. When Buddha is in *Ghoṣitārāma* in Kauśāmbī the female elephant Bhaddavatikā comes to see him and complains against her master Udena. She says, "Formerly he honoured me, looked after me, saying: To thee I owe my life, my kingdom and my wife; now he neglects me because I am old and incapable of rendering any service." Buddha then goes to see the king and asks, 'where is *Bhaddavatikā?*' 'I do not know' answers Udena. Buddha takes him to task for this sort of ingratitude, and since then Udena has to pay attention to her as before.

Jain Literature

In the *KPP* the episode begins with the story of Abhayakumāra. It is supposed to illustrate the evils of licentiousness as in the case of Pradyota — *Paradārye Pradyotakathā.* It runs as follows: Vāsavadattā, the princess of Ujjayinī was well-versed in all arts. Her father Pajjoya desires to bring Udayana to isntruct her in music.

He is caught by means of a mechanical elephant. The prisoner is asked to teach the princess, with the warning, *mama dhuyā kāṇā. sā tumaṁ datthūṇa mā lajjau ti.*

"My daughter is quint-eyed. Let her not be ashamed of you." She is told, *vajjihāo koḍhio,* 'The teacher is a leper.' The lessons begin with a curtain between them.

One day she intentionally commits a mistake and thus the whole mystery is revealed. The love-affair is known to Kāñcanamālā, a nurse of Vāsavadattā.

Once the elephant Nalagiri gets wild and Udayana alone brings it under control. After sometime Pajjoya invites Udayana and Vāsavadattā to the park in order to give a musical performance as desired by Abhayakumāra.

Now Jogandharaino enters Ujjayinī in the disguise of a mad-man. He gives out his *Pratijña* as —

> *yadi tām caiva tām caiva tām caivāyatalocanām*
> *na harāmi nṛpasyārthe nāham yaugandharāyanaḥ.*

He fills four pots with urine and ties these on the back of Bhadrāvatī. A blind man, who could interpret cries heard her cry and said,

> *kakṣāyām badhyamānāyām yathā rasati hastinī*
> *yojanānāṁ śataṁ gatvā tathā prāṇān vimokṣyati.*

Then Udayana, taking his Ghoṣavatī, mounted Bhaddavatī along with Vāsavadattā and Kāñcanamālā. His friend Vasantaka was the driver. He said before the public —

> *eṣa prayāti sārthaḥ kāñcanamālā, vasantakaścaiva*
> *bhadrāvatī, ghoṣavatī, vāsavadattāpyudayanaśca.*

People thought he was going to the park; but the female elephant ran in the direction of Kauśāmbī. When Pajjoya knew this he sent soldiers to catch the fugitives. They pursued on Nalagiri. But at every 25 *yojanas* a pot of urine was broken and Nalagiri wastes time in smelling it. Thus the whole distance was traversed and they reach Kauśāmbī safely.

The story ends by describing how Pajjoya was finally taken as a prisoner to Rājagṛha by Abhayakumāra.

This part of Udayana's history is the most popular in Indian literature. The points which are common to all the versions of the story are as follows:

(1) The king of Ujjayinī was eager to capture Udayana and

bring him to Ujjayinī.

(2) He was entrapped with the help of a mechanical elephant. (According to the *Kanjur* a report is spread that Nalagiri has been lost).

(3) Vāsavadattā was given to him as a pupil.

(4) Yaugandharāyaṇa (Yaugandhara according to *Kanjur*) goes to the rescue of his master.

He stays in Ujjayinī in the disguise of a mad-man. (*DPAK* does not refer to Yaugandharāyaṇa).

(5) The fugitives ride the female-elephant Bhadrāvatī.

(6) They are pursued by Pālaka according to the Kaśmīrī *Bṛhatkathā,* — by Bharata according to the *Kanjur* and by the soldiers according to the *KPP* — riding the elephant Naḍagiri. (The elephant is called Naḍagiri in the Kaśmīrī version, Nalagiri in *BKSS, KPP* and *PY;* and Nadāgiri in the *Kanjur. AK* does not refer to this elephant).

(7) The elephant cannot fight against its mate. (According to the *KSS, BKM* and *PY,* he refused to fight. He loses time in smelling the excrements according to the *Kanjur,* and is smelling urine according to the *KPP*).

According to the *KSS, BKM, BKSS* and *KPP,* Bhadrāvatī dies on the way. According to all the versions of *BK,* she was a superhuman being born as a female elephant. She was *Vidyādharī Māyāvatī* according to the Kaśmīrī version and a *Guhyakī* named Bhadrā according to the *BKSS,* which further informs that Nalagiri was a Yakṣa, Pūrṇabhadra who was guilty of interceding. The *BKSS* further informs us that when she died in the forest of Vindhya, Udayana wept over her loss with such genuine sympathy that she decided to reward him. It is she, who, later on prepares the aerial car to fulfil Vāsavadattā's pregnancy-longing, sends the auspicious dream foretelling the birth of a son; and after saying that their son would be a *cakravartin,* she disappears making a breach in the walls of Kauśāmbī, the part being known as Bhadrāvatī's gate.

It is, however worthnoting that according to the allusion in the *Jātaka,* she is living for a long time after the marriage of Vāsavadattā. Obviously the two narrations, viz., that of *Guṇāḍhya* and the Buddhist one are following two different versions of the story.

Was Pradyota-Mahāsena eager to have Udayana as his son-in-law? We learn so from the *KSS, BKM,* and from the *PY* and *VV* which are based on the same. With this desire, he is propitiating goddess *Caṇḍī* according to the Kaśmīrī version. According to the *VV,* he is propitiating Śiva to have a worthy son-in-law. According to the *AK,* he arrested Udayana simply out of jealousy and then the marriage takes place against the desire of the father, as is obvious from the use of the curtain. The same holds good of the *Kanjur* and the *KPP* also. In the *KPP* he wants to bring Udayana to be a music-teacher only. In the *Kanjur* Pradyota has a genuine grievance agaisnt Udayana when he finds Udayana's ring with Tārā.

The Kaśmīrī version of the *BK* makes Udayana also long for Vāsavadattā before he has to go to Ujjayinī. It would not be out of place to refer here to the following note on Udayana given in *Hindu Classical Dictionary* of Dowson.

Udayana — a prince of Lunar race and son of Sahasrāṇīka, who is the hero of a popular story. He was king of Vatsa and is commonly called *Vatsarāja.* His capital was Kauśāmbī. Vāsavadattā, Princess of Ujjayinī saw him in a dream and fell in love with him. He was decoyed to that city, and there kept in captivity by the king Caṇḍamahāsena, but when he was set at liberty by the minister, he carried off Vāsavadattā from her father and a rival suitor.

Dr. M.R. Kale in his notes on *Meghadūta,* verse 31, gives the story as found in the *KSS* and there includes the following remark: "In the meantime Vāsavadattā saw Udayana in a dream and becoming enamoured of him contrived to inform him of her love."

This part of the story, reminding us of Uṣā-Aniruddha episode could not be traced by me to any available version.

It seems that in the older version of the story there may be no reference to any desire on the part of Vāsavadattā or her father for bringing about the marriage. This embellishment might have been added by the Udayanacarita current near-about Kauśāmbī. When they added this, they had naturally to drop the dramatic part of the story referring to the curtain used during the lessons.

What was the original name of the king of Ujjayinī? *KSS* and

BKM alone give Mahāsena or Caṇḍamahāsena as his name and call the king of Magadha as Pradyota. The *BKSS* calls him Pradyota-Mahāsena. Same is the case with Bhāsa's plays, viz., the *PY, SV* and with the *VV*, *SV* explains the name as follows: *astyujjayinīyo rājā pradyoto nāma. tasya bala-parimāṇa-nivṛttam nāmadheyam mahāsena iti.* The *SV* and *VV* call the king of Magadha as Darśaka, the *VV* refers to him as *māgadho rājā darśakaḥ krūraḥ.* The *BKSS* refers to Padmāvatī as Māgadhī; but the name of her father is not given. The *Kanjur* refers to Bimbisāra as ruling at Rājagṛha at the same time when Pradyota, son of Anantanemi, ruled at Ujjayinī. According to all the Buddhist and Jain versions the name of the king of Ujjayinī is Pradyota. The Chinese *MSVV* calls him Caṇḍapajjota, because he used to get wild if his third call was left unanswered by the sentry.

Obviously his genuine name is Pradyota and Mahāsena may be an appellation as explained by Bhāsa. Somadeva and Kṣemendra seem to have committed a mistake.

The remark from the M.M. quoted in section 1 and the play *VV* refer to one more incident in the life of Vāsavadattā. She was first betrothed to Sañjaya by the father. According to *VV*, the engagement was broken by Pradyota himself, but according to the M.M. by Vāsavadattā. The *VV* refers to Sañjaya as Aśmakeśvara, who is suffering from a disease causing blood vomitting and is much addicted to liquor. The source of this event remains inexplicable. In the Buddhist legend, we find a similar thing about Māgandiyā according to the *AK* and Anupamā according to the Chinese *MSVV*. She was a daughter of a brāhmaṇa who was offered to the Buddha, but refused by him and was later wedded to Udayana. However, the details do not agree with each other. The Buddha is a covetable person. Sañjaya is not so. Māgandiyā or Anupamā is too cruel to be compared with the generous Vāsavadattā.

The Ghoṣavatī *vīṇā* of Udayana, which works miracles like the lyre of Orpheus is referred to in all versions of the story, except the Chinese *MSVV*. But Udayana's skill in music is referred to in the *KSS, BKM,* the Bhāsa plays, the *KPP* and the *Kanjur* only. According to the *AK,* and the *BKSS,* he is well-known for his elephant-charms. In the *BKSS,* he gets Ghoṣavatī from the *Nāgas* in the netherworld and with it he bewitches men and animals. In the *Gandharvadattālābha,* during the musical competition Naravāhanadatta alone could know the song, as it was formerly revealed to him by Udayana. In the *AK,* he received Ghoṣavatī from the sage Allakappa and with three days practice of playing on it he could make the head-elephant kneel before him. In that book, Udayana is to teach elephant-charms to Vāsavadattā as he was arrested with that motive in view. In the *KPP* also Udayana alone could tame the elephant Nalagiri when it gets wild. The same event seems to have been referred to by Kālidāsa in his *Meghadūta* as — *atrodbhrāntaḥ kila nalagiriḥ stambhamutpāṭya darpāt.*

According to all the versions, he used to tame elephants with his Ghoṣavatī. His fondness for elephant-chase is referred to in all the versions, and especially in *PY* and *VV*. The author of the latter play skillfully connects his imprisonment by Pradyota to the curse of Aṅgāraka *muni,* which seems to be an innovation introduced by that anonymous dramatist. He shows how Udayana was interested in elephants since his childhood.

From all these references it is clear that Udayana was more well-known for his skill in taming the elephants. Music must have formed a part of elephant-chase and the *KSS* and *BKM* have shifted the emphasis from elephant-charms to music, to make it more poetic.

Kāñcanamālā is present in the narrations of the Kaśmīrī *Bṛahatkathā,* the *Kanjur* and the *KPP*. In the Kaśmīrī version she is a friend of Vāsavadattā, in the *KPP,* a nurse of Vāsavadattā and in the *Kanjur* a sister of Yaugandhara, going to Ujjayinī in the disguise of a female beggar. In later works like the plays of Śrīharṣa, she is always a friend and maid-servant of Vāsavadattā. Probably the author of *Kanjur* has made her Yaugandhara's sister going in disguise on the analogy of Yaugandhara himself going in disguise. The author seems to be fond of disguise motif. Earlier he has made Udayana escape from Ujjayinī in the disguise of a maid-servant.

In all the versions of this story Yaugandharāyaṇa plays a vital role. His *pratijñā* is given in the play by Bhāsa and in the *KPP* in almost identical words. Somaprabha is utilising some version of the story, which is used by Bhāsa also. Of course Bhāsa's own play would be available to him; but if he is following Bhāsa's version and quoting the *pratijñā* of Yaugandharāyaṇa in Sanskrit from Bhāsa's play we cannot say from where he gets the reference to the pots of urine. It may be in imitation of the exerement mentioned in *Kanjur*. But, from where he is quoting the Sanskrit verses — *kakṣāyām badhya-mānāyām,* and *eṣa prayāti sārthaḥ* — quoted in section 13? Did he use some Sanskrit version of the theory which combined the use of excrements of *Kanjur* with the details given by Bhāsa?

On studying this Udayana-Vāsavadattā episode Dr. D.R. Bhandarkar in his *Lectures on the Ancient History of India* believes that the main events in the story seem to be historical. Of course, so far as the elopement tales are concerned, literature all over the world is rich in them. In Indian literature even our *Purāṇas* are full of such tales as *Rukmiṇī-haraṇa* and *Subhadrā-haraṇa*. In actual history also elopement incidents were very frequent especially in the Rajput history. The episode of Pṛthvīrāja-Saṁyogitā is an instance in point; but we must have sufficient grounds to prove that a king of Kauśāmbī eloped with a princess of Ujjayinī.

(C) Udayana-Padmāvatī Episode

The story in the *KSS* (Lāvāṇaka-lambaka) — Udayana is leading a life of pleasure in company of Vāsavadattā, the responsibility of the state being solely on the shoulders of his ministers. Hence Yaugandharāyaṇa is worried as to how he can be a sovereign king. He knows that Pradyota, the king of Magadha is a powerful rival. He thinks of winning him over by seeking the hand of his daughter Padmāvatī, on behalf of Udayana. But Pradyota would not give her as long as Vāsavadattā is alive. Hence he thinks of spreading a rumour that Vāsavadattā is burnt in fire. He starts with the plan. Vāsavadattā and her brother Gopālaka are taken in confidence. Yaugandharāyaṇa explains how Udayana would not die of grief seeing that Gopālaka is not much aggrieved. In order to prepare grounds for the rumour they must go out of Kauśāmbī. Lāvāṇaka, which is near Magadha is the place selected. They persuade Udayana to go there saying that it is suitable for hunting. When they are about to leave Nārada arrives and says, "Follow the counsel of your ministers and you will attain prosperity." He foretells:

> *kañcitkālaṁ ca te duḥkhaṁ bhaviṣyati na ca tvayā*
> *tatrātimohaḥ kartavyaḥ sukhāntaṁ bhavitā hi tat.*

They then go to Lāvāṇaka and one day when the king is out for hunting they set the tent on fire and a report is spread that Vāsavadattā and Vasantaka were burnt in it. Yaugandharāyaṇa is in the disguise of an old brāhmaṇa. Vāsavadattā appears as his daughter — Avantikā, whose husband, given to vices, has gone somewhere leaving her alone and Vasantaka is a *kāṇabaṭu*. They see Padmavatī in the garden, where Yaugandharāyaṇa hands over Avantikā to her care. Vasantaka also stays there so that Avantikā would not feel lonely. Then Yaugandharāyaṇa leaves under the pretext that he would search for Avantikā's husband. Padmavatī suspects that Avantikā must be belonging to a high-born family. When she arranges *amlānamālātilaka* for the queen — she had learnt that art from Udayana — Padmāvatī's mother also suspects that she may be a deity in disguise.

Now when Udayana returns from hunting and learns of the mishap he falls in a swoon, but then consoles himself saying, "Nārada had formerly blessed Vāsavadattā that she would give birth to a son, who would be Vidyādharādhīpa. He has also told me that I shall have to experience misery for some time. Yaugandharāyaṇa (it is clear that he has now returned to Lāvāṇaka) and Gopālaka do not seem much aggrieved. This may be some strategy of the ministers." When Pradyota knows of the fire-accident he desires to give his daughter to Udayana, as it was formerly desired by Udayana's ministers. Pradyota's proposal is accepted by Udayana on the advice of Yaugandharāyaṇa. He says to himself *pracchāditaitadarthaṁ syāddevī jātucit*. The wedding takes place in Magadha on the seventh day. Once again Avantikā arranges *amlānamālātilaka*. Udayana feels suspicious. The next day they return to Lāvāṇaka. Avantikā also is accompanying Padmāvatī. She cannot stand separation any longer, goes to Gopālaka's room and clings to his neck out of helplessness. This is intentionally reported to Padmāvatī by the ministers. In the meanwhile Udayana inquires about '*the mālātilaka*' and getting suspicious goes to Gopālaka's room. Padmāvatī follows and there the reunion takes place. Yaugandharāyaṇa gives out the plan and assures of Vāsavadattā's chastity.

> *magadheśasutālābhāttava sāmrājyakāṅkṣiṇā*
> *kṛtametanmayā deva devyā doṣo na kaścana.*
> *iyaṁ tvasyāḥ sapatnyeva pravāse śīlasākṣiṇī*
> *ityuvāca vatseśaṁ dhīro yaugandharāyaṇaḥ.*

Even then Vāsavadattā thinks of *Agniśuddhi*. Yaugandharāyaṇa prays to *Lokapālas*. "Please stand witness to her chastity or I shall end my life." A divine voice proclaims to that effect. Then all proceed to Kauśāmbī.

The *BKM* gives a similar account. The prophecy about Padmāvatī is more explicit there. Yaugandharāyaṇa informs Rumanvān and others *cakravartivadhūḥ sā hi bhāvinīti śrutam mayā*. The reasons for Udayana's consenting to the marriage-proposal is given as follows:

> *priyaṁ prāpsyasi tām prāpya śrutveti sacivānnṛpaḥ,*
> *amanyata nijodvāhaṁ virahānaladuḥsahaḥ.*

The *BKSS*, in the fourth *Sarga* (verses 13-20) relates how Udayana has no child, though he has two wives Vāsavadattā and Padmāvatī. The marration is brief and proceeds in a manner, which presupposes the acquaintance of the readers with the personages referred to.

Padāmavatī is repeatedly called Māgadhī, but her father's name is not mentioned. Later on in the *Madanamañcukālābha* Padmāvatī is found associating herself with the affair of Kaliṅgasenā.

The *SV* of Bhāsa has this episode as the main theme. The story in brief is as follows:

Udayana defeated by Āruṇi is staying at Lāvāṇaka nearby. When he is out on chasing expedition, a rumour is spread that Vāsavadattā and Yaugandharāyaṇa were burnt in fire. This was the beginning of a strategic plan of the astute politician Yaugandharāyaṇa. He wanted to bring about the mariage of

Udayana with Padmāvatī, the sister of Darśaka, king of Magadha. Yaugandharāyaṇa and Vāsavadattā leave the place secretly and now Yaugandharāyaṇa, disguised as an ascetic and Vāsavadattā, as an ordinary girl from Avantī proceed towards Rājagṛha. They meet Padmāvatī in a *tapovana* on the way. When she asks the ascetics to choose whatever they wanted Yaugandharāyaṇa takes advantage of the offer and requests her to protect his sister, i.e., Vāsavadattā till her husband, who has gone on a long journey, returns.

A young student from Lāvāṇaka informs us how much Udayana mourned over Vāsavadattā's death. In the Second Act we know that Darśaka has offered his sister to Udayana who had come to Rajagṛha on some business. In the Third Act Avantikā is weaving the wedding garland for Padmavatī. In the bifocal scene in Act IV Vasantaka puts a simple question to Udayana, Whom do you like better, Vāsavadattā or Padmāvatī?" This acutely reminds Udayana of Vāsavadattā and he bursts into tears, while saying, *vāsavadattābadhaṁ na tu tāvanme mano harati*. His answer clearly proves that even after his marriage with Padmāvatī he cannot forget his dear Vāsavadattā. In Act V Padmāvatī is suffering from headache. Udayana, accompanied by Vasantaka, goes to *Samudragṛha* to inquire of her health. While waiting for Padmāvatī, Vasantaka's narration lulls him to sleep and Vasantaka leaves in order to bring his upper garment. Avantikā comes to *Samudragṛha* to comfort Padmāvatī. The sleeping king is mistaken by her for Padmāvatī and she lies down by his side. As Vasantaka's narration referred to Ujjayinī Udayana's sub-conscious mind is revolving about in Ujjayinī and in dream he addresses his beloved *priye vāsavadatte*. Vāsavadattā, realising her mistake, thinks of going away; but she cannot help answering the questions of the dreaming king. Then she hurriedly places his hanging hand on the bed and goes away. The king wakes up only to be lost in grief of separation. Towards the end of the Act we learn that Darśaka has sent his army to fight against Āruṇi. In the last Act Ghoṣavatī, which was lost, somehow comes to Udayana's hand and his grief of separation from Vāsavadattā is aggravated. Meanwhile Āruṇi is defeated by Darśaka's army. Messengers bringing congratulations from Ujjayinī also hand over by way of present the portraits of Vāsavadattā and Udayana, with which Mahāsena had celebrated the marriage. Padmāvatī is struck by the close resemblance between Vāsavadattā's portrait and Avantikā. Yaugandharāyaṇa, disguised as an ascetic comes and demands back his deposit. Vāsavadattā comes, her veil is removed and thus the lovers are reunited. The whole party then thinks of a trip to Ujjayinī.

Tāpasavatsarāja of Anaṅgaharṣa calls the king of Magadha as Darśaka. According to the ruse of Yaugandharāyaṇa, Udayana is in the disguise of an ascetic and Vāsavadattā appears as a nun. The marriage with Padmāvatī, the daughter of Darśaka is brought about. When both Udayana and Vāsavadattā are attempting suicide Yaugandharāyaṇa stops them and then the reunion is brought about.

Padmāvatī has no place in the Buddhist and Jain literature. But in the Buddhist literature two more wives of Udena are referred to.

The *AK:* Sāmavatī was the daughter of a merchant of Bhaddāvatī, who was a friend of the merchant Ghoṣaka of Kauśāmbī. Due to an epidemic in Bhaddāvatī, the family comes to Kauśāmbī. Her parents soon die of hunger. She then comes to Ghoṣita (Ghoṣaka). Udena sees her and asks for her hand. First the offer is rejected but later on Udena succeeds in persuading Ghoṣita, and then the wedding takes place.

(Then occurs the story of Vāsuladattā)

Udena had one more wife, Māgandiyā, the daughter of a brāhmaṇa. She was offered by her parents to the Buddha who refused her hand. Then the parents renounce this world and Māgandiyā is handed over to her uncle Māgandiyā, who hands her over to Udena. Now Māgandiyā has a grudge against the Buddha, while Sāmavatī is a devotee of the Buddha. When the Buddha is in Kaúsāmbī, she sees him through a crevice in the wall. Māgandiyā poisons the ears of Udena against her, and tries various tricks to prove that she has illegal relations with the Buddha. When Udena tries to shoot her, the arrows return to the bow and hence Udena recognises her power. She is then given permission to invite the Buddha. Ānanda with 500 monks comes and preaches her and her maids. When Udena was away Māgandiyā with the help of her uncle burns Sāmavatī along with her 500 maids by setting fire to the harem. Udena, when he returns, kills Māgandiyā and her relatives.

The *MSVV* of the Chinese, gives a similar story, with a few deviations. When the city Roruka is destroyed Śyāmāvatī, daughter of a merchant named Bhīru comes to Kauśāmbī with the num Śailā, who hands her over to Ghoṣita, minister of Udena, who founds Ghoṣitārāma. Udayana and many other kings seek her hand; but she chooses king Hatthālavaka of Aṭavī. That king becomes a convert. Even then Śyāmāvatī devotes herself to service of the monks in Aṭavī. When Hatthālavaka dies she returns to Kauśāmbī and marries with Udayana. She is a devotee of the Buddha.

Now the brāhmaṇa Mākandaka had a beautiful daughter Anupamā. She was refused by the Buddha. Udayana sees her and the marriage takes place. Then follows a similar account of her jealousy and of the arrows turning useless and of the fire. When the fire breaks out Śyāmāvatī rises in the air, delivers a sermon and then falls in the flames.

The same story occurs in the Chinese *DP* and the Chinese *Tripiṭaka*.

Prof. Lacote connects this story with that of Padmāvatī. He says, "From the story of Anupamā he has built up, in transforming it, that of Padmāvatī."

He points out that the criminal fire, set by Anupamā leads to the innocent fire at Lāvāṇaka in Padmāvatī's story.

About Śyāmāvatī (Sāmavatī) Prof. Lacote says, "She was very holy and there was no room for her in a love romance."

But I do not think that there is any connection between the two stories except for the accidental correspndence of fire. Such innocent fire is associated with Udayana in Śrīharṣa's *Ratnāvalī* also. But it would be too far-fetched to connect cruel and vicious-minded Māgandiyā or Anupamā with Padmavatī, who is very kind and generous. The portrait of Padmāvatī, as delineated by Bhāsa, Somadeva and Kṣemendra would agree more with Śamavatī or Śyāmāvatī.

In addition to the character of Padmāvatī we can note the following points in Udayana-Padmāvatī episode:

In the *KSS* and the *BKM* the reason for going to Lāvāṇaka is hunting only. If that is so why did the party go back to Lāvāṇaka and not to Kauśāmbī after the marriage in Rājagṛha, knowing fully well that the tent at Lāvāṇaka was burnt down? Bhāsa has improved upon this by making Udayana leave Kauśāmbī, as he has been deprived of the kingdom by Āruṇi. In the *SV*, Udayana cannot return to Kauśāmbī till Āruṇi is defeated.

Bhāsa shows many deviations from the story of Padmāvatī as given by Somadeva and Kṣemendra. These are too well-known to be repeated here. In most of the cases Bhāsa has made the story more poetic and dramatic.

But as regards the prophesy about Padmāvatī, Kṣemendra is more explicit than Bhāsa. Yaugandharāyaṇa of Bhāsa simply says, "I have heard from the seers that she will be my master's wife", while, Kṣemendra makes him say, *cakravartivadhūḥ sā hi bhāvinīti śrutaṁ mayā.*

About the name of the king of Ujjayinī, we have discussed the point earlier. If Pradyota is the name of the king of Ujjayinī, naturally that cannot be the name of Magadha king. Bhāsa and following him the anonymous author of *Vīṇāvāsavadattā* give Darśaka as the name of Magadha king. Somadeva and Kṣemendra refer to Magadha king as Padmāvatī's father. Bhāsa makes Darśaka her brother. Similarly Yaugandharāyaṇa, as an old brāhmaṇa, introduces Avantikā as his daughter in the Kaśmīrī *BK*. Bhāsa's Yaugandharāyaṇa introduces her as his sister. In both the cases the relation of father-daughter is substituted by brother-sister.

Does it mean that Bhāsa has intentionally deviated from the story of the *BK* as was available in his days, which was later recorded by Somadeva and Kṣemendra? Or is he following some version of the *BK* different than that used by Somadeva and Kṣemendra? It is not possible to decide the point with the material available so far.

When compared to the Buddhist versions of the *BK* it is clear that Padmāvatī is absent in the Buddhist versions while Sāmavatī and Māgandiyā are not found in the Sanskrit versions. The two versions seem to follow two independent developments of the *BK*, which must be having some common source in earlier stages. Prof. Lacote has discussed in details the common points between the Sanskrit and the Buddhist versions.

(D) Udayana and Other Heroines

In addition to the well-known heroines Vāsavadattā and Padmāvatī, Udayana's romance with Ratnāvalī and Priya-darśikā has been recorded by Śrīharṣa.

The plot of *Ratnāvalī* — Ratnāvalī, the princess of Siṁhala, was to be a wife of a sovereign king according to the prophesy of seers. Hence Yaugandharāyaṇa sought her hand for the sake of his master. When the bride's party was travelling towards Kauśāmbī, it met with a ship-wreck. A merchant from Kauśāmbī found Ratnāvalī ship-wrecked and inferring from her jewelled necklace that she must be a princess, he handed her over to Yaugandharāyaṇa. He presented her to queen Vāsavadattā, introducing her as Sāgarikā, a girl from the ocean. The queen was always on the guard that she should not be seen by Udayana. In spite of her precautions Sāgarikā sees Udayana at the *Madanamahotsava* and the expected result follows. She then draws Udayana's resemblance on a picture-board. A *Sārikā*-bird is responsible for bringing Udayana and Vasantaka to that *kadalīgṛha,* where the first meeting of the hero and the heroine takes place. When Vāsavadattā comes there the king is found with the picture-board and she realises that what she feared has already begun. In the Third Act Vāsavadattā is to be deceived by making Sāgarikā wear the queen's robe and Susaṅgatā wear that of Kāñcanamālā. Thus they are going to keep an appointment with the king. All this is known to Kāñcanamālā, who informs Vāsavadattā of it. Vāsavadattā herself goes to the place of appointment and the king is caught red-handed. After some time Sāgarikā dressed as Vāsavadattā comes and is about to hang herself out of the unbearable pangs of love. Udayana steps in to stop her and waxes eloquent over her charms, when once again queen Vāsavadattā steps in. Now Sāgarikā and Vasantaka who is mainly responsible for the mischief, are taken captive. The queen spreads the report that Sāgarikā has been sent to Ujjayinī. In despair Sāgarikā sends from the prison her jewelled necklace to the king through Susaṅgatā. A news is received that the king of Kosala has been defeated by

Rumanvān. Soon a magician Śrīkhaṇḍadāsa, who is desirous of giving a magical performance presents himself before the king. When the show is going on the prime-minister and the chamberlain from Siṁhala, who were formerly accompanying the princess during the journey to Kauśāmbī, appear on the scene. The show is abruptly stopped. They narrate about the ship-wreck and loss of the princess. Vāsavadattā laments over the loss of her cousin. That was the relation between Vāsavadattā and Ratnāvalī. Now there is an uproar from behind the curtain, which is due to a sudden fire that has broken. Vāsavadattā remembers that she has kept Sāgarikā in prison in the harem and repents for it. Udayana rushes in to save her. The moment the lovers embrace each other in confusion, the fire disappears all of a sudden. Now only we can realise that it was a part of the magic-show. At the end when Sāgarikā comes on the scene, the party from Siṁhala recognises her. Now Vāsavadattā does not hesitate in giving her over to Udayana and the play ends happily.

The story of Priyadarśikā runs as follows:

King Dṛḍhavarman of Aṅga had a beautiful daughter Priyadarśikā. Her hand was repeatedly sought by the king of Kaliṅga, but Dṛḍhavarman betrothed her to Udayana. Indignant at this insult the king Kaliṅga, attacked Aṅga and took Dṛḍhavarman a captive. Priyadarśikā is given in charge of the old chamberlain, who takes her to the forest-king Vindhyaketu. As ill-luck would have it Vindhyaketu is attacked by an unknown enemy, who also sets fire to that region. Meanwhile the marriage between Udayana and Vāsavadattā has taken place and Rumanvān and Vijayasena are successful in their military expedition against Vindhyaketu. Among the things robbed off there is a beautiful girl — supposed to be Vindhyaketu's daughter. She, known as Āraṇyikā, is now in charge of Vāsavadattā. As in the story of *Ratnāvalī*, here also Udayana and Āraṇyikā fall in love with each other. A mimic representing Udayana-Vāsavadattā episode is composed by the *Parivrājikā Sāṅkṛtyāyanī* and is to be enacted before the queen. Āraṇyikā is to play the role of Vāsavadattā and Manoramā, a maid-servant of Vāsavadattā that of Udayana.

Manoramā and Vasantaka cleverly manage to make Udayana play his own role therein. Vāsavadattā who is witnessing the play suspects some mischief. She goes to the king's chamber to find if he is there. Vasantaka, who is sleeping there, gives out the secret in his sleep. The result is imprisonment of Āraṇyikā and Vasantaka. Soon a message is received that Dṛḍhavarman, the husband of Vāsavadattā's aunt is in the prison of the king of Kaliṅga. Udayana informs that he has already sent his General Vijayasena to fight against Kaliṅga. Soon Vijayasena enters along with Dṛḍhavarman's Kañcukin. The Kañcukin brings a message of gratitude from Dṛḍhavarman and informs that princess Priyadarśikā has been lost since Vindhyaketu's defeat. At this moment Manoramā hurriedly enters saying that Āraṇyikā has drunk poison in diappointment.

Vāsavadattā repents for her cruelty and orders that she be brought there immediately, so that Udayana could cure her with his magic spells. Āraṇyikā, who is on the verge of death is brought. The chamberlain recognises her as Priyadarśikā. She is cured by Udayana and then the marriage follows.

The *KSS* — (towards the end of *Kathāmukhalambaka).* The princess Bandhumatī is presented by Gopālaka to Vāsavadattā. Vāsavadattā keeps her in the harem and she is known as Mañjulikā. Udayana marries her in the *Gāndharva* form of marriage. Vasantaka is mainly responsible for this. When Vāsavadattā knows the love-affair she puts Vasantaka and Mañjulikā in prison. The *Parivrājikā Sāṅkṛtyāyanī* intervenes and then Vāsavadattā offers her to Udayana. Udayana had another love-affair with Viracitā, a maid-servant of the harem.

In *Madanamañcukālambaka* we get the following story: King Kaliṅgadatta of Takṣaśilā gets a daughter, who happens to be an *Apsaras* Tārādattā born on the earth due to a course. She is named Kaliṅgasenā. When her friend Somaprabhā comes to know that Kaliṅgasenā has been betrothed to Prasenajit of Śrāvastī, she informs her that the only suitable match for her was Udayana, the king of Vatsa. By this time Vāsavadattā has given birth to Naravāhanadatta. Somaprabhā informs how that king is *rūpalubdha* and desires for her but cannot say so openly for fear of Vāsavadattā. Now Kaliṅgasenā is anxious to be united with Udayana. Somaprabhā takes her to Udayana through air. Udayana informs Yaugandharāyaṇa how she has approached him for *Svayaṁvara*. Yaugandharāyaṇa knows that if he marries that extraordinarily charming girl he will forget everything else and hence he delays the marriage with the help of astrologers. In the meanwhile a Vidyādhara named Madanavega enters her apartment every night in the disguise of Udayana and when Kaliṅgasenā is pregnant he leaves her. Udayana allows her to stay in Kauśāmbī. She gives birth to a son, who is taken away by *Prajāpati* and replaced by a daughter, whose form Rati has taken. She is named Madanamañcukā and later married to Naravāhanadatta.

The same story occurs in the *Madanamañcukā-guccha* of the *BKM*. Moreover, after the marriage of Udayana-Vāsavadattā, Udayana is referred to as *gūḍham rajanikākāmī*.

In the available parts of the *BKSS* this episode is absent though Naravāhanadatta-Madanamañcukā episode has been described in greater details. At the *Yauvarājyābhiṣeka* of Naravāhanadatta a courtesan named Kaliṅgasenā is present with a young girl. Udayana takes her in his lap and the brāhmaṇa Ādityaśarman utters some indistinct words. Udayana then sends back the mother and the child with presents.

All these stories point out that Udayana had amours with other ladies also even after his marriage with Vāsavadattā and with Padmāvatī. In the Buddhist versions also this trait in the character of Udayana is present. He was married to Sāmavatī and Māgandiyā (Anupamā) as has been already referred. According to the Chinese *MSVV*, he is so licentious that as soon as he knows that Pradyota has given permission to the ladies in his harem to move out at night he goes to Ujjayinī, in spite of Yaugandhara's warning.

The heroines of Śrīharṣa, viz., Ratnāvalī and Priyadarśikā are not present in any of the available version of the *BK;* but these seem to have been suggested from the *BK*. Bandhumati, presented by Gopālaka to Vāsavadattā in the *KSS* agrees very well with Ratnāvalī presented by Yaugandharāyaṇa and Priyadarśikā by Rumanvān to Vāsavadattā. This also corresponds to Mālavikā presented to queen Dhāriṇī by her brother Vīrasena in the *M.* of Kālidāsa.

Many of the motifs used by Śrīharṣa can be traced to different versions of the *BK*.

Similar to the story of the ship-wreck in *Ratnāvalī*, we find the story of Sāgaradiṇṇā in the 5th *Lambaka*, viz. *Gandharvadattālābha* in the *BKŚS*. Naravāhanadatta wins in the musical competition instituted by Gandharvadattā, daughter of the merchant Sānudāsa. When Naravāhanadatta hesitates to marry her, Sānudāsa says, "She belongs to the same caste as you are or even to a higher one." After the marriage he narrates her story. When Sānudāsa was working as a diamond-expert and was on voyage he met with a ship-wreck. He swam and reached a desert-coast. There he found a woman, naked and famished, who too was ship-wrecked. She related her own story. She was Samudradiṇṇā, daughter of a merchant Sāgara from Rājagṛha. Sāgara had commercial dealings with a merchant, named Mitravarman of Campā. He had asked Samudradiṇṇā for his son. Meanwhile Mitravarman was dead and his son Sānudāsa, had been assassinated by highway-men while he was travelling along with a *caravan*. In despair Sāgara was proceeding to the country of Yavanas to see his father-in-law. They met with a ship-wreck and Samudradiṇṇā alone had been carried to the coast by a current. Sānudāsa now reveals his identity. Samudradiṇṇā finds a large quantity of pearls in the oysters and then the marriage is celebrated there only. A second time Samudradiṇṇā was drawn away by the current in a storm. Later on during his series of adventures Sānudāsa happens to come to the hermitage of Bharadvāja. One day a party of young maids comes down in an arial chariot. Bharadvāja takes one of them in his lap and says, "My daughter Gandharvadattā ! Henceforward Sānudāsa shall be thy father." Gandharvadattā is thus his adopted daughter, her real parents are Bharadvāja and Suprabhā, a *Gandharvakanyā*.

The motif of ship-wreck can be easily traced to this story (Āraṇyikā who was lost during the expedition against Vindhyaketu is a modification of the same). The name Samudradiṇṇā agrees very well with Sāgarikā. It is a Prakrit form of the name Samudradattā.

Sānudāsa is working as a diamond-expert. Moreover Samudradiṇṇā finds pearls in oysters. This might have suggested the jewelled necklace of Sāgarikā.

Disguise-stories are very common in literature. There may be some such story in the *BK* available to Śrīharṣa which would explain Sāgarikā dressed as Vāsavadattā and Āraṇyikā as Vāsavadattā in the mimic play or it may be an innovation introduced by Śrīharṣa.

Lāvāṇaka fire in the Kaśmīrī *BK* explains the magic fire in *Ratnāvalī.*

Heroines committing suicide is also a popular feature in Indian tales. In the *BKSS,* Madanamañcukā is hanging herself due to pangs of separation from Naravāhanadatta. Śrīharṣa has used this motif in all the three plays. Sāgarikā and Malayavatī attempt to hang themselves; while Āraṇyikā is drinking poison.

The prophesy about *Ratnāvalī* is exactly like that about Padmāvatī in the *BKM.*

The imprisonment of Sāgarikā and Vasantaka in the story of *Ratnāvalī,* and that of Āraṇyikā and Vasantaka in the *PD* agrees exactly with that of Mañjulikā and Vasantaka in the *KSS.* It reminds us of the imprisonment of Mālavikā also. As in the story of *KSS* in the *PD* also *Parivrājikā Sāṅkṛtyāyanī* is intervening. (In the *MA* the Parivrājikā is named Kauśikī). In the *Ratnāvalī* that part is played by the magician Śrīkhaṇḍadāsa.

(E) The Birth of Naravāhanadatta

The *KSS* describes this in details in Naravāhanadatta-*janmalambaka.* Piṅgalikā with her two sons enters the palace. Now Vāsavadattā gets impatient to get a son. Nārada advises them to propitiate Śiva. They do accordingly. Vāsavadattā becomes pregnant. She sees in her dream herself seated in the sky and being waited upon by singing Vidyādharīs. Yaugandharāyaṇa then fulfils her *dohada* by means of *yantra, mantra, indrajāla,* etc., In dream Śiva assures her that he will protect her embryo. At an auspicious moment the child is born. A divine voice proclaims, "This is Naravāhanadatta, an incarnation of Kāmadeva. He will be a sovereign of Vidyādharas." It was followed by *Puṣpavṛṣṭi.*

The *BKM* gives a similar story, with minor deviations in the fourth *guccha.*

The *BKŚS* gives it in the second *Lambaka,* Naravāhanadatta is giving an account of himself at the request of the sages. Udayana has two wives but no child. Udayana longs for a son. Piṅgalikā has two sons by Viṣṇu's grace. This induces Vāsavadattā and Udayana to implore gods. General penances in honour of Kuvera are ordered. Padmāvatī, whose health is delicate, is exempted. She is to consider Vāsavadattā's son as her own. Udayana and Vāsavadattā get an identical dream that God Kuvera presents them with a jewel in his garden. The jewel is suddenly transformed into a lion's cub that enters Vāsavadattā's womb. The brāhmaṇa Ādityaśarman interprets the dream saying that Udayana's son will rule over the empire of Vidyādharas. Vāsavadattā gets a strange longing to travel in an aerial car. (See section 4). Yaugandharāyaṇa asks the artisans to prepare one; but they refuse saying that the Greeks alone know that art. A brāhmaṇa does not believe in this excuse. He says that they are intentionally keeping back the secret. Hence Yaugandharāyaṇa puts the artisans to torture. A stranger saves them by building the car.

(It is Bhadrāvatī herself. See section 15) Udayana gets in it with his wives and retinue, makes an aerial *pradakṣiṇā* round the earth, pays a visit to Ujjayinī and then returns to Kauśāmbī. Naravāhanadatta is born with 32 auspicious marks in due course. The four ministers also get sons.

In the Buddhist legend Naravāhanadatta has no place. But there are few reference to Udayana's son. According to the Tibetan tradition, as given by Schiefner, Rāṣṭrapāla was Udayana's son and he joined religious state. According to *Karmaśataka, Śaraṇa* was the son of Udayana Sauvīra. But according to Prof. Jacobi Udayana of Suvīra is different from Udayana of Kauśāmbī.

In Jain literature Naravāhanadatta's adventures form the central topic of *Kathākośa;* but the hero is named Dīpaśikha, a Vidyādhara and not Naravāhanadatta. Naravāhanadatta is the real hero of the *BK*.

The interesting points in the narration of his birth are as follows:

(1) According to the Kaśmīrī version, he was born by the grace of Śiva, according to the Nepālī by the favour of Kuvera. In Indian mythology Kuvera is not such an important god,

though he is the Lord of wealth.

(2) Though in the *KSS* we learn that Yaugandharāyaṇa fulfilled Vāsavadatta's *dohada* with *yantra, mantra* and *indrajāla,* it is made more explicit in the Nepālī version. The Greeks are associated with that art. Why is this interesting reference missing in the Kaśmīrī version of the *BK?* Yavanas have been referred to in Sanskrit literature very often since ancient days.

(3) According to the Kaśmīrī version Mṛgāvatī and Sahasrānīka retired to the forest after installing Udayana on the throne. According to the *BKSS,* Mṛgāvatī is still with them when Vāsavadattā feels the strange pregnancy-longing.

(F) Udayana's End

In the *KSS* (*Mahābhiṣeka-Lambaka-Tarangas* 110, 111) we learn that Udayana, Vāsavadattā and Padmāvatī attend the coronation of Naravāhanadatta as *Vidyādharacakravartin* on the mountain Ṛṣabha. After some days Udayana learns through *Prajñapti* that Caṇḍamahāsena of Ujjayinī is dead, Gopālaka is living in Kauśāmbī and has passed over the kingdom to Pālaka. Udayana now thinks seriously of the instability of the worldly affairs. He goes to the mountain Kalañjara along with Vāsavadattā, Padmāvatī and his ministers. Udayana takes his Ghoṣavatī and throws himself down from a precipice. Others follow him. A *vimāna* comes and takes them all to heaven.

The *BKM* gives the same account in brief.

Buddhist Literature

The Chinese *MSVV,* Udayana was a poor wretch. In his former birth, when he was a brāhmaṇa, he had let loose his dogs on a *Pratyekabuddha* collecting alms. Hence now he meets a miserable death. In the Tibetan *Kanjur,* Udayana fulfils the desire of taking revenge on Pradyota (See section 12). Pradyota is taken a prisoner and made to work as a weaver. Udayana intentionally presents him in that condition to Vāsavadattā. She decides to avenge this. She manages to set Pradyota free and pushes Udayana into a pit, where he is eaten by ferocious dogs. His ministers punish her by burning her alive.

But according to the Tibetan tradition, Udayana was converted by the Buddha. According to one tradition in Tibet, Udayana of Benares got a statue of the Buddha prepared with yellow sandalwood.

Hiuen-Tsang records that an artist, who visited heaven in order to see the Buddha, prepared a statue for Udayana.

According to the canonical texts also, Udayana is a pious king. *Saṁyutta-Nikāya* refers to Udayana being instructed by Bharadvāja. When Piṇḍola Bharadvāja does not salute Udayana he feels offended and leaves angrily. The sage curses him, as a result of which he loses his memory for six months and after that when he regains his memory he has an ardent faith in the teachings of the Buddha. Then he teaches law in Kauśāmbī.

According to *Jātaka* 375 (Fausboll), when Piṇḍola Bharadvāja is in the Ghoṣitārāma, Udayana goes there along with the ladies of his harem. Udayana goes to sleep due to drunkenness. When he gets up he finds the ladies surrounding the monk. Getting angry he attempts to throw red ants towards him. Bharadvāja is uninjured. He rises and goes to the Buddha in Jeṭhavana to tell him of the incident.

According to the Chinese *DP* Udayana is a pious king.

Jain Literature

According to the Jain tradition, Pradyota wanted to steal away Jina's statue from Udayana Suvīra and hence a battle followed. But as Udayana Sauvīra is not the same as our Udayana the tradition is not important for us.

The story of *Domuho-rāyā* given in Devendra's commentary on *Uttarādhyāyanasūtra*, IX has many points common with that of Udayana. That king finally becomes a *Pratyekabuddha.*

Thus Udayana has a happy end in the *KSS* and in Pāli canonical texts. In the *Kanjur* and in the *Mūla-sarvāstitvavāda-vinaya,* the narration is to the credit of Pradyota and as such is bound to be harmful to Udayana.

Finally as Prof. Lacote says, "Udayana's life is made up of gallant adventures and dramas of love. Buddhism has adopted the personage and given him an honourable place among the contemporaries of the Buddha. It was for Guṇāḍhya to make him the prototype of romance and comedy."

Nariman, Jackson and Ogden, the learned editors of *Priyadarśikā,* have said, "We can only conjecture what caused legend to gather, around the figure of Udayana, but even in the canonical Pāli writings there are hints of amorous traits that would make him a suitable hero of romantic adventures."

All this bears sufficient testimony to Śrīharṣa's remark: *loke hāri ca vatsarājacaritam.*

References

1. *Vāsavadattā,* Preface, p. 11, V.S.S. Sukhthankar, Humphrey, Milford, Oxford, 1923.
2. Essay on Guṇāḍhya and the Bṛhatkathā (in French) by Félix Lacôte — Translated into English by Rev. A.M. Tabard, In *Journal of the Mythic Society,* Bangalore, 1923.

16

Utprekṣās of Bāṇabhaṭṭa

As expected by the standards of Sanskrit literary criticism of his period Bāṇa makes a profuse use of all figures of speech like *Śleṣa, Upamā, Rūpaka, Utprekṣā, Virodhābhāsa, Apahnuti*, etc. In all these figures *Utprekṣā* seems to be his special favourite. His special fondness for this figure can be noticed even with a casual reading of his works, the *Harṣacarita* and the *Kādambarī*, e.g., in the first *Ucchavāsa* of the *HC* he has used not less than 157 *Utprekṣās*.

Definition and Scope

As the name itself indicates this figure gives the fullest scope to the flights of a poet's imagination (*ut* + *pra* + *ikṣ* — to look up intently.) Rhetoricians point out that imagination is the soul of *Utprekṣā*. *Sambhāvanamathotprekṣā prakṛtasya pareṇa yat* — Mammaṭa. *Bhavet sambhāvanotprekṣā prakṛtasya parātmanā* — Viśvanātha. In English the name of this figure is rendered as 'Poetic Fancy'. In giving *Utprekṣās* a poet is soaring in the heights of the heaven, much above the world of the mortals. Hence the *Utprekāas* used by a poet give a fair estimate of the range of his imaginative power. The field of Bāṇa's fancy is very extensive indeed.

Any object or person would serve as the basis of his *Utprekṣās*. He can use this figure with advantage in the description of feminine beauty as while describing Sarasvatī, Yaśomatī, Rājyaśrī, Vilāsavatī, Mahāśvetā, Kādambarī, etc., in depicting the scenes of nature as the sun-set, the moon-light, the

Spring, the Autumn, etc., in delineating the personality of a monarch like Harṣa, a king on death-bed like Prabhākaravardhana, a prince like Candrāpīḍa, an ascetic like Divākaramitra, and in describing a horse like Indrāyudha, a parrot like Vaiśaṁpāyana, a lake like Acchoda and a city like Ujjayinī. His high imaginative power can be seen in the wide range of the objects and situations conceived in his *Utprekṣās*. These include the fluid of the fire of wrath, the charter giving one an authority to curse others, silk-turban of the king Sumeru, a crystal spot with a treasure of gems, the white tongue of the moon, the shoots of curiosity, the ghost of youth, chowries of the king Summer, horripilation of the forest, regions of the Milky Ocean, a day put on the swing, the anklets of Divasaśrī, the exhausted sun, the Saptarṣimaṇḍala visiting the earth, Madana engaged in austerities, the water-hostels with the wood-land-nymphs serving nectar, drops of sweat of the moon, betel-juice in the mouth of Lakṣmī, the earth preparing for *satīgamana* and even the Goddess of Glory being offered as sacrificial animal.

Imaginative Power of Bāṇa

His power of interpreting things and situations of daily occurrence in exquisitely poetic terms with his *Utprekṣās* and thus 'giving to airy nothing a local habitation and a name' is really remarkable. He interprets the jingling of Sarasvatī's anklets as muttering of hymns by two pupils. Her lip has become red due to the lac-dye of the feet of lady-lores. The red hue of the eyes of enraged Durvāsas is, according to Bāṇa, an offering of his own blood to the deity of wrath. The *yoga-paṭṭaka* of Sāvitrī is the flow of Gaṅgā, made to coil round her body through the power of austerities. The rising moon has become red due to the blood of her deer, slain by the lion on the Rising mountain. In Bāṇa's imagination the river Gaṅgā becomes an ivory-gate closing the hell or the white silk-turban of the mountain king Sumeru.

Dadhīca's white body having a *yajñopavīta* is now the mountain Mandara, chained by Gaṅgā for having disturbed her lord in the process of *Amṛta-manthana*. The inner leaf of *ketakī* in Mālatī's hair appears to Bāṇa as the tongue of the moon, licking her cheek, through the greed for beauty. Sarasvatī's fingers placed over her heart, when she is listening to Mālatī's words become, in Bāṇa's language, the shoots of curiosity bursting out of her heart. Reflection of the moon in her cheek is the moon-messenger whispering in her ear. In summer ladies wash the tresses of their hair and hold these in the hand to be dried up. Bāṇa sees these as the chowries of the king summer. The ear-rings worn by the servant of Prabhākaravardhana are the sun and the moon come to inquire whether there existed anyone equal to Harṣa. Clusters of stars seen in the evening are the drops of water scattered by the sages in the *Sandhyāvandana*. The dew-drops form the perspiration of the moon on his touching the Lady-Night. The dark spot on the moon is the charcoal of the fire of grief of all people on the demise of Prabhākaravardhana.

The overflowing stream of Bāṇa's *Utprekṣās* does not spare even the terrific aspects of life. The red lotuses near the temple of Caṇḍikā are fancied to be the eyes of the buffaloes killed by the Śabaras. The lines of white ashes on the forehead of Bhairavācārya are fancied to be his skull-bone split up by the burning of *Guggulu*. The dark lines on the forehead of Prabhākaravardhana are the lines drawn by Yama to count the remaining days. Bāṇa's fancy often refers to the offering of blood, flesh, living beings, etc., He can use *Utprekṣās* freely in describing, the scorching heat of summer, the forest-coflagration, the hurricane, and even the moment of death.

Utprekṣās — Pregnant with Meanings

A critical study of Bāṇa's *Uptrekṣās* will show that they possess some distinct peculiarities:

(a) Like the *Upamās* of Kālidāsa they fit in the context very appropriately. His poetic power fancies one and the same situation variously according to the context. In the first *Ucchavāsa* of the *HC*, ruddy twilight of the evening is fancied as the marks of the lac-dye applied to the feet by the Vidyādharīs. When Bāṇa visits Harṣa's palace the evening-twilight appears as a flood of minerals in which the sun-boat is immersed. On the day of Rājyaśrī's wedding it is fancied to be the banner of marital happiness. When Candrāpīḍa returns home the evening-twilight is described as the *Aravinda-madhu-rasa*, which the sun had drunk throughout the day, and which is now being vomitted due to the exhaustion of having traversed the sky. After Sarasvatī is cursed the red rising moon appears as the mass of blood dripping from her own deer slain by the lion on the Rising mountain. After Candrāpīḍa's meeting with Kādambarī the moon is represented as being red due to the lac-dye of Rohiṇī's feet, when the latter kicked him. Similarly in the first *Ucchavāsa* of the *HC*, the white moon in heaven is an ivory-conduit filling the ocean with the milk of the cows. When reflected in Sarasvatī's cheek she is the moon-messenger of the Cupid. Again when reflected in Yaśomatī's chest she appears as the white parasol of the future emperor Harṣa. The same white moon is the parasol of Indra, welcoming Prabhākaravardhana to heaven. After Harṣa's *Digvijaya* and Rājyaśrī's recovery the same white moon is described as a goblet of pearls presented to him by the Lady-Night, or a pearl-glass for drinking glory presented by the Destiny. Similarly the rays of teeth of Durvāsas cause an obstruction to the speech that is about to run away in fear. The rays of teeth of Jābāli are wiping off the dirt of sin. While the glow of Bhairavācārya's teeth is the crescent moon of Śiva, issuing out of his mouth, Śiva being ever present in his heart.

(b) As Kālidāsa's *Upamās* are full of suggestion Bāṇa's *Utprekṣās* also are characterised by suggestivity. With one *Utprekṣā*, pregnant with meaning, Bāṇa can say what would otherwise require a few lines for proper expression, e.g., he describes Sarasvati as *saṅkrānta-kamalāsanakṛṣṇājinapratimām sāmamadhuragītākarṇanāvatīrṇaśaśihariṇamiva kapolasthalīm dadhānām*. The reflection of *Brahman*'s *Kṛṣnājina* in her cheek is imagined to be the deer in the moon descending there in order to listen to the sweet music of *Sāmaveda*. This implies that her cheek was as bright as the moon and also suggests that in the assembly of Brahman or Brahmā there was a holy atmosphere, the recitation of *Sāmaveda* constantly going on. When Bāṇa fancies Dadhīca wearing his *Yajñopavīta* to be Mandara chained by Gaṅgā, his majestic form stands before our eyes and we regard his *yajñopavīta* as sanctifying as the river Gaṅgā. When

Mālatī, wearing a pearl-necklace and a fine garment, is imagined to be the autumnal sky with bright stars and a thin veil of clouds, Mālatī's exceptionally bright white complexion and the soothing effect of her message are suggested. In looking upon the rosary of beads thrown away by the enraged Durvāsas as *Varṇamālā*, the letters of the alphabet are suggested to be the partisans of Sarasvatī which further implies her nature as the Goddess of Learning. Bāṇa uses a number of beautiful *Hetūprekṣā* and *Phalotprekṣās*, thus interpreting simple things in a highly poetic manner. The simple fact that the rays from Sarasvatī's nails were shooting downwards is interpreted by Bāṇa as Sarasvatī being directed the way to the world of the mortals. The red rays of the crest-jewel on the forehead of Harṣa appear to Bāṇa as the mark of the lac-dye of Lakṣmī's feet, when he bowed down to propitiate her, she being offended since Harṣa had shown preference to Sarasvatī. The setting of the sun has been represented as his running away lest he would lose his sovereignty at the hands of Harṣa. The red glow of Divākaramitra's body, spread in all quarters appears to Bāṇa as his teaching the quarters to assume red-robe. In these *Utprekṣās*, Bāṇa attributes the feelings of the character in the story to the object of his fancy. The setting sun is described as hanging his head low through grief on hearing Mahāśvetā's account, and therefore leaving his day's work. Here the feelings of Candrāpīḍa have been attributed to the sun. When Gṛhavarman is eager to see Rājyaśrī's face, the flames of fire are described as eager for her sight. Fear of gods and sages present in the heaven has been transferred to the speech of Durvāsas, that has been fancied as running away in fear. Similarly the wrath of Durvāsas has been transferred to the matted locks. The red sun entering the setting mountain is represented as doing so out of dejection on Prabhākaravardhana's death, the dejection of the subjects being transferred to the sun.

(d) Moreover throughout Bāṇa's *Utprekṣās* we come across a particular feature, which is known in English as 'Transferred epithet'. Even in the first *Ucchavāsa* of the *HC*, we come across many illustrations of this feature, e.g., *itaraśravaṇena ca vikasitasindhuvāramañjarījuṣā hasateva prakaṭitamadā*. Here in 'smiling ear' smile is transferred from Sarasvatī to her ear. In *adhomukhībhutenopadiśyamānamartyalokāvataraṇamārgeva nakhamayukhajālakena, adhomukhībhutatva* is transferred from Sarasvatī to the rays of her nails. In *acchācchenābharanadyutīnām nivahena diśāmiva darśanamārgalagnena cakravālenānugamyamānām* intense desire to see Dadhīca is transferred from Sarasvatī, Sāvitrī and other ladies to the circle of the quarters. When Sarasvatī is gazing at Dadhīca her glance is described as *avaśeva, avaśatva* being transferred from her mind to her glance. In *galatāvataṁsapallavena śrotuṁ śravaṇena dhāvamānen, dhāvamānatva* has been transferred from Sarasvatī's mind to her ears.

Blending with other Figures of Speech

Bāṇa gives beautiful *Saṁsṛṣṭi* and *Saṅkara* of *Utprekṣā* with other Figures of Speech. Of course *Atiśayokti* or exaggeration is bound to be present in every *Utprekṣā*. Hence that should be left out of consideration. (i) Since Bāṇa has a liking for *Śleṣa* we find that figure in numerous *Upreksās* of his, puns on words like *kara, pāda, guṇa, rāga,* etc., being very common. (ii) The blending of *Utprekṣā* with *Rūpaka* is very popular with him. To him the Eastern quarter with moon-light appears as whitened with the powder of pearls from the temples of the elephant of darkness burst open by the moon-light. The river Gaṅgā is fancied as the decorative paintings on the forehead of the heaven-paramour. (iii) He is also fond of mixing *Utpreksā* with *Apahnuti*, e.g., under the pretext of her complexion, Mālatī is fancied to be bringing with her the whole of the clear water of *Soma*. (iv) As in the description of Mālatī, he often gives the mixture of *Utprekṣā* and *Bhrāntimān*. The green pencils or rays of emerald in her bracelet are looked upon as *Sthalakamalinīs* persuing her mistaking her for Lakṣmī. Thus Bāṇa heightens the charm of his *Utprekṣās* by mixing these with many such Figures of Speech. Viśvanātha must have these and such other beautiful illustrations before him when he remarks about *Utprekṣā* — *alaṅkārāntaroṭthā sā vaicitryamadhikaṁ bhajet*.

The height to which Bāṇa's unfettered fancy can soar can be seen from the fact that in describing one simple thing he can heap *Utprekṣā* upon *Utprekṣā*. The river Gaṅgā appears to him as the cast-off slough of the sky-snake, the decorative painting on the forehead of the heaven-paramour, stall for merchandise of merit, ivory-gate closing the hell, white silk-turban of the king Sumeru, fine-textured banner of Kailāsa-elephant, the trodden road to salvation, ring of the wheel of the *Kṛta* era, etc. Similarly the Acchoda-lake is fancied as the jewelled mirror of *Trailokya-Lakṣmī*, *Aṭṭahāsa* of Śiva changed into liquid, autumnal cloud in melted form, Vaidūryagiri in the form of water, the first creation now remaining under the pretext of that lake. The white parasol presented to Harṣa by the king of Prāgjyotiṣa has given Bāṇa a scope for series of *Utprekṣās*. He sees it as the Milky Ocean turned into a circle, a swan remaining silent in order to listen to the jingling of the anklets of Harṣa's glory, *Aṭṭahāsa* of Śiva, the birth-day of the moon, the blooming of Viṣṇu's naval-lotus, etc.

With his *Utprekṣās* Bāṇa often produces a complete picture of the situation before our eyes, e.g., Mālatī with a white layer of sandal paste and a thin fine garment is imagined to be a lotus-plant, the stalks of which are clearly visible in transparent water. Here Mālatī's delicate form is compared with a lotus-plant and her thin garment with water. Similarly her petticoat with variegated spots, shining inside her fine *sārī* is fancied to be a crystal spot with a treasure of gems.

Themes Appreciated by Bāṇa

An analysis of Bāṇa's *Utprekṣās* shows that he is fond of certain objects and topics, which have been oft-repeated in his *Utprekṣās*. (a) Scenes of nature — the evening twilight, the sun-set, the moon-rise, bright moon light, the autumnal sky, the river Gaṅgā, the soft Malaya-breeze, the lotuses — day lotuses as well as the night lotuses — the humming of the bees, etc., (b) Feminine beauty — the bright white complexion where the moon or the neighbouring object is reflected, the red hue of the palms, feet and extremely red lower lip, bright rays from the teeth and from the nails, musical voice, bashfulness, etc.

Bāṇa would describe the physical beauty of a beautiful lady like Sarasvatī or Kādambarī from the head to the toe throwing *Utprekṣā* after *Utprekṣā*. Then he would use another series of *Utprekṣās* to bring out the fact how the natural beauty is enhanced by their toileting, dress and ornaments. In the materials of toilet he would refer to the lac-dye, collyrium, snadal-paste, saffron-marks, decorative painting on the cheeks, use of betel-leaf, etc. In their dresses he describes the white silken garment, a very fine-textured thin garment, occassionally red garment and petticoat with variegated colours. In the decorations and ornaments he mentions bracelets, necklaces, ear-rings, sprouts and flowers used as ear-decorations, anklets, *Kaṇṭhasūtra,* etc. All ornaments are studded with gems of variegated colours. (c) Mythological allusions — Bāṇa seems to be particularly fond of the legend of *Amṛta-manthana,* different aspects of which have been frequently referred to in his *Utprekṣās,* Dadhīca has been fancied as the mountain Mandara. Foam in Indrāyudha's mouth is conceived as nectar that he had drunk while in the ocean. Mahāśvetā is imagined as *Kṣīrodadhi-devatā,* etc. The description of the Goddess Śrī appearing before the king Puṣpabhūti is replete with allusions to this legend. The episode of *Madana-dahana* also is very favourite with Bāṇa. Other incidents from *Purāṇas* and epics have been spread throughout his *Utprekṣās.* His poetic fancies speak of the snake Kāliya being defeated by Kṛṣṇa, the birth of Brahmā from the lotus, the incident of *Gaṅgāvataraṇa,* Rāma and Sītā staying in Pañcavaṭī, the Rāhu-Ketu episode, birth of the moon from Atri's tears, Agastya drinking the ocean, the slaughter of Kṣatriyas by Paraśurāma, the Nandaka sword of Viṣṇu, Śiva's bull, Pārvatī's lion, Yama's buffalo, etc. In the description of the harems of the various kings he seems to refer to the Female Rule of Pramilā described in the *Mahābhārata.* In short, as Prof. Agarwal points out, Bāṇa has a thorough knowledge of the *Purāṇas* and the epics.

Glimpses of Social Life

Even a study of Bāṇa's *Utprekṣās* can give some glimpses in the society of his days. A study of his *Utprekṣās* from this point of view fully corroborates the conclusions of Dr. K.R. Potdar in his *Contemporary Life as revealed in the works of Bāṇa.* Of course one must repeat here the introductory lines from that learned scholar — In trying to get a picture of contemporary life from literary works, one can be certain that one cannot know everything about it. There are definitely limitations. Such works are written for the display of the poetic skill of the author, and hence references to social customs are scattered and scanty. Besides, in a work like *Kādambarī*, which depicts the life of superhuman beings in parts, a clear idea of the ordinary social life naturally becomes difficult. But at the same time one thing is clear, viz., the description even of an imaginary society will necessarily be coloured by the description of the contemporary society".

(A) *Royal Life* — Bāṇa was closely acquainted with the royal life and hence his *Utprekṣās* refer to all details in the life of a king or a prince. (i) Administration — *Mudrā*, the royal seal; *Śāsana-paṭṭa*, giving a grant or a command; *Ājñāvalaya*, issuing a command; *Paṭṭabandha*, which consisted in the king tying a turban on the head of a person by way of honour or reward, the king attending the assembly for giving justice, all this has been referred to in Bāṇa's *Utprekṣās*, e.g., the deer-skin is fancied to be the *Śāsana-paṭṭa*, giving Durvāsas an authority to curse others. The pieces of ice on the head of the lordly elephant Darpaśāta are fancied to be his *Paṭṭabandha*. The beating of drums for various purposes has been referred to in the *Utprekṣās*. March-drums, festive-drums, proclamation-drums, etc., have found their place throughout Bāṇa's *Utprekṣās*. (ii) Military — The three parts of the army, viz., the elephants, the horses and the foot-soldiers are taken as basis for many *Utprekṣās*. The *Utprekṣās* used when Harṣa starts for his *Digvijaya* refer to all details of a military march. They refer to the swords, the spears, the armours, the bows and the arrows, encampment, tents and all minute details. The religio-military ceremony of *Nīrājana* repeated so often in the *Utprekṣās* is a special favourite of Bāṇa. (For the description of the ceremony — see Dr. Potdar's essay page 31). The flames of fire in the houses of the *Saptarṣis* are fancied as performing *Nīrājana* for the *Dharmasādhana*. Even the fire of fever is fancied as performing *Nīrājana* for Prabhākaravardhana for his conquest of the next world. (iii) Among the things associated with a king, Bāṇa's *Utprekṣās* allude to the golden throne, the crown, the foot-stool, the white-parasol, the chowries, the sword, and the golden bracelet on the left fore-arm, the crest-jewel and the ring. The sapphire-ring in the *Yajñopavīta* of Rājavardhana also can suggest an *Utprekṣā* to Bāṇa (iv) Festivals — The *Utprekṣās* used while describing the festivities after the birth of Candrāpīḍa or Harṣa give a fair idea of the merry-making in the royal families. Reference is made to decorating the palaces and the roads, sprinkling the roads with saffron water, musical concerts being held, and music and dancing being given by the courtesans. The *pūrṇapātra* presents given to the servants and gifts munificently distributed to the brāhmaṇas and to the poor also form topics of Bāṇa's *Utprekṣās*. Similar mirth is described in the *Utprekṣās* used in the course of describing Candrāpīḍa's *Yauvarājyābhiṣeka* and Rājyaśrī's wedding.

Puṣyābhiṣeka, a ceremony peculiar to royal families (Refer to Dr. Potdar's essay page 31) also has been included in the *Utprekṣās,* e.g., the elephant Darpaśāta is imagined to be the festive day of *Puṣyābhiṣeka.*

Gambling and hunting popular in the royal families and archery, a compulsory subject in a prince's curriculum, have also provided topics for Bāṇa's *Utprekṣās.*

(B) *Society in General:* (i) Religious attitude — These were the days when Buddhism was getting royal support and yet the old brāhmaṇical religion had not been eclipsed by the former. Throughout Bāṇa's *Utprekṣās,* we can notice a reverence for the *Vedas,* the institution of sacrifice and the *Dharmaśāstra* rites. The daily rituals like *Sandhyāvandana* have been frequently referred to in the *Utprekṣās,* e.g., the stars are looked upon as the drops of water offered by the *Saptarṣis* while performing *Sandhyāvandana.* Performance of sacrifices like *Koṭihoma* has been referred to in many *Utprekṣās.* Even the Viśvajit sacrifice has been alluded to in the course of *Utprekṣās* used to describe the king Harṣa. Obsequial rites like offering sesame and water, performing *śrāddha,* etc., also have been referred to, e.g., the pale moon is looked upon as the boiled rice offered to the deceased king Prabhākaravardhana.

Worship of idols of different deities was necessary part of religious practices and hence has been referred to in numerous *Utprekṣās.* Worship of the sun was hereditary in Harṣa's family. In the language of poetic fancy Bāṇa describes how Prabhākaravardhana worshipped the sun with a white turban on his head, after drawing circle with saffron paste and repeating certain *stotras*. Bāṇa looks upon the day-lotuses also as observing the vow of propitiating the sun. Presence of heretic sects seems to have been alluded to in some *Utprekṣās*. Wrong doctrines in the lands of Śrīkaṇṭha are fancied to have been washed away by the smoke of sacrificial fires. How Buddhism was respected by the royal family of Sthāṇvīśvara is obvious from the regard shown by Harṣa to Divākaramitra. How the Buddhist monks were spreading their religion far and wide is hinted by Bāṇa in his *Utprekṣās* like the following — The red hue of Divākaramitra's body spread in the quarters is fancied as his teaching the quarters to wear red-robe.

People seem to be undergoing various types of vows like the *Pāśupata*-vow practised by Mahāśvetā, numerous vows and worships practised by Vilāsavatī and Yaśomatī. *Dinakarārādhanavrata, Dhūmrapānavrata*, etc., have been also alluded to in Bāṇa's *Utprekṣās*. Offering of human blood, flesh and living beings form topics of some *Utprekṣās*. (ii) Asceticism seems to be prospering in those days. Even a *Kārpaṭika* like Bhairavācārya was highly respected by Puṣpabhūti. The *Utprekṣās* used while describing Bhairavācārya would give a detailed picture of such an ascetic. With his dark woollen blanket he is fancied as practising residence in the nether-world. The fact that round globes of conches were hanging down from his matted locks of hair, is looked upon as his having arrested the Siddhas. Similarly his forehead being marked with ashes, burning of *Guggulu* and incense, drawing mystic circles, offering variegated-coloured banners to Śiva, his knowledge of *Śiva-Saṁhitā*, his iron-bracelet, crystal ear-rings, bundle of magic-threads with various herbs and conch-shells in it, rosary of beads, thick beard, his power of bringing snakes near himself, his *Viśākhika*-staff, oblation of black sesame offered by him, use of different *Mudrās* by him, all this has been included in Bāṇa's poetic fancy. (iii) Social Customs — Birth of a son was celebrated with great enthusiasm. In this context the *Utprekṣās* refer to all the minute details like placing of the *Sarṣapa* seeds on the head of the child to ward off evil, besmearing *Gorocanā*-pigment, using an ornament known as *Vyāghranakhapaṅkti* to protect the child from evil eye, etc. When the eight-year old Bhaṇḍi comes to Sthāṇvīśvara the *Utprekṣās* speak of the tuft of his hair, the side-locks and the coral necklace. He seems to have come soon after his *Upanayana*.

Marriage — In the description of Rājyaśrī's marriage, Bāṇa's poetic fancies refer to the evening time, which is supposed to be auspicious for wedding, to the red chowries moved by the side of the bridegroom, the *Vaikakṣaka* garland worn by him and to the dropping of the parched grains in the sacred fire. The practice of *Svayaṁvara* might have been followed in a few cases. The *Ekāvalī* presented to Harṣa by Divākaramitra is fancied to be the *Svayaṁvaramālā* of the Pṛthvīvadhū.

The practice of *Satīgamana* or Self-immolation, after the husband's death was highly honoured in the society and has been referred to in the *Utprekṣās* of Bāṇa, e.g., the *Digdāha*, i.e., the quarters becoming red before the death of Prabhākaravardhana has been fancied as the earth preparing for *Satīgamana*. While describing the event of Yaśomatī's self-immolation Bāṇa's *Utprekṣāss* speak of her wearing red garment and white silken shawl, besmearing the body with saffron-unguent, with her lower lip reddened due to chewing of betal-leaf, her wearing an *Āprapadīna Mālā* in the neck and a lotus on the ear, her putting on all ornaments like *Kaṇṭhasūtra*, and carrying with her a picture-board with her husband's resemblance drawn on it, and his *prāsayaṣṭi*, the spear. (iv) Superstitions and beliefs — The people were far more superstitious than what we are now. Before undertaking a distant journey, before starting on a military march or before beginning any new undertaking they used to consult astrologers and palmists. They were also guided by superstitions about good and bad omens. Bāṇa's *Utprekṣās* refer to moving of the flames to the right, throbbing of the left eye in the case of the ladies and the right eye in the case of men, etc. as being good omens. While describing the event of Prabhākaravardhana's death, Bāṇa's *Utprekṣās* speak of many ill-omens like the cries of the black crows, the earthquake, *digdāha*, appearance of dark clouds in the sky or a spot on the disc of the sun, etc.

Belief of the people in the significance of dreams, in the efficacy of magic and incantations, belief in ghosts and evil spirits also has been alluded to in the *Utprekṣās*. (v) The occupations like that of a farmer, a gardner, a magician, a musician, a dancer, an alchemist, a physician, etc., and the instruments and implements used for these professions have been referred to throughout the *Utprekṣās.* A ploughshare, a water-wheel, a weighing balance, a lute, etc., form topics of many *Utprekṣās.* (vi) General health of the society seems to be good. The *Utprekṣās* of Bāṇa speak of strong and sturdy men, of ladies having a healthy complexion, of boys and even princes and kings going to gymnasium, enjoying hunting, horse-riding, elephant-driving, etc. Medical science seems to have been developed considerably. The *Utprekṣās* refer to remedies and medicines for various illnesses. Among the diseases *Rājayakṣmā* Tuberculosis and *Dadruroga* leprosy have been frequently referred to in his *Utprekṣās.*

In short, a general picture of the society in Bāṇa's times can be conjectured even with the help of his *Utprekṣās,* not to say of his works as a whole.

Admiration of Bāṇa's Imaginative Power

The charm underlying Bāṇa's flights of imagination has been highly admired by Sanskrit Classical poets and modern scholars, Eastern as well as Western. Prof. S.K. De describes Bāṇa's imagination as prodigal and defends Bāṇa for his lack of sense of proportion in art with the words,[1] "The lack of proportion is due partly to largeness of handling and partly to a prodigal imagination which prefers lawless splendour to decent insipidity."

This scholar attributes the entire charm in Bāṇa to his picturesque imagery. If scholars like Prof. Weber find fault with Bāṇa's exquisitely ornate and elaborate diction, Prof. De defends[2] Bāṇa's position by saying, "But he (Bāṇa) is attractive if attention is confined at a time to the marvellous richness of his fancy revealed in one or two of his episodes and descriptions." This scholar further continues,[3] "What we have here (in Bāṇa) is the sheer delight of voluminous expression, the largeness of tumultuous fancy, and the love of all that is grand and glorious in fact or fiction."

Prof. A.B. Keith[4] remarks "Among his few verses is a fairly good example of lively fancy."

Shri Hamsaraja Agrawal,[5] says,

> *paurāṇikīnām vārtānām mahān khalu jñānavibhavaḥ bāṇasya āsit, adbhutā ca asya utprekṣāśaktiḥ abhūt.*

Bāṇa really deserves all praise that has been bestowed upon him by Indian tradition. Jayadeva rightly calls him 'The five-arrowed Cupid staying in the heart of the *Kavitākāminī*.'

About his *Utprekṣās* one would feel like remarking — *Utprekṣā bāṇabhaṭṭasya* on the lines of *Upamā kālidāsasya.*

References

1. *History of Sanskrit Literature*, p. 232, University of Calcutta, Calcutta, 1947.
2. *Ibid.*, p. 238.
3. *Ibid.*, p. 239.
4. *A History of Sanskrit Literature*, p. 327, Oxford University Press, 1st Edition, 1920, 5th Edition 1956.
5. *Saṁskṛta Sāhityetihāsa*, Part II, p. 3, Śakti Prakāśana, Ludhiana, 1951.

17

Good and Bad Verbal Borrowing According to Rājaśekhara

A POET or a writer, to whichever language he belongs, can always borrow ideas and expressions from another author. Borrowing is thus a common feature of literature as such. In Sanskrit literature Bāṇa (7th cent. A.D.) in his introductory verses in the *Harṣcarita* had already alluded to borrowing on the part of poets. Vāmana (8th cent. A.D.) has discussed borrowal under *anyacchāyāyoniḥ arthaḥ*. Ānandavardhana (9th cent. A.D.) has dealt with it in his *Dhvanyāloka*, chapter IV. But Rājaśekhara (9th to 10th cent. A.D.) is the first Sanskrit critic to discuss the problem of borrowing in all its aspects. He has devoted three full chapters, viz., chapters XI to XIII to his *Kāvyamīmāṁsā* to consider various aspects of borrowing. In chapter XI he discusses *śabdaharaṇa* (verbal borrowing) and in chapters XII and XIII he deals with *arthaharaṇa* (borrowing of ideas).

Types of Borrowal of Ideas

As far as his discussion of *arthaharaṇa* is concerned it has been put in clear words and there is no reason for any divergence in the interpretation of chapters XII and XIII. It is clear that according to him there are 4 types of borrowal of ideas: (1) *pratibimbakalpa*, (2) *ālekhaprakhya*, (3) *anyadehitulya*, and (4) *parapurapraveśasadṛśa*. He considers the first type as *parityājya* and the rest as *anugrāhya*. There also the degree of goodness varies directly with the originality on the part of the borrower and hence these three types are arranged by him in ascending order of importance. His ideas of *arthaharaṇa* have been studied and often repeated by later Sanskrit critics like Kṣemendra (11th cent. A.D.), Bhoja (11th cent. A.D.) and Hemacandra (12th cent. A.D). Modern commentators and Hindi translators have unanimously explained these ideas. Dr. V.M. Kulkarni has made a thorough study of the topic in his learned article on 'Sanskrit writers on Plagiarism' published in the *Journal of the Oriental Institute*, Baroda, 1954-55. But as far as *Rā's* views on *śabdaharaṇa* are concerned I feel that these have not been properly understood by the modern scholars and a careful and critical study of the same is necessary. In the following lines there is one such attempt to interpret chapter XI of *Rā's Kāvyamīmāṁsā*.

Originality of Ideas

According to *Rā*, originality of ideas is the touchstone of poetic genius. Among various poets, composing their works on the same theme each one is bound to catch some different ideas. That being so every poet is sure to display some originality of ideas in his composition, even when he is borrowing the material from another source. But this cannot be said about the words used by a poet. As Ānandavardhana[1] has already said: *nahi vācaspatinapyakṣarāṇi padāni vā kadācidapūrvāṇi ghaṭayituṁ śakyante*. Every poet cannot coin new words for himself and say in the manner of Jagannātha,[2] *śabdo mayātra nihito na parasya kaścit*.

Therefore, *Rā* rightly treats *śabdaharaṇa* and *arthaharaṇa* at two different levels. He cannot insist upon absolute originality in the process of *śabdaharaṇa* as he does for *arthaharaṇa*. *Rā* knows fully well that *apūrvapadaghaṭanā* is not to be expected from every poet. Nevertheless, he does expect some originality on the part of a poet, who is using words from some other source. *Rā* firmly believes that even while borrowing words and expressions from another poet there is ample scope for a poet to supply flashes of his originality.

Keeping this in mind we can analyse *Rā*'s views on *śabdaharaṇa* as follows:

If a later poet uses an expression used by an earlier one

exactly in the same sense and in the same context, without any change of idea, it is a bad borrowing (*parityājyaṁ haraṇam*). On the other hand if he shows at least a little of originality while utilising the former expression, it is a good borrowing (*anugrāhyaṁ haraṇam*).

Types of Borrowing

In the beginning of chapter XI he first defines *haraṇa*, mentions its two types as *parityājya* and *anugrāhya*, and then enters into the details of *śabdaharaṇa*. From the point of view of quantity he divides it in five types as follows:

(a) Borrowing of a word, (b) Borrowing of a quarter of a verse, (c) Borrowing of a half-verse, (d) Borrowing of a full verse, and (e) Borrowing of a composition as a whole.

(a) *Borrowing of a word:* The ancient teachers had said that borrowal of one word is not defective. This is obvious. Any two compositions, compared at random, are bound to have so many words in common. *Rā* has, however, to add a modifying clause to this rule, viz. "Provided the word, is not paronomastic." Obviously he is of the opinion that a *śliṣṭa-śabda* should not be borrowed. Here both the Hindi translators of *Kāvyamīmāṁsā*, viz. Shri Gangasagar Rai and Shri Kedaranath Sharma Sarasvat, have understood the clause *anyatra dvyarthapadārthāt* in exactly opposite sense. They translate it as "If the word is paronomastic in the source." According to their interpretation a *śliṣṭaśabda-haraṇa* is *anugrāhya* for *Rā* but I follow the explanation given by Shri Madhusudan Mishra in his Sanskrit commentary on the *Kāvyamīmāṁsā*. He has said there, *dvyarthapadaharaṇe tu doṣa eva*. Using the *śliṣṭa* words exactly in the same senses without any change of context shows absolute lack of originality. *Rā* then discusses this *parityājya ekapādaharaṇa* in all its details: (i) *Śliṣṭapadaharaṇa* as in the verse *mā gāḥ pāntha* . . . borrowing the words *durākṛṣṭaśilīmukham* and *kirātam* from another verse, (ii) *Śliṣṭapadaikadeśaharaṇa* as in the verse *kopānmānini* . . . borrowing *māṁsa* from another verse, (iii) *Śliṣṭasya yamakena haraṇa* as in the verse *dalayatā viśikhaiḥ* . . . borrowing the words *niravadhīritamākulamasuram* from an early verse, (iv) *Śliṣṭasya praśnottareṇa haraṇa* as in the verse *kim karoti* . . . borrowing *karṇāyatekṣaṇam* from another verse, (v) *Yamakasya yamakena haraṇa* as in the verse *cakrāni dahatā* from an earlier verse.

After this, *Rā* takes up the topic of borrowal of non-paronomastic words more than one. In this regard his teachers had said that such words can be borrowed in succession up to the extent of three words only, and never, more. They illustrated — *sa pātu vo yasya hatāvaśeṣaḥ* . . . as a faulty borrowing since it has borrowed four words from an earlier verse, viz., *sa pātu vo yasya jaṭākalāpe*.

But here also *Rā* differs from the ancient teachers and seems to say, "It is not the quantity of the borrowed material that matters. It is the manner in which it is utilised that decides the point."

Refuting the opinion of the ancient teachers that three *aśliṣṭa* words can be borrwed in succession, but not more than that, *Rā* says, *ullekhavān padasandarbhaḥ pariharaṇīyo na. pratyabhijñāyātaḥ pādo'pi. tasyāppi sāmye na kiñcana duṣṭam syāt.*

In the interpretation of the above passage I beg to differ from all the interpretations offered so far.

(1) The *G.O.S.* Edition (First 1916) reads the text as follows:

> *ullekhavān padasandarbhaḥ pariharaṇīyo napratyabhijñā-yātaḥ pādo'pi. tasyāpi sāmyena kiñcana duṣṭam syāt.*

The first edition does not add any note about the meaning of this passage.

(2) In his Sanskrit commentary *Madhusūdanī* published in the *Chowkhamba Sanskrit Series,* Banaras, *Samvat* 1991, Pandit Madhusudan Mishra has explained the passage as follows: (He amends the readings in two places and reads the passage as: *ullekhavān padasandarbhaḥ pariharaṇiyo na pratyabhijñāyataḥ pādo'pi. tasyāpi sāmye na kiñcana duṣṭaṁ syāt*)

> *neti ācāryairyaduktaṁ tanna iti granthakāraḥ. yataḥ pratibhānavān yasyāviṣkaraṇe pratibhāyāḥ kṣayo bhavati sa padasandarbhaḥ padasamudāyaḥ pariharaṇiyaḥ. yasya padasandarbhasya prādurbhāvakaraṇe anyena svapratibhā vyayīkṛtā sa tu parityājyaḥ, na svīkartavya iti bhāvaḥ. pratyabhijñayātaḥ sa evayamiti pratyabhijñāya yātaḥ*

> *prāptaḥ pado'pi na pariharaṇīyaḥ, tam na pariharet svīkuryadeva. tasya pratyabhijñāptasya kintu ullekhatāśūnyasya padasya sāmyespi sādṛśye'pi na kimapi duṣṭaṁ syāt.*

Upon the readings as pinted in the *G.O.S.* Edition, Shri Mishra comments:

> *atra mudritapustake napratyabhijñāyātaḥ iti akāraghaṭitaḥ pātho'papāṭhaḥ: tathā sāmyeneti tṛtīyāntatayā bhrāntaḥ pāṭhah. sāmye iti saptamyantaḥ pāṭhastathā na iti niṣedārthaka nakāra pṛthak.*

Following this the translation of the passage will be as follows:

> A construction of words, containing a poetic flash should be avoided (from borrowal), but not even one full quarter (need be avoided) from (an ordinary) easily recognisable verse. Even with its similarity there is no defect.

According to this interpretation *ityuktavānuktiviśeṣaramyam rāmanujanmā virarāma mānī* is a borrowal, which is free from defect since there is no poetic flash in it. But *prasaradbindunādāya* is an instance of *parityājyaharaṇa,* because it has borrowed *śaṅkarakṣīrasindhave,* an expression containing a poetic flash from an earlier verse : *namaḥ saṁsāranirvāṇa. . . .*

(3) The *G.O.S.* Third edition, revised and enlarged by K.S. Ramaswami Sastri, in 1934 reads the text as follows:

> *ullekhavān padasandarbhaḥ pariharaṇīyaḥ pratyabhijñāyātaḥ pādo'pi. tasyāpi sāmyena kiñcana duṣṭam syāt.*

In the notes added at the end Shri Sastri explains that according to this *ullekhavān padasandarbhaḥ* should be avoided. So also a full quarter from an ordinary verse should be avoided. He remarks that following this reading we shall have to say that both *ityuktavānukti . . .* and *śaṅkarakṣīrasindhave . . .* are instances of plagiarism.

Further he also suggests that the passage can be also read as:

> *ullekhavān padasandarbhaḥ pariharaṇīyaḥ. na pratyabhijñāyātaḥ pādo'pi. tasyāpi sāmye na kiñcana duṣṭam syāt.*

He then explains it as explained by Shri Mishra above, and says that according to this *ityuktavānuktiviśeṣa* . . . is not an instance of plagiarism.

This explanation, given by Shri Mishra has been followed in the Hindi translation given by Shri K.S. Sarasvat and Shri G.S. Rai. Dr. V. M. Kulkarni also seems to follow the same explanation, since he has remarked *Rā's* opinion in this regard is that any striking expression of an earlier poet should not be borrowed by later poets.

(4) I understand the passage as follows:

> *ullekhavān padasandarbhaḥ pariharaṇīyaḥ na. pratyabhijñāya ataḥ pādo'pi (svīkaraṇīyaḥ). tasyāpi sāmye na kiñcana duṣṭaṁ syāt.*

I would translate it as follows:

> A noteworthy construction of words need not be avoided. With due recognition of its debt (one can borrow) even a quarter from it. Even with its similarity, i.e., even with that much similarity there is no harm.

I do not think that *ullekha* means *pratibhāna*. It is just *nirdeśa: ullekhavān* means the same as *ullekhanīya*. I do not think that *Rā* advises poets to avoid such noteworthy expressions of earlier poets.

At the end of the chapter he has said: *ullikhecca kiñcana prācyam manyatāṁ sa mahākaviḥ*. One who restates something from the older poets is also a great poet according to him. It is our common experience that certain lines from a well-known song or a verse become so popular that many authors use them in their composition in various contexts. Of course such an expression being well-known they have absolutely no intention of claiming it as their own. They use it by way of a quotation. Sometimes they employ it to give some unthought of meaning in order to create humour, or to give some sarcastic remark. It is in this manner that Kālidāsa's well-known *Arthāntaranyāsa — eko hi doṣo guṇasannipāte nimajjatīndoḥ kiraṇeṣvivāṅkaḥ* has been used by a modern poet in his composition. *eko hi . . . dāridryadoṣo guṇarāśināśī. Rā* knows that such expressions are very attractive and an author feels tempted to employ them in his own composition. *Rā* means to say that there is no harm in using words from such expressions even to the extent of one full *pāda*. But *Rā*, insists on honesty on the part of the borrower. The borrower must duly recognise his debt to the original drawn upon by him. I do not think that *pratyabhijñāyātaḥ* means *atyantaprasiddhaḥ* but *ullekhatāśūnyaḥ. Rā* must have known cases of such *anugrahyaharaṇa.* In the latter half of the eighth century the Jain poet Jinasena composed his *Pārśvābhyudaya,* giving the biography of Pārśvanātha, the 23rd *Tīrthaṅkara.* In this work the whole of Kālidāsa's *Meghadūta,* consisting of 120 verses has been used by way of *Samasyāpūraṇa.* At the end of the work Jinasena honestly says, *taccoditena jinsenamunīśvareṇa kāvyaṁ vyadhāyi pariveṣṭitameghadūtam.* A similar use of the *Meghadūta* was later made by Vikrama in his *Nemidūta,* by Caritrasundaragaṇi in his *Śīladūta,* by Merutuṅga in his *Jain Meghadūta* and so on. In the instance given by *Rā* the expression *śaṅkarakṣīrasindhave* must have been used by the poet giving the verse *prasaradbindunādāya* by way of quotation only.

After this *Rā* deals with *pādataḥ haraṇa, ardhavṛttataḥ haraṇa,* etc. one by one.

As regards (b) *pādataḥ haraṇa* or *ekapādaharaṇa* and (c) *ardhavṛttataḥ haraṇa* or *dvipādaharaṇa (samasta* and *vyasta). Rā* says that the ancient teachers called it as *svikaraṇa* (adaptation), but he calls it as *haraṇa* only.

Now arises the problem: is this *haraṇa anugrāhya* or *parityājya* according to him? His own wording is vague. The modern interpreters of *kāvyamīmāṁsā* have not explained the point clearly. They have simply translated the vague clauses as they appear in the text.

Then coming to *tripādaharaṇa* as in *araṇye nirjane . . . tanvāṅgī yadi labhyeta Rā's* own remark is *pāda evānyathākaraṇam na svīkaraṇam pādonaharaṇaṁ vā.* Shri Madhusudan Mishra comments upon this: *atra vāśabda evārthakaḥ. athavā na etat svīkaraṇaṁ na vā haraṇam.* Thus he is not sure whether this is *anugrāhya* or *parityājya.*

After that *Rā* illustrates *pādāṁsonaharaṇa* in *yā vyāpāravatī . . . premṇaḥ samānaṁ sukham,* and then *padāṁsonaharaṇa* in *asakalahasitatvāt . . . .* According to him all these are like *tripādaharaṇa,* i.e., *na svīkaraṇam pādonaharaṇam vā.* Hence whether all these cases of *haraṇa* are *parityājya* or *anugrāhya* has not been clearly said by *Rā.* and has not been explained by his commentators and translators.

In the notes to the Third *G.O.S.* Edition, Shri K.S. Ramaswami Sastri has suggested that these are the cases of plagiarism according to *Rā* and in many cases the Hindi translations seem to follow the same opinion. Dr. V.M. Kulkarni also refers to all such cases as 'plagiarism' according to *Rā.*

But I feel that *Rā* does not want to condemn, all such cases as plagiarism or *parityājya haraṇa.* If it were so *tu* in *yattu parakīyam svīyamiti* has no significance. According to me up to that point *Rā* has discussed *anugrāhya haraṇa* and then he turns to *parityājya haraṇa* from the remark *yattu parakīyam . . .*

(i) This is supported by one remark in Shri Mishra's Sanskrit commentary. He introduces this passage *yattu,* etc. saying, *nanu yadyevam nāpaharaṇamanumanyate tat kidṛśo haraṇapadārtho vivakṣita ityāha — yattu . . .*

(ii) This is also supported by Hemacandra's remarks in his *Kāvyānuśāsaṇa,* chapter I, and by his own *Viveka* on it. In his *Vṛtti* on *Chāyādyupajīvanādayaḥ śikṣāḥ* in *Sūtra* 10 he remarks: *ādiśabdāt padapādādīnāṁ ca kāvyāntarādyathaucityamupajīvanām.* In his *Viveka* on this portion he has quoted a considerable portion from *Rā's Kāvyamīmāṁsā,* XI. Having discussed all varieties of *śikṣā* including *samasyāpūraṇa* he says, *evaṁ mahākavyārtha-carvaṇaparakṛtakāvyapāṭhādyāḥ śikṣā abhyūhyāḥ.*

Thus according to him all these methods of borrowing seem to be *anugrāhya.* However, he does not approve of the borrowal of all the four quarters remarking, *pādacatuṣṭayopajīvane tu paripūrṇam cauryamiti tanna nirdiśyate.*

(iii) Bhoja (11th cent. A.D.) in his *Śṛngāraprakāśa* discusses these cases under a figure of word which he calls as *paṭhitī*. Obviously according to him this is something *anugrāhya*.

(iv) Kṣemendra (11th cent. A.D.) in his *Kavikaṇṭhābharaṇa* advises a poet to be *chāyopajīvī, padopajīvī, pādopajīvī,* etc. Hence according to him also *padopajīvana* and *pādopajīvana* are not bad. Hence according to *Rā ekapādaharaṇa, dvipādaharaṇa, tripāda-haraṇa, pādāṁśonaharaṇa* and *padāṁśonaharaṇa* would all come under *parivartana* of *artha* or *arthāntarasaṅkramana*. He says, *uktayo hyarthāntarasaṅkrāntā na pratyabhijñāyante svadante ca.*

A poet who uses this manner of borrowing is called a *parivartaka* (a transformer) by him. (d) A poet who borrows the whole verse (*vṛtta*) and construes it in an altogether different manner as applicable to a quite different topic is also a very good *parivartaka* according to him. In the verse illustrated by him, viz., *subhru tvaṁ kupiteti* . . . the borrower has used it in connection with a defective sight, while in the original it was used for propitiation of a beloved.

All commentators are agreed upon the fact that *Rā* considers a verse which utilises three quarters from three different verses adding one original quarter and thus changing the context altogether is as good as original composition. His illustration for this is *kimiha . . . kimapi . . . vipākaḥ. Rā* calls such a poet as a *saṅgrāhakakavi* (an assimilator).

After having dealt with all such cases of *anugrāhya haraṇa, Rā* turns to *parityājya haraṇa* in *yattu parakīyamiti* . . . According to him the following are the cases of *parityājya haraṇa* or plagiarism: (1) Passing on the words and expressions of another poet as one's own by taking undue advantage of circumstances like *ayamaprasiddhaḥ*, etc. earlier mentioned by Avantīsundarī, (2) Using the expression of an earlier poet exactly in the same meaning and the same context, without the slightest change, e.g., *urudvyayam sarasakadalīkāṇḍasabrahmacāri* . . . in the verse *urudvayaṁ kadalakāṇḍalayo mṛgākṣyāḥ* . . ., (3) Purchasing another's composition and passing it under one's own name. The division (e) from quantitative analysis will be included here.

A poet who uses the borrowal of any one of the above three types is called *Ācchādakakavi* (a concealer) by *Rā*.

Conclusion

Thus on a careful study of *Rā's Kāvyamīmāṁsā,* XI we can summarise his views on *śabdaharaṇa* as follows: According to him (A) *Uttamaharaṇa* or the best borrowing will be (i) that of a *Sangrāhaka-kavi,* who assimilates different quarters from different verses with an original quarter of his own and (ii) that of a *parivartaka* who uses the same verse for a quite different topic. (B) *Anugrāhyaharaṇa* or good borrowing will be (i) Borrowal of *ullekhavān padasandarbhaḥ,* with a very honest acknowledgement of the source. (ii) *Ekapādaharaṇa, dvipādaharaṇa, tripādaharaṇa, pādamśonaharaṇa, padāṁśonaharaṇa* from an earlier verse, provided it is utilised to convey an original idea. The goodness of this type of borrowal varies in direct proportion with the originality displayed in its employment. (C) *Parityājyaharaṇa* will be (i) *Śliṣṭaśabdaharaṇa* (ii) *Uktīnām tathaiva haraṇa,* i.e., when the same expressions is used in the same context, without the slightest originality. (iii) Passing on other's expressions as one's own. (iv) Purchasing a composition of another poet and publishing it as one's own.

References

1. *Dhvanyāloka,* IV 15 *Vṛtti.*
2. *Rasagaṅgādhara,* Introductory verses, No. 6.

18

Apavārya and *Janāntikam* in Theory and Practice

WHILE reading classical Sanskrit plays we come across the stage-directions *Apavārya* and *Janāntikam*. If somebody asks, "What is the difference between the two ?" it becomes difficult to answer. The annotations on these terms as found in the various editions of the plays are often confusing. Even the dictionaries do not make the difference quite clear, e.g., Apte's Dictionary (Pune 1957) explains *Apavārya* as 'apart, aside to another'. 'It is speaking in such a way that the only person addressed may hear it'. Then it gives the definition from the *S.D.*, VI.

Tadbhavedapavāritam rahasyam tu yadanyasya parāvṛtya prakāśyate — VI.138. *Tripatākākareṇānyanapavāryāntarā kathām.*

Janāntikam is explained as secret communication, whispering or speaking aside to another and the definition from *S.D.*, VI is given as — *tripatākākareṇānyānapavaryāntarā kathām, anyonyāmantraṇaṁ yat syājjanānte tajjanāntikam,* VI.139. Thus here *tripatākākareṇānyānapavaryāntarā kathām* is common in both. Hence, here is an attempt to understand what exactly the two stage-directions denote.

Distinguishing Characteristics According to Sanskrit Critics

First let us see what the works on dramaturgy have to say about them (1) the *Nāṭyaśāstra* of Bharata (about 3rd cent. A.D.)

discusses the dramatic speeches in chapter XXV. The two terms are defined as follows:

> *Apavāritam —*
> *nigūḍhabhāvasaṁyuktamapavāritakam smṛtam.*
> *Janāntikam —*
> *kāryavaśādasrāvayaṁ pārśvagatairyajjanāntikaṁ tat syāt.*

Apavāritam is some speech containing a secret thought and *Janāntikam* is some speech which is not to be heard by persons standing by the side, for some dramatic purpose. How are these speeches to be spoken? Bharata recommends:

> *hastamantarataḥ kṛtvā tripatākaṁ prayojayet,*
> *janātikam prayoktavyamapavāritakaṁ tathā.*

Thus both these varieties are to be spoken after screening or excluding others with a *Tripatākāhasta.* According to him *Patākāhasta* means holding up the hand with all four fingers raised up. When the *anāmikā,* i.e., the indicating finger is turned down it becomes *tripatākāhasta.* Thus the speaker of both these speeches excludes other characters on the stage from hearing it by raising up the palm with three fingers spread up (near the cheek, to the right or left according to the position of the characters to be screened). Bharata's definition of *Apavāritam* is not very clear. How does he distinguish it from *Ātmagatam,* which, according to him, is *hṛdayasthaṁ vacaḥ*? M.M. Ghosh translates *Apavārya* as 'concealed speech' and *Janāntikam* as 'private personal address'.

(2) Abhinavagupta (950-1020 A.D.) distinguishes between the two as follows:

> *sarveṣāṁ yannigūhyate eka eva śṛṇuyāditi tadapavāritam.*
> *janāntikamekāntikatvam caikasyaiva nigūhyate iti viśeṣaḥ.*

Apavāritam is to be heard by one and concealed from all the rest, while *Janāntikam* is to be heard by all and concealed from one. Bharata's definitions do not warrant this distinction. On the contrary he uses a form of plural *pārśvagataiḥ* for the persons who are not supposed to hear *Janāntikam.*

(3) Dhanañjaya (974-96 A.D.) the author of *Daśarūpa* is the first critic to make clearcut distinction in all varieties of dramatic speech. Having divided dramatic speeches in three categories, viz., *prakāśam*, *svagatam* and *niyataśrāvyam* he defines *niyataśrāvya* as a speech which is to be heard by certain characters on the stage, while certain others are excluded from hearing it. Then it is divided further as — *dvidhānyannāṭyadharmākhyam janāntama-pavāritam*. He makes it clear that these two varieties are presented on the stage artificially (*nāṭyadharma*) and not as we find them in practical life (*lokadharma*). He defines the two aside speeches as follows:

> *rahasyam kathyate'nyasya parāvṛtyapavāritam* (65)
> *tripatākākareṇāṇyanapāvaryāntarā kathām,*
> *anyonyāmantraṇaṁ yat syājjanānte tajjanāntikam* (66)

Thus the speaker of *Apavāritam* takes a turn and communi- cates some secret to somebody else (*anyasya — anyasmai*). The speaker of *Janāntikam* temporarily breakes the course of conversation by exluding some characters from hearing him by means of *Tripatākākara* and then holds a mutual conversation with the other character for whom the speech is intended. In fact though not stated specifically the phrase *antarā kathām* goes with *Apavāritam* also.

What Dhanañjaya means is expounded further by his brother Dhanika in his *Avaloka* as follows:

> *yasya na śrāvyam tamantarā ūrdhvasarvāṅgulikaṁ vakrānāmikaṁ tripatākālakṣaṇaṁ karaṁ kṛtvānyena saha yanmantryate tajjanāntikam. parāvṛtyānyasya rahasya-kathanamapavāritam.*

Nṛsiṁhabhaṭṭa, in his *Laghuṭīkā* on the *Avaloka*, remarks.

Anyena saha kathayan tataḥ parivṛtyānyakarṇe yat kathayati tadapavāritam. But the word *anyakarṇe* is wrongly placed here, for then *Apavāritam* will not differ from the stage-direction *karṇe*.

What Dhanañjaya says about *Apavāritam* and *Janāntikam* can be put as follows:

Apavāritam — (1) The speaker breaks the course of

conversation by turning in the direction of the addressee. (2) He only communicates the secret in his mind to this character and the implication is that. (3) He does not expect the addressee to respond.

Janāntikam — (1) The speaker breaks the course of conversation by means of a *Tripatākākara*. (2) Then he holds a mutual conversation with the person for whom the remark is intended. (3) The conversation takes place to one end of the group of characters present on the stage (*janānte*). In *Kārikā* 65 he calls the speech *Janāntam*.

All later theorists repeat Dhanañjaya's views only.

(4) *Nāṭakalakṣaṇaratnakośa* of Sāgaranandin (Somewhere between 920 and 1100 A.D.) defines the two terms in Section XVI verses 2267-69.

About *Janāntikam* he says, *vañcayitvaikamanyo'nyam dvābhyām yat khalu paṭhyate.*' According to him it takes place in a group of three, where one is deceived by the other two. This is not correct. More characters can be present on the stage when *Janāntika* conversation takes place.

(5) *Nāṭyadarpaṇa* of Rāmachandra and Guṇacandra (1100-75 A.D.) defines these two terms in *Viveka* 1 verses 12, 13. Nothing new is added to Dhanañjaya's definitions.

The *Vṛtti* explains the terms as usual and gives the derivations of the two terms as follows:

Apavāritam — *apavāryate bahūnām pracchādyate iti apavāritam.*

Janāntikam — *janānāmekasyaiva gopyatvāt bahūnāmantikam, srāvyatayā nikaṭam janāntikam.*

Thus the view of Abhinavagupta is repeated here.

(6) *Bhāvaprakāśa* of Śāradātanaya (1175-1250 A.D.) repeats the definitions given by Dhanañjaya *ad verbatim*.

(7) *Sāhityadarpaṇa* of Viśvanātha (14th cent. A.D.) deals with these stage-direction in chapter VI, verses 138, 139. Nothing new is added.

Tarkavāgīśa Bhaṭṭācārya explains *janāntikam* as *janānte, janasamīpe.*

(8) Vasantarājīya, quoted by *Kāṭayavema* in his commentary on *Mālavikāgnimitra* is placed by scholars in about fourteenth century A.D. The author explains *niyatasrāvya* as *ekena vijñeya* known to one only, implying that such conversations take place in groups of three only; but he defines *Apavārita* as *parairalakṣya-vyāpare kathito'rthaḥ* using the form of plural *paraiḥ*. Hence the point about the number of characters seems to be insignificant.

(9) *Nāṭakacandrikā* of Rūpagosvamin (about 1490 to 1575 A.D.) follows Dhanañjaya in the divisions of *Nāṭyoktayaḥ* and in the definitions of these two stage-directions.

Thus according to all Sanskrit critics *Apavārya* and *Janāntika* have some definte distinguishing characteristics.

Different Views of the Practising Sanskrit Dramatists

We know that practice always precedes theory. It is worthwhile analysing critically the *Apavārya* and *Janāntika* remarks in Sanskrit plays from this point of view, in order to verify whether the theorists have framed their rules on the basis of the practice followed by the Sanskrit playwrights.

Bharata's *Nāṭyaśāstra* presupposes some dramatic compositions; but unfortunately most of these are lost to us. Aśvaghoṣa's play is available in fragments only. Hence the first playwright of whom we can think in this context is Bhāsa.

Here we cannot enter into the critical problem about the chronological relationship between Bharata and Bhāsa; but we know that among all classical dramatists at the most Bhāsa alone could be known to Bharata. Let us, therefore, study the aside-remarks in Bhāsa plays in this light.

(1) Bhāsa has used very few aside-remarks (A) *Apavārya* remarks, where the speaker does not get or expect a response are three — in *Avimāraka* Act III, in *Pañcarātra* Act II and in *Cārudatta* Act III. (B) *Apavārya* remarks which get a response are three — in *Pañcarātra* Act II, in *Cārudatta* Act I and in *Cārudatta* Act II. (C) *Apavārya* remark which does not seem to be addressed to any one and which is as good as *Ātmagata* — in *Dūtavākya* Act I. In fact the *Apavārya* in *Pañcarātra* Act II, noted under (A)

above can better be put here, unless it is interpreted as addressed to Yudhiṣṭhira. (D) There is only one *janāntika* remark in *Cārudatta* Act III where Maitreya expects a reply from Radanikā.

As already noted Bharata's definitions of the two terms are not very clear. Probably the remark in *Avimāraka* Act III in (A) in *Pañcarātra* Act II and in *Dūtavākya* in (C) would be *Apavārya* according to Bharata. The rest would go under *Janāntika.*

Many Sanskrit plays belonging to the period between Bharata and Abhinava-Dhanañjaya are fortunately available. We can analyse the aside-remarks in these plays to find out whether the rule laid down by these critics are in consonance with the practice followed in these classical plays.

Love-plays in Sanskrit afford ample scope for aside-remarks. Hence all the three plays of Kālidāsa, *Mṛcchakaṭika* of Śūdraka, the two *Naṭikās* of Śrīharṣa and *Mālatimādhava* of Bhavabhūti are replete with aside remarks.

(2) Kālidāsa's plays:

(A) *Apavārya* remarks not expecting a response from the addresse — 5 — 1 in *M* Act. I. 2 in *Vi* Act II. 1 in *V.* Act III. 1 in *V.* Act V and 1 in *A. Śā* Act II.

(B) *Apavārā* remarks meeting with a response — 2 — 1 in *M.* Act I, 1 in *M.* Act III.

(C) *Apavārya* remarks which are as good as *Svagata* — 3 — 2 in *A. Śā.* Act V, 1 in *A. Śā.* Act VI.

(D) *Janāntika* remarks with mutual conversation — 11 — 3 in *M* Act II, 2 in *M,* Act V, 1 in *Vi.* Act II, 1 in *A. Śā.* Act I, 1 in *A. Śā.* Act III, 1 in *A. Śā.* Act, IV, 2 in *A. Śā.* Act VI.

(E) *Janāntika* remarks not expecting a response — 5 — 1 in *M.* Act III, 1 in *M.* Act V, 1 in *Vi* Act I, 1 in *A. Śā* Act II, 1 in *A. Śā.* Act V.

(3) Śūdraka's *Mṛcchakaṭika:*

(A) *Apavārya* remarks not expecting a response — 1 in Act I.

(B) *Apavārya* remarks with a response — 2 — in Act I, Act V.

(C) *Apavārya* which is as good as *Svagata* — 1 in Act X.

(D) *Janāntika* remarks with a conversation — 5 — 2 in Act I, 1 in Act V, 2 in Act IX.

(E) *Janāntika* remarks without a response — 2 — Act V, Act IX.

(4) Śrīharṣa's plays:

Śrīharṣa has used in all 23 *Apavārya* remarks, *Janāntika* not being used by him at all. Obviously he has included the technical *Janāntika* in his *Apavārya*.

(A) *Apavārya* remarks without a response — 11 — 3 in *R.* Act II, 2 in *R.* Act III, 2 in *R.* Act IV, 1 in *P.D.* Act III, 1 in *P.D.* Act IV, 1 in *N.* Act I, 1 in *N.* Act II.

(B) *Apavārya* remarks with a response — 7. Out of these 4 have the stage-direction *Apavārya* again for the responder. 2 in *R.* Act II, 2 in *R.* Act III, 1 in *R.* Act IV, 1 in *N.* Act II, 1 in *N.* Act III.

(C) There is 1 remark in *R.* Act IV which is as good as *Svagata.*

(5) Viśākhadatta's *Mudrārākṣasa* is full of *Svagata* remarks; but it has no aside speech. For this political play an aside remark is not possible even when three or more characters are present on the stage. In Act I when Cāṇakya, his pupil and the door-keeper are present, Cāṇakya is not likely to take either in his confidence. When Malayaketu—Bhāgurāyaṇa and Rākṣasa—Karabhaka are present it is a bifocal scene. Again when Malayaketu—Pratīhārī and Bhāgurāyaṇa—Kṣapaṇaka are present in Act V it is a bifocal scene. Later in this Act Malayaketu, Rākṣasa, Siddhārthaka and Bhāgurāyaṇa are present on the stage. A lesser dramatist would have made Siddhārthaka and Bhāgurāyaṇa speak aside; but in this play of political intrigues no two agents of Cāṇakya know each other as belonging to the same party.

(6) Bhaṭṭanārāyaṇa's *Veṇīsaṁhāra:*

(A) *Apavārya* remark without a response — 1 in Act II.

(B) *Janāntika* remarks, which are as good as *Svagata* — 2 in Act I.

(7) Bhavabhūti's plays:

(A) No *Apavārya* remark without a response.

(B) *Apavārya* remark with a response — 1 *MVC* Act VII.

(C) *Apavārya* remarks which are as good as *Svagata* — 9 — 1 in *MVC* Act I, 1 in *MVC* Act IV, 1 in *MVC* Act V, 1 in *M.M.* Act II, 2 in *M.M.* Act IV, 1 in *M.M.* Act VI, 1 in *URC* Act I, 1 in *URC* Act IV.

(D) There are not less than 11 *Janāntika* conversations:
2 in *MVC* Act I, 1 in *MVC* Act V, 3 in *M.M.* Act II, 1 in *M.M.*

Act III, 2 in *M.M.* Act IV, 1 in *M.M.* Act VIII, 1 in *M.M.* Act X.

(E) *Janāntika* remarks without a response — 2 in *M.M.* Act I.

(F) *Jnāntika* remark which is good as *Svagata* — 1 in *M.M.* Act III.

Analytical Survey of the Plays

As already seen, 'mutual conversation' is the real point of distinction between *Apavārya*, in which it does not take place and *Janāntika* in which it takes place. The above analysis shows that in the plays of the playwrights from Bhāsa to Bhavabhūti[1] 12 *Apavārya* remarks are without any response from the addressee, while 6 have such response. 28 *Janāntika* remarks have mutual conversation, while 11 do not have it. Thus in general *Janāntika* seems to be used when the speaker expects a reply. Otherwise the stage-direction *Apavārya* is used. In some particular cases *Janāntika* has been used even when no response is expected, probably out of exigencies of stage. We can say that Dhanañjaya seems to have framed his definitions of these varieties of *Niyataśrāvya* on the basis of these plays.

Abhinavagupta says that *Apavārya* is kept away from more characters and intended for one only while *Janāntika* is intended for all excepting one. The view is repeated by Rāmacandra and Guṇacandra. A critical survey of the plays in the foregoing lines proves that this is not correct. When more than three characters are present on the stage *Apavārya* is used in 14 cases, while *Janāntika* in 17 cases. The context shows that mostly all these remarks are intended for one character only in all these cases.

Technical Stage Direction: Different Methods

Even in the use of these technical stage-directions each individual playwright has his own method. Śrīharṣa does not use *Janāntika* and has *Apavārya* even for mutual conversation. He has twice used *Apavārya* for a mere gesticulation, without any word. In *R.* Act II the picture-board falls down from the Vidūṣaka's hand while Vāsavadattā and Kāñcanamālā are present. The stage direction now is — (*rājā apavārya vidūṣakamaṅgulyā tarjayati*). Again in Act III Vasantaka receives Vāsavadattā and Kañcanamālā whom he has mistaken to be Sāgarikā and

Susaṅgatā in disguise. The stage direction is *Kāñcanamālā — (apāvarya aṅgulyā tarjayantī)*. Some dramatists have a fancy to use *Apavārya* in the place of *Svagata*. Bhavabhūti has committed this mistake at least 9 times. Occasionally other playwrights also have done this. Bhavabhūti makes two characters make an aside-speech together; which sounds very awkward. In *MVC* Act IV Vasiṣṭha-Viśvāmitrau make *Apavārya* remark together, in which they speak about Rāma's glory being known to Paraśurāma. To whom is this addressed? Do they address each other with the selfsame words? The same can be said of the *Apavārya* in *MVC* Act V when Sugrīvan Bibhīṣaṇau recite one verse *apavārya* where they speak how Vālin's calamity cannot be avoided. Again in the same Act Sugrīva Bibhīṣaṇau make a *janāntikam* remark to *Śramaṇā*.

Post-Bhavabūti Sanskrit Plays

After Bhavabhūti Sanskrit drama faces a period of decandence. In this period these lesser dramatists tried to fit their plays in the technicalities of Sanskrit drama. As such we expect them to frame their aside remarks also so as to suit their technical definitions. By way of sample survey of these plays the aside remarks in the following plays have been analysed: (1) *Bālarāmāyaṇa* of Rājaśekhara (10th cent. A.D.), (2) *Caṇḍakauśika* of Kṣemendra (10th cent A.D.), (3) *Anargharāghava* of Murāri (11th cent. A.D.), (4) *Kundamālā* of Vīranāga or Diṅnāga (about 11th cent. A.D.), (5) *Subhadrādhanañjaya* of Kulaśekharavarman (somewhere between 950 and 1150 A.D.), (6) *Rukmiṇīharaṇa* of Vatsarāja (12th cent. A.D.), (7) *Prasannarāghava* of Jayadeva (13th cent. A.D.), (8) *Vidagdhamādhava*, a devotional play by Rūpagosvāmin (16th cent. A.D.), (9) *Amṛtodaya*, a philosophical play by Gokulanātha (1650 A.D.), (10) *Bālamārtaṇḍavijaya*, a play in praise of king Mārtaṇḍavarman of Travancore by Devarājakavi (18th cent. A.D.), (11) *Pṛthvīvallabha*, a historical Gujarati play by Shri K.M. Munshi — translated into Sanskrit by Shri Limaye — (20th cent. A.D.).

The analysis of these aside remarks gives the following results:

(A) *Apavārya* without response — 20

(B) *Apavārya* with response — 9
(C) *Janāntika* with conversation — 9
(D) *Janāntika* without response — 9

Thus the *Apavāryas* generally follow Dhanañjaya's definition, though not very carefully. A *Janāntika* seems to have been used both with and without response without any distinction. The dinstinction laid down by Abhinavagupta about *Janāntika* being concealed from one only, also is not practised. Thus these later playwrights are not at all particular about the distinction of these two varieties of *Niyataśrāvya*. *Kundamālā, Prasannarāghava* and *Amṛtodaya* have no *Janāntika* like Śrīharṣa. Murāri seems to be very careless in making any distinction between these two stage-directions. When a remark is to be concealed from more than one character he has used *Apavārya* once and *Janāntika* on another occasion. When Rāma is pointing out various spots to Sītā from the *Puṣpaka* he uses *Apavārya* while pointing out Praśravaṇa mountain, but *Janāntika* while pointing the river Godāvarī. Yet playwrights like Rūpagosvāmin seem to be quite careful about the distinction between *Apavārya* and *Janāntika* as defined by Dhanañjaya. However, in general the distinction seems to have been ignored in this period.

Views of Sanskrit Commentators

Sanskrit commentators of the classical Sanskrit plays have explained these two stage-directions in their commentaries (1) Kāṭayavema in his commentary of the *M.* gives the definitions of Dhanañjaya for both. For *apavārya* he quotes from Vasantarājīya. He explains *Janāntika* as *janasyābhiṣṭasyāntikam, samīpe yadabhiṣṭajana eva sṛṇuyāditi kṛtvā tatsamīpe ucyate.* This description holds good of both the stage-directions. (2) Raṅganātha in his *Prakāśikā* on *Vi.* gives Viśvanātha's definitions for both and also quotes Sāgaranandin. (3) Jagaddhara, in his commentaries on the *M.M.* and on *V.S.* quotes the definitions of Bharata. (4) Tripurāri in his commetary on *M.M.*, (5) Pṛthvīrāja in his commentary on *Mṛ* and (6) Rāghavabhaṭṭa in his commentary on *A. Śā* quote the definitions given in the *Daśarūpa.*

Thus they do not add anything new to the distinctions

between these two stage-directions.

Modern Scholars' Views

In the modern editions of Sanskrit plays modern scholars have annotated these terms (1) Monier-Williams in his edition of *A. Śā* (O.U.P. 1876) has annotated *Janāntika* without referring to the mutual conversation and has quoted the definition of *Janāntika* in *S.D.* (2) Shri M.R. Kale in his edition of *Ratnāvalī* (Bombay 1921), gives a note on *Apavārya,* which is in fact a note on *Janāntika*. Śrīharṣa's *Apavāryas* include *Janāntikas* also. Hence this note is all right for Harṣa's plays and not in general. In his edition of *Vi.* he explains both clearly in English, but does not refer to the mutual conversation in *Ja.* However he gives the definitions from *D.R.* for both. (3) Prof. A.B. Athalye and Prof. S.S. Bhave give a short but clear note in their edition of *Vi.* (Bombay 1932) — "The difference between the two is not well-defined. However, it appears that *Apavārya* is used only for a small speech, where some secret is given out, while *Janāntika* is used for a sort of mutual whisper, by stopping the course of conversation." These scholars point out that there is mutual conversation in *Janāntika*; but they have not pointed out clearly the difference in the gesticulations for both. (5) Prof. A.B. Gajendragadkar (3rd edition of *A. Śā.* Bombay 1941) has annotated *Nāṭyoktayaḥ:* in Appendix-A (p. 402), He explains the gesticulations for both in details and says, "The difference between *Janāntika* and *Apavārya* mainly lies in the particular gesticulations that accompany them." He continues — "The idea in *Janāntika* is more or less negative, i.e., to exclude certain characters, while in *Apavārya* it is positive, i.e., to indicate the character or the characters for whom the speech is meant." (6) Prof. R.D. Karmarkar (3rd Edition of the *URC*, BORI, Pune 1954), repeats Prof. Gajendragadkar's view that the difference lies in the manner of utterance only. (7) Dr. G.K. Bhat and Dr. R.N. Gaidhani (Marathi edition of *Veṇīsaṁhāra*, Pune 1957) have given a note on *Apavārya,* which is really a note on *Janāntika*. This is probably due to oversight but (8) Dr. G.K. Bhat has given a very clear note on these two terms in his Marathi edition of *Mālavikāgnimitra* (Kolhapur, 1962). After having explained the

Tripatākākara gesticulation in details he says about *Janāntika*, "Through this gesticulation other characters are given a hint that they have to remain aloof and the spectators also can get an idea that here is a private conversation between the two characters." *Apavārya* has been explained as follows: "When a character turns his back upon other characters on the stage, faces the audience and reveals some secret in the plot, then the dramatic speech called *Apavārya* is used." He further remarks: "It seems that the difference between the two can be noted as follows: *Janāntika* is a private conversation between two characters and when a character makes a speech, as if having taken the audience in confidence, it is *Apavārya*; but this distinction is not observed meticulously in the writing of Sanskrit plays."

Critical Analysis

Each one of these annotations is clearly bringing out certain features of these stage-directions. Putting together all that has been said about *Apavārita* and *Janāntika* by ancient Sanskrit critics like Bharata and Dhanañjaya, the evidence produced by the practice on Sanskrit stage from Bhāsa to Bhavabhūti and even later, the remarks of ancient commentators like Kāṭayavema and Jagaddhara, and the annotations in the editions of Sanskrit plays by eminent scholars, we can explain clearly the two types of *Niyataśrāvya* as follows: Both stage directions are used when three or more characters are present on the stage.

(A) *Apavārya* or *Apavāritam* — This stage direction is used when one character wants to communicate some secret instruction or information in his or her mind to certain other character, concealing it from other or others. The speaker does not expect any response from the addressee. In order to achieve his or her purpose the character takes a turn, which should be easily noted by the spectators as being a turn and then gives the intended instruction or information.

(B) *Janāntikam* — This stage-direction is used when the speaker wants to disucss or decide about some secret in his or her mind with certain other character, concealing it from other or others. The speaker holds up his or her palm, with its fingers excepting the indicating finger spread up in front of the face near the cheek — right or left according to the position of the actors on the stage — in order to exclude the characters beyond the backside of the palm from hearing it. The speaker does not turn the neck much so as to be noticeable by the spectators. Then the two — or rarely more — carry on their mutual conversation. When it is over, the *Tripatākākara* is removed. Sometimes the conversation does not take place; but the speaker begins with a *Tripatākākara* expecting a response. *Janāntikam* can be better understood as *janānām pātrāṇāmante* 'to one side of the group of characters' and not *Janānāmantike* as *Abhinavabhāratī* and *Nāṭṭyadarpaṇa* take it.

In *Apavārya* no doubt there is a secret in the mind of the speaker, but not that he communicates it 'as if having taken the audience in confidence.' For then it would not differ from *Svagata. Apavārya* does not necessarily reveal 'a secret in the plot'. There are many *Apavārya* remarks which in no way contribute to the development of the plot, e.g., *Vi.*, Act I Urvaśī says *Apavārya* to Citralekhā, *abhijātam khalvasya vacanam.* On the other hand *Svagatas* also can contribute to the development of the plot, e.g., *Svapnavāsavadatta,* Act I Vāsavadattā's *Ātmagata* remark, *ham. iha māṃ nikṣeptukāma āryayaugandharāyaṇaḥ. bhavatu, avicārya kramaṁ na kariṣyati.*

Abhinavagupta distinguishes the two as *Apavārya* being concealed from many and *Janāntika* from one only. This is not warranted either by theory or practice. *Apavārya* is not necessarily 'a short remark' as understood by some scholars. The foregoing analysis in section 3 proves that even *Apavārya* speeches can be lengthy e.g., Mālatī's long sppech on the news of her engagement to Nandana in *M.M.*, Act III. The difference between the two stage-directions, thus does not 'mainly lie in the particular gesticulations that accompany both.'

Prof. Gajendragadkar is right when he says that the idea in *Janāntika* is more or less negative, while in *Apavārya* it is positive. When the *Tripatākākara* is raised up the spectators know that the speech is not to be heard by the characters to the back of the palm. The speaker of *Apavārya* takes a visible turn and faces the addressee. The spectators know that it is meant for him or her only, whom the speaker faces.

It is true that the distinction between the two stage-directions is not meticulously observed in the writing of Sanskrit plays, yet in general the practice follows the essential conditions of the two. Sometimes the stage-direction *Apavārya* or even *Janāntikam* is used when the remark is in fact *Svagata,* while sometimes *Janāntika* is used in place of *Apavārya*. In some of these cases at least it is due to the exigencies of the stage, e.g., in *V.S.*, Act I Draupadī and Buddhimatikā are sitting in a corner, their presence not being noted by Bhīmasena. Now Draupadī makes 2 *Janāntika*[2] remarks. I feel this is so because in the sitting posture it is difficult to take a visible turn for *Apavārya*. It is easier to use the *Tripatākākara*. Same is the case when the judge makes a *Janāntika* remark to the assessors about Cārudatta in *Mr.* Act IX.

Thus the critical analysis of the 'asides' in Sanskrit plays unfolds many interesting points about the two stage-directions.

References

1. Śrīharṣa's plays have *Apavārya* only. Hence they are left out for this calculation.
2. (i) Draupadī — *tadekānte upaviṣṭā bhūtvā śṛṇomi tāvannāthasya vyavasitam. nātha, aśrutapūrvam khalvīdṛśam vacanam. tatpunaḥpunastāvadbhaṇa.*
   (ii) *nātha, na lajjanta ete. tattvamapi tāvanmā vismārṣīḥ.*

19

The Process of *Rasaniṣpatti*

THE Kevalādvaitins maintain that the world was never created and *Jagadutpatti* cannot be discussed from a metaphysical point of view. Similarly the exponents of *Rasa* maintain that *Rasa* is not created and really speaking *Rasaniṣpatti* does not take place. What springs up in good literature is not *Rasa* but its relish, *carvaṇa*. Hence we are analysing the process of *Rasacarvaṇā-niṣpatti*.

The word *Rasa* in the sense of the highest bliss was known to the *Upaniṣrds* also; but it is Bharata, the author of the *Nāṭya-śāstra*, who, for the first time, has used it in the context of the literary compositions.

Since no dramatic device can be effective without *Rasa (na rasādṛte kaścidarthaḥ pravartate*). Bharata had to discuss it in the context of drama. He gives his oft-quoted, much discussed *Rasasūtra*:

> *vibhāvānubhāvavyabhicārisaṁyogadrasaniṣpattiḥ.*

He accepts *Rasaniṣpatti* as an established fact and does not bother to analyse the process. Bharata must not have dreamt that this short aphorism was going to inspire many a Sanskrit commentator and was going to bring to light numerous expositions on the topic. After Bharata, many ancient commentators must have tried to throw light on this *Sūtra*. Unfortunately, their dissertations have been irrevocably lost to us. Thanks to the intellectual giant, Abhinavagupta that the views of some of them are at least partially preserved for us. The earliest available commentary on the *Nāṭyaśāstra* is *Abhinavabhāratī* of Abhinavagupta. He had referred to *Rasa* in a number of places in the *Abhinavabhāratī* and the *Dhvanyālokālocana*. In his commentary on the *N.S.* chapter VI he had discused the problem of *Rasaniṣpatti* in details. This scholarly exposition had such a strong impact upon the literary critics like Mammaṭa, Hemacandra and Viśvanātha that all of them have simply reproduced his views. Māṇikyacandra, the author of *Saṅketa* pays him a compliment in this regard as *sarvasvaṁ rasasyāsya bhaṭṭapādā hi jānate*.

Before giving his own theory Abhinava mentions and refutes the views of some of his predecessors as follows:

Lollaṭa — *Sthāyins* are the permanent emotions inherent in every human being in a subtle undeveloped form. When a *Sthāyin* comes in contact with the respective *vibhāvas, anubhāvas* and *vyabhicāribhāvas* it becomes fully developed (*upacita*) and the resultant is *Rasa,* the aesthetic-delight (*sthāyyeva vibhāvādibhi-rupacito rasaḥ*). During this process the *Sthāyin* develops different relations with the different constituents of *Rasa* as follows: *sthāyin-vibhāva*; *utpādya-utpādaka-bhāva,* because *vibhāvādis* produce *upacita-styāyin. Sthāyin-anubhāva; gamya-gamaka-bhāva,* since the *upacaya* is inferred through *anubhāvas; sthāyin-vyabhicāribhāva; poṣya-poṣaka-bhāva,* because *vyabhicārins,* develop and expedite *Raśa.* This *Rasa,* 'the *upacitasthāyin*' really belongs to the character of the original story like Rāma, Duṣyanta or Bhīma. Yet the actor presents everything with full concentration and hence a peculiar charm *(vastusaundarya*) is developed. Hence now the spectators superimpose the *Rasa* on the actor. It is this superimposition that leads to their delight.

This theory of Lollaṭa is known as *Utpattivāda,* because according to him *Upacaya* of *sthāyin* is produced by *vibhāvādis* Lollaṭa is called a *Mīmāṁsaka.* Modern scholars explain this saying that he is *uttarmīmāṁsaka,* i.e. *Vedāntin.* For he speaks of the superimposition of *pātrasthāyibhāva* on the *naṭa* just as a *Vedāntin* speaks of the *Adhyāsa* of *jagat* on *Brahmaṇ.* To my mind he can be called a *Mīmāṁsaka* because in his spirit to deny *vyañjanā* he includes it under *Abhidhā,* accompanied by *Arthāpatti* which he describes — as farflung process of *Abhidhā.*

Lollaṭa's explanation of *Rasaniṣpatti* did not appeal to other critics like Śaṅkuka, who pointed out numerous flaws in it. The most noteworthy defect is as follows:

How does this *Rasa* come to be relished by the spectators, when it is in no way connected with them?

Śaṅkuka explains the *Sūtra* as follows:

The *Sthāyibhāva* really belongs to the character in the original story. The actor imitates the *anubhāvas* of this *sthāyin* very skillfully, by dint of his training and practice. On the basis of their own experience the spectators in the playhouse have already established a *Hetu-sādhya-bhāva* between the *anubhavas* and the *sthāyin* that the particular *anubhāvas* reveal a particular *sthāyin*. Now when they witness the paraphernalia of *Rasa*, i.e., *vibhāvas, anubhāvas* and *vyabhicāribhāvas* on the stage they know that all this is artificial. Yet the efficient acting of the actors creates such a verisimilitude that the spectators get lost into the performance and accept the *vibhāvādis* as genuine. Now they infer the *sthāyibhāva* in the *naṭa*. They feel that this *sthāyibhāva* is similar to that of the *pātra*. In order to distinguish it from the original *sthāyibhāva* they call it *Rasa* (*ratiranukriyamāṇā śṛṅgāraḥ*). This inference of the spectators is different from ordinary inferences *vastusaundaryabalāt* due to the peculiar charm of the whole situation. It is something like visualising a horse on seeing the picture of a horse, in which the horse is not real, illusory, similar or doubtful (*Citraturaganyāya*).

Anumāna is the very pivot of Śaṅkuka's theory. Hence it is called *Anumitivāda* and he is designated as a *Naiyāyika*.

This explanation of the *Rasasūtra* also was subjected to acid-test by later critics. Following are most noteworthy defects in it:

(1) Imitation implies that the imitator has thorough knowledge of the original matter to be imitated. How can an actor imitate a charactor like Rāma and Duṣyanta?

(2) *Rasa* is a matter of direct experience. How can it be relished through an *anumāna?*

(3) An inference wrongly formed on the basis of something similar to the middle-term leads to a fallacy and not to the conclusion of a similar *sādhya*. If one sees fog, similar to smoke and infers the existence of fire, it will only lead to a fallacy and

not to the conclusion of something similar to fire. How can the spectators infer similar *sthāyibhāva* in the actor?

After Śaṅkuka, Bhaṭṭanāyaka came forward to explain the process of *Rasaniṣpatti*. Till now the *sthāyin* was located in the *pātra* or the *naṭa*, while the relish is enjoyed by the spectators. It is Bhaṭṭanāyaka, who, for the first time, treats *Rasa* as an experience belonging to the spectators. He started analysing how a dramatic performance appeals to the spectators. He could observe two stages:

(1) The spectators happen to disconnect the entire performance from the aspect of particular space, time and substratum.

(2) Then it enters the innermost recesses of their hearts. He called the first phenomenon as *Sādhāraṇīkaraṇa* generalisation or universalisation. The second is what Abhinava calls as *tanmayībhavana*. He could realise that this *sādhāraṇīkaraṇa* cannot be effected by *Abhidhā*. At the same time he did not want to accept *vyañjanā*. Therefore, he called this process of imaginative absorption as *bhāvakatvavyāpāra* (A process which brings into existence (causal of *bhu* to be) the generalisation.) This process detaches the whole dramatic scene from all particulars of time, space and person. Now if it remains an abstract generalised concept the spectators cannot enjoy it. Hence Bhaṭṭanāyaka has to bring in another process that would enable the spectators to enjoy it. He calls it *bhojakatvavyāpāra*. (A process of introspective taste which makes (causal of *bhuj* to enjoy) the spectators enjoy the performance). The *sādhāraṇīkṛta* elements on the stage incite a state of mind, predominated by *sattva* in the case of the spectators. Their minds pass through *dṛti* and *vistāra*, when *sattva* mingles with *rajas* and *tamas* respectively. The *sthāyin* of a spectator now rests in its own lustruous blissful consciousness and the spectator enjoys the highest aesthetic experience. Enjoyment of *Rasa* by the spectators is the main foundation of *Nāyaka's* theory, which is therefore known as *Bhuktivāda*. He is called as a *Sāṅkhyavādin* probably because like the *puruṣa* of the *Sāṅkhyas* the actor remains aloof from this enjoyment.

It can be easily observed that this theory of Bhaṭṭanāyaka has really paved the way for Abhinava's *Abhivyaktivāda*. Most of the conclusions of *Nāyaka* are acceptable to Abhinava. The only criticism that he offers is on *Nāyaka*'s statement: *Bhāvanābhāvya eṣa śṛṅgārādiguṇaḥ* and about *Bhojaktvavyāpāra* he inquires — *pratītyādivyatiriktaḥ saṁsāre ko bhogaḥ?*

Thus Bhaṭṭanāyaka had almost touched upon the crux of the problem. An explanation for the *Sādhāraṇīkaraṇa* and *Rasānubhava* was to be offered and the theory was going to be an established fact. With his matchless genius Abhinavagupta came forward to do it and did it very effectively indeed. This great critic modestly says that he is not saying anything new; but is just expounding what his great predecessors have already said. According to Abhinavagupta the power of *vyañjanā* could offer a convincing explanation for both the processes of *bhāvakatva* and *bhojakatva*. It is *vyañjanā* that divests the paraphernalia of *Rasa* displayed on the stage of its particular space, time and individuality. It is an extraordinary process that leads the aesthets through the gateway of suggested sense to the aesthetic *summum bonum* of *camatkāra* or *carvaṇā*. When the whole network is thus *sādhāraṇīkṛta* it at once appeals to the appreciative spectators by a special type of intuitive cognition. This is *Rasa*, the aesthetic experience.

Abhinava's theory is rightly known as *Abhivyaktivāda*. According to him *Rasa* was already present in the minds of the spectators in an *avyakta* form or latent impressions. With the proper stimulant *(ālambanavibhāva)*, excitants (*uddīpanavibhāvas*) and insuants (*anubhāvas*) it blends into the manifest form, enjoyable by all *sahṛdayas*.

Let us illustrate this with the first Act of the *Abhijñānaśākuntala*. Duṣyanta is the *āśraya* of the *rati*, Śakuntalā is the *ālambanavibhāva*. The hermitage in the solitude, the trees, the creepers, the remarks of Priyaṁvadā and Anasūyā, all these act as *uddīpanavibhāvas*. *Rati* of Duṣyanta gets the stimulus at the very first sight of Śakuntalā when he remarks, *aho madhuramāsāṁ darśanam*. Further he admires her charms again and again and goes on thinking of her only. He fears that perhaps she may be Kaṇva's real daughter and then he cannot marry her. Thus the different *vyabhicāribhāvas* like, *abhilāṣā*, *cintā*, *śaṅkā* develop in his mind. Duṣyanta's reactions to all these feelings are seen in his facial expressions, knitting of the eye-brows, horripilation, tremour, etc. With a harmonius blending of the *vibhāvas*, *anubhāvas* and *vyabhicāribhāvas* and with a similar response from

Śakuntalā, Duṣyanta's *rati* develops into *Śṛṅgāra*.

Now let us review this in the light of the stage-performance. There is an actor playing the role of Duṣyanta and three actresses playing the roles of Śakuntalā, Priyaṁvadā and Anasūyā. The spectators come to the play-house. The music, setting, surroundings, etc., gradually make them forget their practical experience. Slowly and gradually their hearts get predominated by *Sattva* and become clean like a mirror, ready to catch any reflection. Now the skilled acting of the actors, the proper setting on the stage, the suitable make-up, the efficient direction of the director, the necessary atmosphere created by the music all these create verisimilitude of the actual happenings on the stage. The suggestive power used by the playwright in the recitative element and the gestures and histrionics on the part of the actors now remove all bonds of space, time and substratum. Now the spectator does not experience *Duṣyantatva, naṭatva* or even his own *prekṣakatva.* It is fully a *sādhāraṇīkṛta* phenomenon. Now the all-powerful suggestive power operates further on and the generalised experience automatically becomes the private experience of each one of the spectators. Each one is immersed into it. Viśvanātha has described this in his *Sāhityadarpaṇa* as follows:

> *parasya na parasyeti mameti na mameti ca,*
> *tadāsvāde vibhāvādeḥ paricchedo na vidyate*

The experience of one spectator meets with *hṛdayasamvāda* of other spectators. There results *ekaghanatā,* uniformity of the sympathetic imaginative experience of all spectators. This happens because latent impressions in the minds of all spectators belong to the same category. The spectators are now forgeful to everything else excepting this wondrous bliss. This is *vigalitavedyāntara ānanda, vedyāntarasparśaśūnya ānanda.* This can be compared to *ātmānanda* of the *Vedānta*:

> *sa yathā priyayā striyā samparisvakto na bāhyam kiñcana veda nāntaram, evam vāre'yamātmā prājñenātmanā sampariṣvakto na bāhyam kiñcana veda nāntaram.*
>
> (*Bṛhadāraṇyakopaniṣad,* IV.3.21.)

Thus the minds of the spectators are unified with their own blissful, shining consciousnesss. This intuitive experience is next to *Brahmānanda* only, differing from it in this much only that while Brahman is *niṣkala, nirañjana, niravadya,* etc., their minds are tinged with a variety of latent impressions. Viśvanātha has described this *Rasāsvāda* as follows:

> *satvodrekādakhaṇḍasvaprakāśānandacinmayaḥ,*
> *vedyāntarasparśaśūnyo brahmāsvādasahodaraḥ.* (III. 2)
> *lokottaracamatkāraprāṇaḥ kaiścit pramātṛbhiḥ,*
> *svākāravadabhinnatvenāyamāsvadyate rasaḥ.* (III. 3)

Bhaṭṭatota goes to the extent of saying that this *rasāsvāda* is even superior to the experience of a perfect *yogin,* because the *yogin* has to achieve the state with great hardships while here the bliss flows spontaneously.

The essence of this aesthetic state is wondrous joy — *rase sāraścamatkāraḥ.* In this engrossed state the spectators feel as if this wondrous joy is just throbbing in front of them, penetrating their hearts through and through and is nailed up within the innermost recesses of their heart. Abhinava has compared this with the blooming of a miraculous flower (*adbutapuṣpa*) whose petals bloom within the wink of an eye, never to fade away. This experience is simply indescribable. It is not the sumtotal of the *vibhāvas, anubhāvas* and *vyabhicāribhāvas;* but something extra-ordinary over and above all of them. It is compared to *ṣāḍavarasa, pānakarasa* or *prapāṇakarasanyāya.*

What is the proof of its experience? The theroists clearly say that the experience of the connoisseurs is the only proof for it. It is *svasaṁvedya,* known through *sacetasāmanubhava* only. It is not a *kārya* resulting from *vibhāvādis,* because unlike other effects it cannot exist without its *nimittakāraṇa.* It is not a *jñāpya,* which is *jñāpita* by *vibhāvādis,* since only an already existing entity can be *jñāpita.* It is not like *savikalpapratyakṣa,* because in this *āsvāda* all distinctions have evaporated. Nor again is this like *nirvikalpa-pratyakṣa,* since this *rasāsvāda* is *ruṣitavikalpasaṁvedana.*

That is exactly the reason why Abhinava and others take pride in describing it as *alaukika.* This experience of aesthetic delight is not an objective phenomenon, but purely a subjective experience, and yet there is *hṛdayasamvāda* of all spectators about this personal experience.

However, it is worthnoting that the spectator identifies himself with the various dramatic situations presented on the stage and yet always maintains an aesthetic distance. No appreciative spectator rushes to the stage to drive way the bee that is hovering around Śakuntalā's[1] face or to give a good beating to the wicked Śakāra. There is 'a transparent and yet adament partition' that separates the spectator from the dramatic character. He does not experience feelings of the characters but rather feels about the feelings. Modern scholars describe this as 'meta-feeling'. That is why Worsfold says in his *Principles of Criticism* — "Actuality, not reality, i.e., reality hightened by concentration is the essence of drama."

Now Bharata had brought in the concept of *rasa* for *nāṭya* only. Later critics like Abhinava extended the theory so as to make it applicable to literature as a whole. Hence Abhinava remarks, *kāvye'pi nāṭyāyamāna eva rasaḥ*.

The abstract images of thoughts and ideas represented by a poet's words play the roles of actors on the stage of a reader's mind. That is why Bhaṭṭatota warns the poets *prayogatvamanāpanne kāvye nāsvādasambavaḥ*.

He glorifies the descriptive art of great poets as follows:

varnanotkalitā bhogaprauḍhoktyā samyagarpitāḥ,
udyānakāntācandrādyā bhāvāḥ pratyakṣavat sphuṭāḥ.

We are reminded of many pen-pictures of the master-poet Kālidāsa, e.g.,

tam vīkṣya vepathumatī sarasāṅgayaṣṭirnikṣepaṇāya padamuddhatamudvahantī,
mārgācalavyatikarākuliteva sindhuḥ śailādhirājatanayā na yayau na tasthau.

(*Kumārsambhava*, V.85)

dhenvā tadadhyāsitakātarākṣyā
nirīkṣyamāṇaḥ sutarām dayāluḥ.

(*Raghuvaṁśa*, II.52)

Thus the subtle process of *Rasaniṣpatti* is based upon the beautiful art of suggestion, which is found in drama, poem, all good literary pieces and in fact in all works of art.

Reference

1. See — *Aesthetic Rapture*, Vol. I, p. 24, by S.L. Masson and M.V. Patwardhan, Deccan college, Poona, 1970.

Glossary

Agnidivyam (Agniśuddhiḥ): According to the *Dharmaśāstra* one of the ordeals which a suspected criminal has to undergo in order to prove his or her innocense. He or she has to enter the fire and come unhurt out of it.

Agnihotram: Offering of the daily oblations into the domestic fire; maintenance of the domestic fire.

Airāvata (Airāvaṇa): The white elephant, which came out of the Milky Ocean at the time of the churning of the ocean. It belongs to Indra.

Ākāśagaṅgā: The cluster of the stars known as the Milky way.

Amṛta-manthana: The incident of the churning of the ocean by the gods and the demons in order to secure *amṛta,* the nectar.

Āprapadīnamālā: A garland which reachess up to the feet.

Aśvamedha-yajñaḥ: At the end of the military conquest this sacrifice is performed by the victorious king. It proclaims his sovereignty.

Brahmodyam: A metaphysical riddle with which the priests entertained themselves during a sacrificial session.

Cakṣurmohinī-vidyā: The magic-lore by means of which one can keep oneself invisible to others.

Cintāmaṇiḥ: The Desire-yielding gem. Whatever wish is pronounced holding it in hand is immediately fulfilled.

Dhanurbhaṅgaḥ: The breaking of the bow. The big bow of Śiva, which was kept at the palace of Janaka, by way of a challenge to win Sītā, was broken into two at the touch of Rāma.

Digdāhaḥ: The atmospheric phenomenon when the weather suddenly changes and all the quarters become red.

Digvijayaḥ: Allover-military-conquest-tour. A prince, accompanied by an army and a sacrificial horse starts on this tour. The horse is let loose in different territories and the land is won. Whosoever catches the horse is supposed to give a challenge and then a battle takes place. At the end the prince returns victoriously and the victory is celebrated by performing *Aśvamedha-yajña.*

Divyadṛṣṭiḥ: Super-human vision, clairvoyance which enables a person to see distant places, the past and the future.

Duḥsvapnaḥ (Duḥsvapnam): A bad dream, which is an ill omen.

Dohadaḥ: Pregnancy longing of a pregnant woman.

Durdinam: A rainy day.

Dvijaḥ: Twice-born, a *brāhmaṇa,* the thread ceremony being looked upon as his second birth.

Gondhagajaḥ (*gandhadvipaḥ*): A powerful elephant in rut, which scares away animals even from a distance by means of the scent of its ichor.

Indrajālam: Magic.

Kalpavṛkṣaḥ: The desire-yielding heavenly tree. Whatever wish is uttered under its shade is immediately fulfilled.

Kāmadhenuḥ (*Kāmadhuk*): The divine desire-yielding cow. Whatever wish is uttered in its proximity is immediately fulfilled.

Kaustubha-maṇiḥ: A gem of that name which was churned out of the Milky Ocean. Viṣṇu wears it on his chest.

Koṭihomaḥ: A kind of sacrifice.

Kṣapaṇakaḥ: A Jain mendicant.

Kṣīrodadhiḥ: The Milky Ocean at the bottom of which Viṣṇu sleeps. It was churned for the sake of nectar.

Mudrāḥ: The various particular positions of the fingers practised by the *Śaiva*-devotees, who are followers of *Tantra* school.

Nīrājanam: The ceremony of waving light around the idol of a deity and then waving it around the face of a person, who starts on important mission.

Pañcāgnividyā: The lore of five fires in the *Upaniṣads*. In the *Bṛhadāraṇyaka* (V.2.10) it explains the theory of transmigration.

Pañcajanāḥ: The five Vedic tribes — Puru, Anu, Yadu, Druhyu and Turvaśa.

Pāśupataṁ vratam: The vow of a follower of *Pāśupata* sect. The followers of this sect are devotees of Śiva.

Pātālam: The under-world.

Paṭṭabandhaḥ: The ceremony of tying a turban. The kings honoured the herces with it.

Praśastiḥ: A poem written in praise of a person, especially on the occasion of a donation.

Proṣitabhartṛkā: A married woman whose husband has gone away on a distant journey and who, therefore, is supposed to observe various restraints.

Pūrṇapātram: A present given to a servant by a member of a royal family for having brought a good piece of news.

Puroḍāśaḥ: A sacrificial cake prepared out of rice-flour.

Rājasūya yajñaḥ: A great sacrifice performed by a universal monarch at the time of his coronation. It proclaims his sovereignty.

Samasyā-pūrtiḥ (Samasyāpūraṇam): A sort of riddle in which one adds three quarters of a stanza to the fourth quarter, which alone is given.

Sandhyāvandanam: The daily worship by a householder in the morning and in the evening.

Saptarṣayaḥ: The seven great sages of the *Purāṇas*, Marīci, Atri, etc. Also the constellation known as the Great Bear.

Sāsanapaṭṭaḥ: Literally a document proclaiming a command, used in the sense of a metal-plate on which the grant of a land is inscribed.

Satīgamanam: The act of a widow following her dead husband on the funeral pyre.

Śrādhakalpaḥ: The portions in the *Dharmaśāstra* dealing with the obsequial rites for the Manes.

Sthalakamalinī: A lotus plant growing on land.

Svadhā: The food of the Manes.

Svarbhānuḥ: The *Vedic* prototype of the demon Rāhu.

Svayaṁvaraṁ: The ceremony in which a bride, generally a princess, chooses her own husband from amongst the assembled youths.

Svayaṁvara-mālā: The garland of flowers and herbs which the bride carries in her hand and puts in the neck of the youth of her choice.

Ucchaiḥśravas: The name of the white horse that was churned out of the Milky Ocean at the time of the *Amṛta-manthana*.

Upanayanam: The thread-ceremony, the ceremony of initiation.

Uśijaḥ: Members of a particular Vedic clan.

Utsūtraṁ-vyākhyānam: Extra explanation given by a commentator, for which there is nothing in the original text.

Vaikakṣaka mālā: A garland worn over the left shoulder and under the right arm.

Vasatīvanī āpaḥ: The water in the *soma-vat* in which the juice of the crushed *soma*-leaves flows.

Vijñaptipatram: Literally a letter of request. It is used in the sense of a letter, sent by a Jain disciple to his preceptor, informing him of the progress of his religious tour.

Viśvajīt yajñaḥ: The name of a particular sacrifice.

Vṛkṣadohadāḥ: Various pregnancy longings imagined by the Sanskrit poets in the case of particular trees.

Vyāghranakha-paṅktiḥ: A locket shaped like a tiger's nails, which is put in the neck of a child in order to avert evil eye.

Yajñopavītam: The sacred thread worn over the left shoulder and under the right arm. A boy starts wearing it at the time of his initiation and is supposed to wear it throughout his life.

Yauvarājyābhiṣekaḥ: The ceremony of coronation of a prince as the heir-apparent.

Yogapaṭṭam: A piece of cloth thrown over the back and the knees of an ascetic during the abstract meditation.

Bibliography

Sanskrit Texts

Abhijñāna Śākuntala, Kālidāsa, e.d. by A.B. Gajendragadkar, New and Secondhand Book Stall, Bombay, 1941.

Agnipurāṇa, *Ānandāśrama Sanskrit Series* No. 41, Poona, 1900.

Aitareya Āraṇyaka, *Ānandāśrama Sanskrit Series* No. 38, Poona, 1898.

Aitareya Brāhmaṇa, University of Banaras, Varanasi, 1942.

Anargharāghava, Murāri, Nirnayasagara Press, (NSP), 1937.

Āścaryacūḍāmaṇi, Śaktibhadra, Balamanorama Press, Madras, 1926.

Atharvaveda, ed. by S.P. Pandit, Govt. Central Book Depot, Bombay, 1898.

Bālarāmāyaṇa, Rājaśekhara, E.J. Lazaru, Banaras, 1869.

Bhāgavata Purāṇa, NSP, Bombay, 1894.

Bhāsanāṭaka-cakra, Bhāsa, ed. by C.R. Devadhar, Oriental Book Agency, Poona, 1962.

Bhāvaprakāśa, Śāradātanaya, *Gaikwad Oriental Series (GOS)* No. 14, Baroda, 1930.

Brahma Purāṇa, Motilal Banarsidass (MLBD), Delhi, 1985.

Bṛhatkathā-Mañjarī, Kṣemendra, *Kāvyamālā Series*, No. 69, Bombay, 1901.

Bṛhatakathā Ślokasaṅgraha, Budhasvamin, e.d. by F.D. Lacote, Impremerie Nationale, Paris, 1908.

Caṇḍakauśika, Kśemīśvara, J. Vidyasagar, Calcutta 1884.

Collection of the Principal Upaniṣads with Śaṅkara's commentary, ed. by H.R. Bhagvat, Ashtekar Company, Poona, 1918.

Daśarūpa(ka), Dhanañjaya, Chowkamba Vidya Bhavan, Varanasi, 1976.

Dhvanyāloka, Ānandavardhana, N.S.P, Bombay, 1890.

Dhvanyāloka, tr. by K. Krishnamoorthy, Karnatak University, Dharwar, 1974.

Gopatha Brāhmaṇa, ed. by Bloomfield, Allahabad, 1975.

Harṣacarita, Bāṇabhaṭṭa, ed. by P.V. Kane, MLBD, Delhi, 1965.

Hymns of the Atharvaveda, Tr. by R.T.H. Griffith, MLBD, Delhi, 1962.

Hymns of the Ṛgveda (eng. tr.), R.T.H. Griffith, MLBD, Delhi, 1970.

Jaiminīya Brāhmaṇa, Kendriya Saṁskṛta Vidyāpītha, Tirupati, 1967.

Kādambarī, Bāṇabhaṭṭa, Oriental Book Agency, Poona, 1951.

Kaṇva Saṁhitā, Vaidika Saṁśodhana Maṇḍala (VSM) Poona, 1985.

Kapiṣṭhala Saṁhitā, Meherchand Lacchmandass, Lahore, 1968.

Kathāsaritsāgara, Somadeva, NSP, Bombay, 1930.

Kauṣītakī Brāhmaṇa, Lindner, Jena, 1887.

Kāvyādarśa, Daṇḍin, Meherchand Lacchmandass, Lahore, 1975.

Kāvyālaṅkāra, Bhāmaha, *Bombay Sanskrit Series*, No. 65, Bombay, 1909.

Kāvyālaṅkāra-Sūtravṛtti, Vāmana, NSP, Bombay, 1953.

Kāvyamīmāṁsā, Rājaśekhara, Oriental Institute, Baroda, 1934.

Kumārasambhava, Kālidāsa, Sahitya Akademi, Delhi, 1962.

Kundamālā, Dinnāga, MLBD, Delhi, 1937.

Mādhyandina Saṁhitā, Svādhyāya Maṇḍala, Vapi, 1927.

Mahābhārata (Text Only), Vyāsa, Bhandarkar Oriental Research Institute (BORI), Poona, 1971.

Mahāvīracarita, Bhavabhūti, ed. by R.R. Ambardekar, Adresh Prakashana, Bombay, 1971.

Maitrāyaṇī Saṁhitā, F.A. Brockhaus, Leipzig, 1923.

Mālatīmādhava, Bhavabhūti, ed. by Devdhar and Suru, Fergusson College, Poona, 1935.

Mālavikāgnimitra, Kālidāsa, ed. by G.K. Bhat, New and Secondhand Bookstall, Kolhapur, 1961.

Matsya Purāṇa, NSP, Bombay, 1897.

Mṛcchakaṭika, Śūdraka, ed. by M.R. Kale, Bookseller's Publishing Company, Bombay, 1962.

Mudrārākṣasa, Viśākhadatta, ed. by Devdhar Bedkar, Keshav Bhikaji Dhavale, Bombay, 1948.

Nāṭakacandrikā, Rūpagosvamin, *Chowkhamba Sanskrit Series,* No. 97, Banaras, 1964.

Nāṭakalakṣaṇa-ratnakośa, Śagaranandin, OUP, London, 1937.

Nāṭyadarpaṇa, Guṇacandra and Ramacandra, *GOS,* No. 49, Baroda, 1929.

Nāṭyaśāstra, (Vols I-IV), Bharata (With Abhinava Bhāratī, *GOS,* Nos. 36, 68, 124, 145 Baroda, 1956-64.

Padma Purāṇa, Parts I-V, MLBD, 1988-90.

Prasannarāghava, Jayadeva, NSP, Bombay, 1922.

Priyadarśikā, Śrīharṣa, ed. by Nariman *et. al.*, Indo-Iranian Series, No. 10, University of Calcutta, Calcutta, 1965.

Raghuvaṁśa, Kālidāsa, NSP, Bombay, 1892.

Rāmāyaṇa, Vālmīki, Gujarati Printing Press, Bombay, 1912.

Ratnāvalī, Śrīharṣa, ed. by Devadhar and Sapru, Oriental Book Agency, Poona, 1925.

Ṛgveda Saṁhitā, with Sāyaṇa's commentary, VSM, Poona, 1951.

Ṛksūktaśatī, ed. by H.D. Velankar, Bharatiya Vidya Bhavan (BVB), Bombay, 1972.

Rūpakaśataka, Vatsarāja, *GOS,* No. 8, Baroda.

Ṣaḍviṁśa Brāhmaṇa, Kendriya Saṁskṛta Vidyāpītha, Tirupati, 1967.

Sāhityadarpaṇa, Viśvanātha *Kashi Sanskrit Series,* No. 145, Varanasi, 1967.

Śakuntalā, Monier-Williams, Oxford University Press (OUP), 1876.

Sāmaveda Saṁhitā, (Eng. tr,) R.T.H. Griffith, Cosmo Publication, New Delhi, 1978.

Sāṅkhyāyana Brāhmaṇa, Lindner, Jena, 1887.

Śatapatha Brāhmaṇa, Bibliothica Indica, Calcutta, 1902.

Śatapatha Brāhmaṇa, Volumes I-V, (Eng. tr.) J Eggeling, *Sacred Books of the East (SBE)* Nos. 12, 26, 41, 43, 44, MLBD, Delhi, 1963-66.

Subhadrāharaṇa, Kulaśekhara, *Trivandrum Sanskrit Series*, Trivandrum, 1912.

Suśruta Saṁhitā, Suśruta, Meherchand Lacchmandass, Lahore, 1941.

Taittirīya Āraṇyaka, *Ānandāśrama Sanskrit Series*, No. 50, Poona, 1927.

Taittirīya Brāhmaṇa, Godbole, N.S., Poona, 1898.

Taittirīya Saṁhitā, VSM, Poona, 1968.

Unmattarāghava, Bhāskara, NSP, 1925.

Uttararāmacarita, Bhavabhūti, ed. by G.K. Bhat, Popular Book Depot, Surat, 1953.

Vakrokti Jīvita, Kuntaka, ed. by S.K. De, Firma K.L. Mukhopadhyaya, Calcutta, 1961.

Veṇisaṁhāra, Bhaṭṭa Nārāyaṇa, ed. by A.B. Gajendragadkar, New and Secondhand Books Stall, Bombay, 1935.

Vīṇā-Vāsavadattā, Kuppuswamy Shastri Research Institute, Madras, 1962.

Viṣṇu Purāṇa, N.S.P., Bombay, 1887.

Yajurveda Saṁhitā, Svādhyāya Maṇḍala, Vapi, 1927.

Critical Works

Agarwal, H., *Saṁskṛtasāhityetihāsa*, Shakti Prakashana, Ludhiana, 1951.

Akshay Kumari Devi, *Evolution of the Ṛgvedic Pantheon*, Vijay Krishna Brothers, Calcutta, 1938.

Bergaigne, A., *Le Religion Vedique*, Eng. tr. by V.G. Pavanjpe, *The Vedic Religion*, Ārya Saṁskṛti Prakāśana, Poona, 1969.

Burnouf, E., *Commentary sur Yasna*, Royal Printing Press, Paris, 1883.

Colbrooke, *Miscellaneous Essays*, Higgin Bothem and Co., London, 1892.

Dandekar, R.N., *Vedic Bibliography*, Volume I, Karnatak Publishing House, Bombay, 1946; Vol. II, University of Poona, 1961; Vol. III, BORI, 1973; Vol IV, BORI, 1976.

Das, A.K., *Ṛgvedic Culture*, R. Cambray and Company, Calcutta, Madras, 1925.

Dasgupta S.N. and De, S.K., *History of Sanskrit Literature: Classical Period*, Calcutta University, Calcutta, 1961.

De, S.K. *History of Sanskrit Poetics*, Firma K.L. Mukhopadhyay, Calcutta, 1960.

De, S.K., *Sanskrit Poetics as a study of the Aesthetics*, OUP, Bombay, 1963.

De, S.K., *Some Aspects of Sanskrit Literature*, Firma K.L. Mukhopadhyay, Calcutta, 1950.

Dikshitar, V.R., *Purāṇa Index*, Madras University, Madras, 1925.

Dowson, *A Classical Dictionary of Hindu Mythology, Religion, etc.*, Kegan Paul Ltd., London, 1950.

Dwivedi, H.P., *Meghadūta Eka Purānī Kahānī*, Hindi Ratnakar, 1971.

Fallaize, E.N., *Encylopaedia of Religion and Ethics*, T and T Clark, Edinburg, 1967.

Geldner, K.F., *Der Ṛgveda*, Volumes, I-III, *HOS*, 33-35, OUP, 1951.

Gnoli, R., *Aesthetic Experience According to Abhinavagupta*, Chawkhamba Sanskrit Studies, Varanasi, 1968.

Griswold, H.R., *The Religiòn of the Ṛgveda*, OUP, London, 1923.

Hillebrandt, A., *Vedishe Mythologie*, Eng. tr. by S.R. Sarma, *The Vedic Mythology*, MLBD, Delhi, 1987.

Holmberg, *Mythology of All Races*, Vol. IV, Gen. Editors Gray and Moore, Marshal Jones Company, Boston, 1927.

Hume, R.E., *Thirteen Principal Upaniṣads*, OUP, 1958.

Kane, P.V., *History of Sanskrit Poetics*, MLBD, Delhi, 1971.

Kangle, R.P., *Daśarūpavidhāna*, Maharashtra Sāhitya Saṁskṛti Maṇḍala, Bombay, 1974.

Kangle, R.P., *Rasabhāvavicāra*, Maharashtra Sāhitya Saṁskṛti

Maṇḍala, Bombay, 1973.

Keith, A.B., *History of Sanskrit Literature*, OUP, 1956.

Keith, A.B., *Mythology of All Races*, Vol. VI General Editors, L.H. Gray and G.D. Moore, Marshal Jones Company, Boston, 1917.

Keith, A.B., *The Sanskrit Drama*, OUP, 1959.

Krishnamachariar, R., *Classical Sanskrit Literature*, Tirupati Devasthāna Press, Tirupati, 1937.

Krishnamoorthy, K., *Dhvanyāloka and its Critics*, Kavyalaya Publications, Mysore, 1967.

Krishnamoorthy, K., *Essays in Sanskrit Criticism*, Karnatak University, Dharwar, 1964.

Kuhn Adalbert, *Der Herabkunft des Feuers und des Göttertranks*, Ferd Dummlers' Verlagbuchhandlung, Berlin, 1983.

Kulkarni, V.M., *Studies in Sanksrit Sāhityaśāstra*, B.L. Institute of Indology, Patna, 1983.

Lacote, Félix, *Essai sur Gunāḍhya et le Bṛhatkathā*, Eng. tr. "An Essay on Gunāḍhya and the Bṛhatkathā" by A.M. Tabord, In *Journal of the Mythical Society*, Bangalore, 1928.

Ludwig Alfred, *Der Ṛgveda*, Vols. I-IV, F. Temsky, Prag, 1876-81.

Macdonell, A.A. and Keith, A.B., *Vedic Index of Names and Subjects.*, MLBD, Delhi, 1958.

Macdonell, A.A., *Vedic Mythology*, Indological Book House, Varanasi, 1963.

Mackenzie, Donald, *Indian Myth and Legend*, Gresham Publications, London, 1913.

Malsekara, G.P., *Dictionary of Pāli Proper Names*, John Murray, London, 1958.

Modi, J.J., *Anthropological Papers*, Anthropological Society of Bombay, Bombay, 1911.

Mukhopadhyay, G.M., *History of Indian Medicine*, Calcutta University, Calcutta, 1929.

Nève Félix, *Essays Sur le Mythe des Ribhavass* (Eng. tr. Davane, G.V., *"An Essay on the Myth of the Ṛbhus"*), Ajanta Publications, Delhi, 1985.

Oldenberg, H., *Ṛgveda Noten,* Vols. I & II, Weidmannsche Buchhandlung, Berlin, 1909, 1912.

Pargiter, F.E., *Ancient Indian Historical Tradition,* MLBD, Delhi, 1962.

Patwardhan, M.V. and Massen J.L., *Aesthetic Rapture,* Parts I & II, Deccan College Post-graduate and Research Institute, Poona, 1976.

Potdar, K.R., *Sacrifice in the Ṛgveda,* BVB, Bombay, 1953.

Raghavan, V., *An Introduction to Indian Poetics,* Macmillan and Company, Madras, 1970.

Raghavan, V., *A Study of Some Concepts in the Alaṅkāraśāstra,* Adyar Library, Adyar, 1942.

Rahurkar, V.G., *Seers of the Ṛgveda,* University of Poona, Poona, 1964.

Renou Louis, *Etudés Vediqués at Paniniennés,* Vols I to XV, E.E. Beccard, Paris, 1955-65.

Sorensen, *Index of the proper names in the Mahābhārata,* MLBD, Delhi, 1963.

Tilak, B.G., *Orion,* Tilak Brothers, Pune, 1893.

Velankar, H.D., *Ṛgveda Maṇḍala* VIII, BVB, Bombay, 1963.

Velankar, H.D., *Ṛgveda Maṇḍala* III, University of Bombay, Bombay, 1968.

Velankar, H.D., *Ṛksūktaśatī,* BVB, Bombay, 1972.

Vyas, B.S., *Saṁskṛta Kavi Darśana,* Chowkhamba Vidya Bhavan, Banaras, 1958.

Winternitz, M., *A History of Indian Literature,* Vol. I, University of Calcutta, Calcutta, 1962.

Zimmer, H.R., *Hindu Medicine,* Johns Hopkins, Baltimore, 1948.

Articles

Chakravarty, A.K., "Samudra in the Ṛgveda", In *IHQ,* Vol. XII, 1932.

Chakravarty Chintaharana, "Origin and Development of *Dūtakāvya* Literature in Sanskrit", In *IHQ,* Vol. III, 1927.

Shende, N.J., "*Aṅgirasas* in the *Vedic* Literature", In *Annals of the Bhandarkar Oriental Research Institute,* Poona, No. XXXI, 1951.

Index